Gone to the Dogs

Gone to the Dogs

Robin Page

ROBINSON
London

Robinson Publishing Ltd
7, Kensington Church Court
London W8 4SP

First published by Robinson Publishing Ltd 1994

A copy of the British Library Cataloguing in Publication
Data for this title is available from the British Library.

ISBN 1–85487–288–5

Typeset by Hewer Text Composition, Edinburgh
Printed in Great Britain by Mackays of Chatham

Contents

For my Parents
For my Dog
For my Friends – man and beast
and for the 'Friends' of the
Countryside Restoration Trust

Preface

I did not expect to write this book. In *A Peasant's Diary* I wrote: 'My father was a farmer. I am a peasant. Tomorrow I could be an endangered species.' I really thought my time had come; the mighty John Seldom Glummer – sorry, John Selwyn Gummer – was Secretary of State for Agriculture and seemed to have as much understanding of the plight of the small farmer, as I have knowledge of nuclear fission. The interesting point about this of course is that the Prime Minister, no less, invited Mr Gummer to be Minister of Agriculture, yet nobody has invited me to run Britain's nuclear power industry; I wonder why? I could learn as I go along, as the politicians do.

The great and good Mr Gummer wanted a world trade agreement. Part of that agreement would entail the disappearance of thousands of small farmers throughout Britain. My brother and I could have been two of them; yes, I really felt endangered. I was about to become a statistic and was thinking of writing a book about barn owls, and another on Africa, but then my life suddenly changed. Yes, Mr Gummer was moved away from the Ministry of Agriculture; but it was more profound than that: I was also asked if I would present a television programme – one of my favourites – *One Man and His Dog*.

The invitation came out of the blue and created a problem. Over the years I have not been happy with the way the countryside and countryside interests have been shown on television – the BBC, ITV and assorted satellites are all guilty. What few programmes have appeared have usually been patronizing, critical and incomplete. Many have simply been urban journalists giving their warped views of the countryside, commenting on things they do not like and people they do not understand. Consequently country people, a minority in their own country, have been ignored, and on the few occasions when they have not been ignored, they have usually been misrepresented.

I thought; I consulted Bramble my dog, and accepted. If I liked the programme, why not take part in it? If I grumbled that real country people were ignored, why not take the opportunity of being a real country person in television's virtually only real country programme? The money was important too, not to make me rich, but every penny earned away from the farm means not cash in the bank, but a new sheep trailer or a load of fencing stakes: survival.

Consequently the arrival of *One Man and His Dog* meant that in a very real way I had gone to the dogs. The last eighteen months have been momentous ones in a number of ways. Not only did cameras arrive, but other events on the farm have contrived to change my life, and these I have recorded here. The changes have been sudden and unexpected: otters returned to the farm (an event that I did not expect to occur in my lifetime); a new charitable trust, The Countryside Restoration Trust, that I founded with friends, took off in an astonishing way. There were other incidents too, involving tears and laughter, happiness and concern. I continue to visit Africa whenever possible and even when I am in sunny Cambridgeshire I find it difficult to ignore the problems of that torn yet beautiful continent – so Africa has again intruded.

Some of the chapters have appeared in my fortnightly Farmer's Diary column in the *Daily Telegraph* and other articles have also been reproduced from *The Field*, *Country Living* and *Heritage* magazines. I would like to thank all these publications for permission to reproduce those pieces here. But a sizeable portion of the book is new, written especially for this volume.

Even more so this time I am grateful to my family and friends for helping me through. Two thousand letters for the Trust to attend to, articles to write, a brother to help, programmes to make, trees to plant, otters to protect, meetings to attend, cricket to play: all have meant that at times I have appeared to be travelling in ever decreasing circles, but my mother and father, sister Rachael, brother John, Ellen, Lena and Edwin have all helped to lighten the load and keep my sanity. Margaret must also be thanked for checking the manuscript and typing, while maintaining a happy smile. There is someone else too who deserves my gratitude: yes, Mr John Selwyn Gummer. This book covers his two new incarnations: his move from Agriculture to Environment, and his change from Church of England to Roman Catholic – his haloes become more numerous and brighter at every turn. We should be grateful to our politicians. They give us such a lot of amusement and material.

Finally I must thank Bramble. As you will read, without him I do not believe I would have gone to the dogs at all – he is much shrewder than he looks.

1

Cold Comfort Farm

It is a cold, white dawn, similar to the one that inspired W.H. Davies to write:

> Come, lovely Morning, rich in frost
> On iron, wood and glass;
> Show all your pains to silver-gild
> Each little blade of grass.

The ground is like rock and the iced grass crunches underfoot. My cheeks tingle and my breath matches the frost; I cannot understand why so many people dislike winter.

A fox trots by the field hedge, leaving small padded impressions of crystallized ice; the dogs are still asleep, so Reynard is unconcerned, making for shelter in the sandy earth. The wind is bitter, cutting and numbing, but it does not impair the perfect clarity of the orange shafts of light from the rising sun. The sunlight holds no warmth, but gives the field a shining arctic aspect. Puddles glisten and already the ice bears. Far off the cry of a lapwing is carried by the wind; it is a distant, plaintive call, one of the welcome sounds of winter.

Where a large hawthorn hedge gives shelter it seems warm. Brambles and long-dead, trailing hops help to hinder the wind, but they too are dusted white. The patterns on the bramble leaves are held like frozen snowflakes, some tinted with mauve where the leaves have died to the same colour as the juice of the long lost berries. A little owl flies in fast undulations to a hole in a willow, while a feathered flurry of long-tailed tits lands in the hedgerow top. The family party works its way along the swaying thorns finding food in apparent emptiness.

At a bend in the brook the water swirls coldly, reflecting only the depth of the season. Bent reeds form moving archways of crystal-clear ice and where the current slows, the water is freezing at the edges, slowly checking the flow. Two mallards fly, the sun catching the cascades of falling water and a lonely snipe spirals upwards. From a tangle of old nettles and fallen branches a wren sings, its song clear as the cold air as it joins the tumble of sound where spring water joins the brook.

A cock pheasant struts from the hedge, aglow with light, and a covey of nineteen partridges whirrs into low fast flight. It is strange that after a bad breeding summer, we should have the largest covey we have seen for several years.

Even with the sun higher it is still too weak to fight the ice in the wind. From a nearby village comes the sound of a horn where huntsmen and their hounds are working a wood. Three foxes run, but the scent is bad over the hard ground and they find easy sanctuary away. With red coats, black hats and steaming horses, the hunt makes a fine sight and it is odd that a growing number of eyes fail to see its beauty or its place in country life.

The sun will get no higher and its light is dazzling; incredibly there appear to be two suns; one a brilliant reflection of the other in the high-up wisps of cirrus ice. Suddenly the wind seems to fall and clouds appear. I hope for snow on frost and a scene similar to that described by Walter de la Mare:

> No breath of wind,
> No gleam of sun –
> Still the white snow
> Whirls softly down
> Twig and bough
> And blade and thorn
> All in an icy
> Quiet, forlorn.
> Whispering, rustling,
> Through the air,
> On sill and stone,
> Roof – everywhere . . .

I love the snow – soft and gentle, or whipped off the fields in deep ridges and drifts. But it is not to be, for as the wind dies, so the build-up of cloud melts away; the light fades and the cold intensifies. Already the cattle drinking trough has frozen over, locking again the flotillas of broken ice, and a long icicle hangs below a once dripping tap.

I decide to split logs of elm and willow, with the axe, as the

2

sun slides behind a long low hill, filling the south-western sky with colour. It helps me to remember the other verses of W.H. Davies's freezing poem:

> Come, rich and lovely Winter's Eve,
> That seldom handles gold;
> And spread your silver sunsets out,
> In glittering fold on fold.
>
> Come, after sunset; come, Oh come –
> You clear and frosty Night
> Dig up your fields of diamonds, till
> The heavens all dance in light!

2

Bleating about Life

I had to go to the Black Hole again the other day. I hate visiting London and do so as infrequently as possible. To me it really is a Black Hole – a bottomless pit containing everything that is wretched, into which everything that is good is eventually sucked if it is not careful. It consumes and devours, specializing in innocence, beauty and people. Those who have the misfortune to live in its urban darkness are dehumanized, and the most evident fruits of its negative forces are vandalism, mugging, pollution and the Houses of Parliament.

On my last visit, a month ago, I thought I had been mistaken. Stepping over drunks on Hungerford Bridge, which crosses the River Thames, I decided to walk along the South Bank. The sun was shining, the wind was blowing the smell of treated sewage away from me and London's river scene looked truly picturesque. It was given a final touch by a tug pulling a barge; it looked traditional, clean and wholesome. I was even prepared to change my views on London.

I need not have bothered. When the tug and barge drew level I saw that the barge was full of sewage waste which was going to be emptied in the Thames Estuary. My original view had been correct all the time. In spite of the current claims that the Thames is a clean river, any person unlucky enough to fall off London Bridge into the water would still need a stomach pump to get rid of the various evil bugs that make salmonella look quite friendly.

In an attempt to show that the Thames is cleaner than it was a few years ago, it is sometimes claimed that salmon now breed there. This is not strictly true. Salmon have been reintroduced into the river through releasing thousands of fry. Some have returned in order to breed and a few, a very few, have passed up river in the exceptional circumstances of a clean tide and current. For the most part, however, the water is simply too dirty and any self-respecting salmon wanting to move upstream would need goggles and a snorkel to navigate through London. One other piece of information should also be addressed to those who claim that the Thames is clean: the river's largest tributary is a twin sewage outlet near Tilbury. Isn't the modern world wonderful.

The London Underground never fails to amaze me. We complain about carting live animals around in cattle trucks, yet happily allow our own kind to be herded together on the Central Line. There is pushing, shoving, wheezing and sneezing. The London Underground must be the most efficient spreader of contagious diseases in the world. At one station graffiti was scrawled all over the wall: 'Do you know why there is never any staff at this station – they're all out mugging.'

From the horror of the Underground I went into Liberty's, that rather exclusive shop in Regent Street, to see how the other half lives. Unfortunately I found myself in a lift with an enormous,

middle-aged American tourist. I do not understand the American perception of beauty, for she was so heavily and hideously made-up that she looked like Coco-the-clown's mother.

She smiled at me alarmingly, and then looking around at the wooden panels on the sides of the lift she said: 'Gee, isn't this quaint – is this lift Tudor?' For the first time in my life I was speechless.

This is not the first time I have heard strange utterances from Americans. In the farmhouse we have some attractive horse brasses around the open fireplace. Again it was an American woman who said: 'Oh what a wonderful collection of bottle-openers.'

On a visit to Masailand in Kenya on one occasion I had the misfortune to be ensconced in a Land Cruiser with an American State Senator – again a woman. We were driving through wide, wild bush country, with a population of possibly two people per square mile. As we passed a small bore hole and drinking trough (for cattle), she asked: 'Is that the sewage pumping station?'

Even better was an American lady overheard at Windsor Castle. As a Jumbo jet flew low overhead, before landing at Heathrow, she enquired: 'Why did they build the castle so near the airport?' Not all American absurdities are spoken by women of course, hence

President Clinton demonstrated his great wit during his inaugural address, when he claimed that America was 'the oldest democracy in the world'. Who knows, on this basis he probably thinks that Christopher Columbus discovered Europe. I must visit America one day soon to discover what sort of society manages to produce such strange people. I hope America is ready for me.

Not all oddities are uttered by Americans. After giving a Swiss friend a traditional English farmhouse meal (pheasant of course), she bit into her After Eight. 'Is this toothpaste?' she asked in astonishment. If only cleaning our teeth could be such a pleasure.

Fortunately my day in London was made more enjoyable by a visit to Conservative Central Office. There, a grey, oleaginous Euro-clone gave me the news that I had been removed from the Tory Party's parliamentary candidates' list. Oh, what a surprise! The decision was not open to discussion or appeal. It is good to know that the Tory Party is keen for democracy to be adopted in Eastern Europe; perhaps it should also look into the possibilities for adopting democracy at Central Office.

My demise has caused no loss of sleep, as the modern, born-again, cash-flow Tory Party seems to have little in common with country people and country values any more. Indeed some leading Conservatives seem to forget that the Tory Party's original strength came from the Shires and it actually absorbed the Country Party, because of their common aims and objectives.

Most traditional rural Tories seem totally disillusioned; the Party appears to have been hijacked by an assorted grey gang of lawyers, accountants, bankers, bonkers and stockbrokers, not forgetting that army of smooth, dark-suited Central Office advisers and researchers. Roll on the day when Parliamentary candidates have to be over thirty-five (to try to ensure that they have done a proper job), resident in their constituencies for at least five years, and chosen by the people who vote for them – not simply exclusive paid-up party members. Actually believing in things might be helpful too; the present gang only seem to believe in what they think will get them elected next time – they are virtually all career politicians; the 'conviction' politician is as rare as snow on a summer day.

But, still, despite the present Tory party being agriculturally and environmentally illiterate, I shall not leave – I will simply not vote. The reign of the grey men can't last for ever.

Kind people who read *A Peasant's Diary* will be relieved to know that I am not going skiing this year, but I have been out in the Fens wearing my new knee braces as a safeguard. Although skating at Bury fen only lasted a day, the generosity of farmer Edward Dow, in flooding his field and allowing free access, was rewarded by his gate being taken off its hinges and his hedge being broken in two places. I suppose the open-access lobby will say that the fences and gates were provocative. Perhaps another year they will even demand warm ice – nothing surprises me any more.

I have come to the conclusion that I need a sheepdog. At the moment we have a unique way of rounding them up: if they fail to come to their usual bucket of food, Father stands by the pen while I act as dog. 'Faster', 'Stop them going over there', 'Watch the one at the back' and 'I told you they would do that' are a selection of his shouts and commands. Of course we already have three dogs. Often Bramble will lurch after the sheep (in the wrong direction) and so is confined to the car. Rinty the labrador retriever does not retrieve sheep, and shows no interest in doing so, and Husky, the ferocious Heinz 57, is not given the chance to get anywhere near the sheep, as he would only produce instantly minced mutton.

So I have to become temporary border collie. As I arrived by the pen wheezing and dripping with sweat after our last imitation of *One Man and His Dog*. I was exhausted. The sheep seemed amused. Their amusement was made still greater when I leant on a metal hurdle. I had not seen the wisp of wire connecting it to the electric fence. There was a blue flash; I left the ground and my wheezing stopped almost instantly. Last year it was my father's turn for red-hot voltage; this year it was mine.

A neighbour tells me that my father is not unique in his method of testing electric fences – simply grabbing it. His old father, of roughly the same vintage, actually spits on his hand, grabs the wire and plunges the index finger of his other hand into the ground as an earth. He apparently seems to enjoy the experience. Perhaps that is why so many farmers of my father's generation still seem so hale and hearty in their late seventies – regular electric shock treatment.

3

Pheasants and Peasants

Although the shooting season is over we are still eating pheasants at regular intervals, thanks to the modern miracle of the deep-freeze. For some reason this has been an excellent year for pheasants arriving in the Page pantry: some free, some picked up off the road, one scooped up from the M11 Motorway before a container lorry could flatten me, and several were purchased at the amazing value of two pounds a brace.

At such a price pheasant ceases to be the rich man's food of popular mythology; it becomes good, cheap and wholesome food, available to everyone, including peasants like me. It is a 'green' food too, genuinely 'free range'. The pheasants live free and contented lives and their end is quick and out in the open – unlike all those miserable hens carted long distances before their execution.

Needless to say, with such green, clean meat available, assorted animal liberation saboteurs are now disrupting shoots to protest about the 'brutality' of this almost natural harvest. Yet nobody protests about, or ambushes, those ugly, overcrowded lorries packed with poultry speeding down our motorways, carrying their cargoes to mass slaughter. It is further proof, if any were needed, that Britain is rapidly becoming one vast, urban-dominated madhouse.

In fact, pheasant is my favourite dinner, especially when presented with stuffing balls, sausages, bread sauce and white sauce; I am beginning to feel hungry as I write. Forget gammon, turkey, trout, soya roast, or delicious nut cutlet; pheasant is my choice and since it is much cheaper than beef I am amazed that it is not on every Sunday dinner table at least once during the winter.

I have to say too that preceding the pheasant there has to be 'light pudding'. I have praised light pudding before, and I will praise it again; in fact I regard myself as a light pudding missionary, trying to spread the habit of happy eating and encouraging the nation's salivary glands. Light pudding is the starter that we have whenever we eat game. The recipe was handed down to my mother from her mother and from her mother before her; when and where it started is lost in the historical mists of the family's gravy vapour, but it is never lost on my plate, and when presented with proper gravy it is almost a meal in itself. The giblets have to be used for the gravy of course. Amazingly, I understand that poultry is now sold giblet-free, no doubt as a result of some European directive produced by a bitter, twisted Euro-bureaucrat with a culinarily retarded wife.

For those who wish to become enlightened (and full) the recipe for between six and eight people is:

8 ozs (225 g) of self-raising flour
Salt to taste
1 teaspoonful of baking powder
3 oz (80 g) of cooking margarine
2 eggs
Milk

Add the salt to the flour, then rub in the margarine. Mix in the beaten eggs. Finally add milk. The consistency should be quite stiff, and certainly not runny. The mixture is baked in a greased 'Yorkshire pudding dish' in a very hot oven for twenty minutes, until it has risen and the top is crisp; alternatively it can be steamed for an hour and a half. Another advantage of this pudding is simple; the action of rubbing the margarine into the flour is a wonderful way of getting your hands clean.

All is not well for the peasant pheasant-eater, however. Old habits

die hard and I suppose that if pheasant becomes too popular then the Mr Gummer of the day will insist that a Ministry vet attend every shoot under European Directive 26/91EZ/794–EC413/1011/Brussels.

Another European directive ought to control my father, as he likes pheasants well hung – so do I, but not hung quite so long as he does. His favourites are just turning green, so that you can shake the feathers out, rather than pluck. I have eaten pheasants in this state with not an incidence of salmonella in sight. I prefer my pheasant plucked not shaken, and shot, not run over by a bus.

Shortly before the shooting season ended I bumped into the trumpet-playing/teaching/writing/shooting/talking/ pheasant-plucking/non-slimming/cigar-smoking John Humphreys. 'Would you like to come beating on our shoot?' he asked. Years ago I had foolishly been a beater in an area of overgrown gravel-pits belonging to another neighbour of mine, the artist Will Garfit. It had been like an army assault course and I vowed never to go beating again. 'I'd love to,' I replied, on automatic pilot.

Fortunately John Humphreys' fenland shoot is a lot easier than Garfit's gravel and I only became stuck in a bottomless bog twice. I suppose I had better explain what a 'beater' is. The beater is a caustic critic of landowners, shooters, the price of beer, the government and the weather, sometimes linking the last three in a sort of heinous conspiracy. The collective noun for a group of beaters is a 'whinge'. They are transported to a distant, bleak part of a farm or estate where they form a line across the land. They then advance, whacking clumps of shrub with their sticks as they direct the pheasants and partridges towards the line of 'guns'.

It was a cold, crisp day with the east wind blowing uninterrupted from the Ural mountains when I arrived for the great Humphreys shoot. The beaters and guns were all friends and if the evidence of my ears is correct, then the enthusiastic dogs had some most unusual and rather coarse names.

What opponents of shooting forget is that sport provides good habitat, not only for pheasants but also for a whole host of other wildlife, because of the cover, spinneys, rough headlands and wetlands left for game. On one drive a short-eared owl flew, with its attractive floating flight, and a gang of widgeon whistled overhead. My wildlife highlight was a small group of whooper swans flying by, their plumage far whiter than the clouds and their calls evocative of wilderness and wild places.

11

My shooting highlight came when a gun let fly at a simple bird with both barrels, and missed with ease. Instead of suffering in silence, beaters doubled up with laughter. 'Perhaps you should only shoot when they're perching,' came one raucous comment; such behaviour would never have been witnessed outside the Fens.

Then I saw a trick that I had not seen for years; an old beater with a large cock pheasant approached a young beater: 'You feel the weight of this boy, it's a beauty.' The young beater immediately took the bird: 'Gosh, it's heavy.' The old beater smiled and refused to take his burden back.

The day ended in the local pub where guns and beaters ate, drank and were merry. It is an old traditional pub, where pheasants are sometimes passed around for a 'guess the weight of the pheasant' jackpot. One day someone even picked up a dead rat from the road; it became a 'guess the weight of the rat' competition.

At the end of a good day and evening one of my fellow beaters came up to me looking serious. 'I think I should tell you Robin, John Humphreys has to go into hospital soon for a serious operation,' he said gloomily. I braced myself for the worst. 'He needs surgery to try to get his hip flask out of his pocket.'

4

Slaughtering the Slaughtermen

I sometimes wonder whether the Prime Minister and his Secretary of State for Agriculture actually live on the same planet as me. John Major talks about subsidiarity and how Britain must be kept free from the bureaucratic flood cascading through Europe from Brussels. The sacred John Selwyn Gummer is more specific: on a visit to our farm in the autumn he said: 'Robin, if you have a problem with petty officialdom – as a last resort, let me know.'

Before Christmas I let Mr Gummer know of the pressure being put on a small slaughterman/butcher in the Prime Minister's constituency of Huntingdon. A farmer friend of Tom Chamberlain had contacted me as he could not get beyond the petty officialdom surrounding the Prime Minister's constituency office. I faxed Mr Gummer informing him of the problem, as the great man had suggested. At the time of writing, well into January, I have not even had an acknowledgement. Since then, Tom Chamberlain of Farcet has gone out of business.

It is true that Tom Chamberlain could have continued trading, as the 1 January deadline for compliance with the Fresh Meat Directive has been put back until 18 April; but he had had enough, and despite the extension he would still have had to pay increased veterinary inspection charges, raised from £14,000 to over £55,000. Perhaps increases like these are required to fund the ever-rocketing expenses of MPs over the last twelve months?

Chamberlain's the Butcher's was a small family business, just too large to benefit from Mr Gummer's derogation for very small slaughterhouses. Not only did it give an excellent service to customers (Tom won 'Sausage Maker of the Year' at the 1992 East of England Show), but it also gave a good service to local farmers. Much of the beef came from extensively grazed cattle

14

from the nearby Nene Washes. Consequently the cattle pleased both environmentalists and the animal welfare lobby, with the animals having to travel between only five and ten miles from field to food basket. Sadly, environmental and animal welfare considerations do not appear to feature in the calculations of the local MAFF officials.

Some of the demands made to Tom Chamberlain seem to have gone beyond both the absurd European directive, and commonsense. The slaughterhouse is about twenty yards away from the butcher's shop, across a small courtyard. He was told that he could no longer carry the meat through the yard, a journey that could be completed on a zimmer frame in ten seconds – he would have to build a refrigerated tunnel. There were many more similar edicts of idiocy; Tom Chamberlain understandably threw in the towel.

Nearby, in Peterborough, the Brown brothers have had similar problems – from the same MAFF official. They run an excellent butcher's shop and, as their meat is traditional and of the highest quality, the recession has missed them completely. Their slaughter-house seems to be almost a model to me, again taking mostly local animals. Yet once more they have had lists of ludicrous alterations dished out to them and have experienced official pressure that seems close to harassment. Fortunately they are small enough to benefit from the two-year derogation and are going to struggle on, in spite of the increased charges; but what will happen after two years?

Of course, these problems are not just restricted to Cambridge-shire. Over the country as a whole hundreds of thriving businesses have been closed down because of the new rules, despite the fact that most vets and environmental health officers believe them to be 'overkill' and 'over the top'. In 1972 there were 1,972 slaughterhouses in the country as a whole. In 1982 the number had fallen to 1,062. At the end of 1992 there were just 510 and with the fall of Tom Chamberlain that number is already out of date.

This situation is made even more intolerable by the fact that only Britain is implementing the absurd Fresh Meat Directive with any sort of determination. In Greece, lambs are still being killed at the roadside, while the French are continuing, as always, as if the regulations do not exist. Indeed, while MAFF officials here are seeing that every wooden handle, wooden worktop and wooden block are removed from British slaughterhouses and butcher's shops, the French are now arguing that wood is more hygienic than the metals and plastics favoured by Gummer's Euro-MAFFIA.

Before Christmas, in answer to a Parliamentary question, Mr Gummer said: 'The Single Market hygiene legislation is not intended to destroy traditional small businesses, which play an important part in the rural economy. My Department has taken a number of steps to ensure that this Directive can be implemented sensibly and without imposing unnecessary burdens.' To the hundreds of successful companies hounded out of business in the last few years these words have a particularly hollow ring. Consequently I have a simple message to Messrs Major, Gummer and the other British Euro-clones intent on destroying British rural industries and farms – subsidiarity should start at home.

5

Seldom Glummer

The big news is that John Gummer has now replied to my letters complaining of the fate of assorted butchers and slaughterers. My problem is that a host of other people have also sent me letters, complaining of John Gummer. Alas! he does not seem to be a very popular man. How I will reply to them all I simply do not know, as my secretary has just decamped to Germany for a year.

I will respond to Mr Gummer's letter however, and now seems as good a time as any. Sadly he does not yet seem to realize the seriousness of the situation – as our traditional butchers, with their hand-raised pies, home-cured ham and traditional sausages, go out of business; so MAFF fiddles as our European competitors are filled with disbelief at our Ministry-inspired commercial suicide.

Mr Gummer's letter is as expected: 'I cannot continue to defend a situation where meat to be exported to France and Germany must be produced to higher standards than meat which is consumed here.' The fact that the French, Italians, Greeks and Spaniards simply ignore many of the same European standards seems to be beyond him.

Correspondents tell me of French outdoor markets they have visited during the summer where meat was piled on to wooden tables, slabs of beef were balanced on fences and where sausages were hanging from trees – without a public health official, vet or Euro-clone in sight. If only our officials and ministers would spend less time in banqueting-halls and conference centres, when in Europe, and more time out and about and seeing what is actually going on, they would then discover that Europe is a two-tier Europe, made up of those countries that keep the rules, and those countries that quite openly break them. Sadly we are one of the countries who keep the rules – however absurd and inappropriate they appear to be.

It is always sad when jokes turn into reality. Hence this little tribute to the EC was funny at first: 'The Germans make the rules; the British keep the rules; the French bend the rules; the Italians ignore the rules, and the Greeks, Spaniards and Portuguese don't know that any rules exist at all.' The humour has long since died, as the jingle now appears to be a statement of fact.

In his letter, dear John Gummer makes other astonishing claims. In his opinion vets now have to be at slaughterhouses to spot 'salmonellosis, listeriosis and leptospirosis'. When I told my vet this he collapsed with laughter: 'Have these ministry vets got X-ray or infra-red eyes then?' he asked. 'You need blood tests and bacteriological tests to determine these.' An assortment of vets, environmental health inspectors and farmers all agreed – all this is nonsense. To be fair, one vet, out of half a dozen, considered that a vet might spot extreme conditions of these ailments in cull cows and casualties – a tiny number of cattle passing through slaughterhouses.

Mr Gummer then excels himself. He claims that vets will spot 'animals which may contain harmful drug residues'. Without exception all the vets I have consulted claim that this is absolute nonsense. Drug residues can only be spotted in blood tests. So my advice to Mr Gummer is simple: please sack your advisers who are writing such silly letters for you and causing so much damage to the farming and meat industries. The other alternative of course is that Mr Gummer could try to get work for which he appears to be more obviously suited – a monk, a valet, or a petrol pump attendant.

As usual, though, I suspect that the real reason for the presence of vets at slaughterhouses has nothing to do with listeriosis or drug residues. I believe that it is all to do with the Ministry's hidden agenda – BSE – Mad Cow Disease. The Ministry is haunted by the fear of BSE-infected cattle arriving on the butcher's slab, leading then to BSE-infected people. But many believe that BSE only arrived in the national cattle herd entirely because of MAFF incompetence anyway; offal from diseased sheep was allowed to be processed and fed to cattle. Herbivores were being turned into carnivores; it was obviously wrong, unnatural, irresponsible and stupid; yet the Ministry allowed it and many think that BSE resulted. Now, to cover their ineptitude, those same Ministry officials are insisting on vets at slaughterhouses to look out for conditions that cannot be seen with the naked eye, apart from BSE. BSE is a Ministry problem; therefore, if vets are required, the Ministry should pay; at the moment these huge and unjustified veterinary charges have been foisted on others.

Double standards can be seen elsewhere too. Mr Gummer

insists that all EC standards should be met in Britain. Yet last year, Compassion in World Farming filmed horrific scenes at Spanish slaughterhouses, showing that EC rules on hygiene and animal welfare were being almost totally ignored. Now, because of the Single Market, Britain is sending sheep to these same slaughterhouses – why? Britain keeps the rules; Spain breaks them. Britain has standards for killing sheep; Spain has different ones: yet Mr Gummer now allows British sheep to be exported to Spain. What hypocrisy.

The Single Market will also have other horrific effects. Before, all livestock leaving the country was inspected at our ports of exit. Over 28,000 animals were found to be unfit to travel. Now, under the new rules, inspections no longer take place, as barriers are down. This year 28,000 injured and sick animals will be suffering and dying, unchecked and uncared for as they are bundled towards the great EC supermarket. Conversely it also means that a large number of sick, dead and dying animals will be shipped, unseen, into Britain. These are very strange days we are living through: deception and self-delusion seem to have become parts of daily life.

By the time this book was put together, this obvious development had already taken place. There were numerous reports of lorries arriving in various parts of Britain containing dead and dying animals. In addition, a variety of diseases that had been eradicated, or had never even been in Britain, were soon imported, causing distress, suffering and disbelief. The politicians however insisted that there were no problems, the rules were good etc. etc. etc. Oh for the day when we can import a new batch of politicians, preferably people who are honest, open and have a sense of vision. It would help too if they entered politics out of conviction, not as a career opportunity.

It would also help if we could export the present bunch, as a job lot, under the same Single Market rules that we export sheep. I doubt, however, whether there would be a buyer.

6

Seed-time and Set-aside

Still the changes in farming seem to multiply: changes that could affect the whole appearance of the countryside. Whether these changes will be long-term or short-term is anybody's guess; even the politicians seem baffled as they lurch from one short-term stop-gap policy to the next.

At the moment, as people are starving in Somalia and the Sudan, the aim is to reduce food production in Europe. The chosen method is set-aside; formerly there was voluntary set-aside; now with the agreed reform of the Common Agricultural Policy (CAP Reform), it is to be compulsory set-aside. Fifteen per cent of all European arable land is to go out of production in an effort to reduce both the surpluses themselves, and the cost of producing them.

For countries such as Britain, not self-sufficient in several basic temperate foodstuffs, such limits to production are an absurdity, but the European super-state has decided. For farmers the set-aside is almost an affront: for years they have been urged to produce more, to adopt new methods, use more fertilizers and sprays, and become more 'efficient'. Some, as they see fifteen per cent of their arable fields turn to 'weeds', will find it hard.

It is thought that some farmers will become even more intensive on their remaining eighty-five per cent of cultivated land, meaning that production is affected hardly at all – we shall see.

Many people have assumed that set-aside will mean an extra fifteen per cent of land for wildlife. Sadly they are wrong, for the idiotic rules that govern most of the non-productive land mean that the fallow land has to be mown or cultivated (bare fallow), just as the skylarks and lapwings are nesting – it will be carnage. It is yet another example of urban politicians and bureaucrats making rules for the countryside, about which they apparently know almost nothing. They see 'agricultural policy' purely as a means of limiting or encouraging production. They seem unable to realize that wildlife and landscape are inseparable from agriculture and should be included in their policies.

Fortunately we have been able to put our set-aside into an experimental environmental scheme: the Countryside Stewardship Scheme, which allows us to take several options sympathetic to wildlife. Sadly this scheme is restricted to a small minority of farmers with special features on their land. Our special feature is our brook.

Over the last three years we have had a form of voluntary set-aside on the farm. One of the birds to have benefited is the 'grey', 'common', or 'English' partridge. Technically it is the grey partridge, although we have always called it by its everyday colloquial name of 'English', to distinguish it more dramatically from its imported, inferior cousin, the 'French', or 'red-legged' partridge. This is not a racist comment: the French partridge really does lack the charm and individuality of the English; sportsmen do not like it either as it often prefers running to flying.

It was intensive farming that almost finished the English partridge. The plough, sprays and disturbance killed its food and destroyed its nesting sites. The Game Conservancy was the organization that helped to save it, discovering that the chicks of the English Partridge need to eat plenty of insects during their early days in order to survive. On the over-intensive prairie lands of East Anglia, formerly the stronghold of the English Partridge, its food was simply sprayed away and the partridge became at risk.

The Game Conservancy persuaded interested farmers to cease spraying the edges of their fields to allow a supply of insects and seeds to survive for the wild birds, and the decline was halted just in time. Our English partridges came back to the farm with set-aside. Now we see them regularly: in summer, skulking cautiously with their chicks, and later in the autumn, in coveys flying at speed over the stubble. It is such a relief to have them back; they are part of an English rural picture that at one time seemed to have been erased for ever.

There are numerous environmentally friendly alternatives to set-aside that could have been used to reduce cereal production. The most obvious method involved nitrogen quotas. Such a method would simply have limited the amount of nitrogen farmers could have used on their crops. This would not only have reduced production, but also the cost of production. Its other advantage would have been that it would have kept the farmers and their employees working on the land, instead of turning some of them on to the dole queues and the rest into wardens for fifteen per cent of non-production.

Another way to have reduced production would have been to encourage spring-sown crops. Such fields of wheat, barley and oats nearly always yield less than those sown in the autumn. Sowing in the spring has other advantages too. Less nitrogen is required and the system benefits wildlife. Autumn and winter stubble provides seeds and shelter for numerous small birds, as well as pheasants and partridges. It also gives the soil a rest through the winter and seems to be more in tune with the natural rhythms of nature.

On many farms these days the ploughman is hard at work the minute harvest is over, turning farm fields into a factory for conveyor-belt cereal production. Spring sowing would slow the process down; it would reduce production as the politicians want and winter would again separate seed-time from harvest; a degree of harmony between farming and nature would, could and should be restored.

7

The Solway Saga

There is a romantic ring about the name of the Solway Firth, and deservedly so, for it is one of Britain's most important estuaries for wildlife, being bettered only by Morecambe Bay and the Wash. Consequently it has drawn naturalists and wildfowlers from all over Britain for many years. Now, the government too has recognized its richness and has designated the Upper Solway Flats and Marshes as a Special Protection Area (SPA), under the EC directive on the Conservation of Wild Birds, and as a Wetland of International Importance under the Ramsar Convention.

In theory this means that virtually 80,000 acres of salt marsh and mudflat receive extra protection. The main reason for the special safeguards is the large number of wintering wildfowl, commonly reaching over 120,000. Often there are more than 43,000 swans, geese and ducks, and 79,000 waders, giving sights and sounds as memorable as anywhere in Europe.

The wintering migrants include the entire population of Spitsbergen barnacle geese, now approaching 13,000 birds. Their story, at a gloomy time for conservation, is one of success. In the late 1940s there were as few as 300 birds, but with the creation of a National Nature Reserve in 1957 at Caerlaverock, on the Scottish side of the Solway, plus, in 1970, a nearby reserve run by the Wildfowl and Wetlands Trust, numbers have been restored. How and why numbers fell in the first place are matters of conjecture. During the early part of the century, with marshes, crofts and mainly small farms providing ideal wintering conditions, there were about 6,000 barnacles. Wildfowling was a traditional pastime around the estuary, harvesting the natural surplus of many types of duck and goose, but it is thought that the sport had little effect on overall barnacle numbers.

However, during the Second World War, there were horrific stories of army personnel shooting at geese; including one incident when barnacle geese were said to have been machine-gunned on their roost. In addition to deliberate acts of hooliganism, there were also tank ranges on the feeding grounds around Caerlaverock, and so the traditional flocks of the Solway experienced difficult times.

The crash in numbers was aggravated by a change in wildfowling availability. With the growing popularity of the motor-car, wild-fowlers arrived on the Solway from far and wide. Once there, they could also keep their mobility and move with the geese, particularly on the Scottish side with its tradition of open access. Because of all the pressures, in 1954, barnacle geese were made a protected species throughout Britain. In 1955 they received similar protection in Spitsbergen as well. Since then improvements have continued, although because of current breeding densities in Spitsbergen, it is thought that numbers could now be at their upward peak.

Although the barnacle goose is undoubtedly one of Solway's great winter attractions (the bulk of the birds are resident between September and early May), there are many more. There are nearly 15,000 pink-footed geese (14 per cent of the Icelandic population), 250 whooper swans (4 per cent of the British wintering population), 1,400 pintail (6 per cent British), 2,300 scaup (57 per cent), 33,850 oystercatchers (12 per cent), 15,300 knot (7 per cent), 4,800 bar-tailed godwits (8 per cent), 6,700 curlew (7 per cent) and 2,100 redshank (3 per cent). In addition there are significant numbers of shelduck, teal, shoveller, goldeneye, golden plover, grey plover, sanderling, dunlin and turnstone.

During the summer the importance of the Solway continues, as a breeding area for lapwing, redshank, oystercatcher, mallard, skylark and meadow pipit, with smaller numbers of dunlin, ring plover, teal, pintail, shoveller, red-breasted merganser and a smattering of both common and arctic terns.

This is not the end of the area's wildlife, for around the edges are farms and woods where barn owls still fly; the otter is common; red squirrels can be seen and the famous salmon rivers of the Eden and the Esk flow, finishing their journeys at the eastern end of the Firth.

In February I paid my first visit to the Solway and it was well worth the trek. I saw huge flocks of dunlin and bar-tailed godwits, flying with their rapid, flowing symmetry; there were oystercatchers, and a large raft of goldeneye where the Eden meets the sea.

Every morning and evening, and midday too, there were geese. Huge flocks; small skeins; wide Vs and straggling family parties, all calling conversationally. The barnacles almost barked as the pink feet whiffled; geese always seem to have so much information to exchange.

At Caerlaverock, in bright sun, a large skein of barnacles came in high, with some tumbling downwards, twisting left and right as they fell, in sheer enjoyment. They reminded me of rooks at play on a hot summer's day. Others glided in slowly; so slowly that it seemed as if they would stall and fall. But they landed so lightly and delicately that they hardly had to bend a knee.

The ever-changing light and wide lowland skies provided more beauty. Bright shafts of sunlight shone into sea mist, picking out oystercatchers in pools of filtered light. One evening too, there were low ridges of wind-whipped cloud, tinted with pink as calling geese flew towards the sun. A pigeon died and feathers flew in that same wind, as a peregrine plucked its prey. In just a short time the Solway gave me experiences that I shall never forget.

But although the Solway Firth is an area of great beauty and attraction there have been problems. Wildfowling has been one of them. So far the area has escaped the worst excesses of Italian and German shooters, brought over to Scotland for shooting holidays – it is impossible to call them 'sporting' holidays. Elsewhere there are depressing stories of foreign shooters leaving dead and dying birds where they fall; of roosting birds being shot and of protected birds being fired at in broad daylight. My most dreadful story, from a reliable source, involved a party of Italians up early for geese. At first light a large flock of starlings foolishly flew overhead. Mayhem broke out; it was like the Somme, with starlings dropping out of the sky as fast as their illegal (in Britain) five-shot repeater shotguns could blast them. Quite unsurprisingly no goose was seen, but the Italians were not disappointed, claiming they had enjoyed one of their best shoots ever.

There is a fear that sooner or later these groups will be brought to the Solway by unscrupulous tour leaders, and their fast-firing guests will not be welcome. The problem stems from Scotland's access laws, which allow anybody with a gun licence to shoot quite freely on the Scottish foreshore (unlike in the rest of Britain), and the ease with which visitors to Britain can get 'visitors' shot-gun permits'. For years the Solway has had its own endemic wildfowling problems and it does not want them added to.

Solway's problem is that its wildfowling is so good that over the years its free shooting has attracted irresponsible wildfowlers who could not tell a donkey from a dachshund, yet alone a barnacle goose from a greylag. Most of the hooligans have come from the north and north-east of England and they have managed to tarnish the reputation of wildfowling.

Last year three barnacle geese were shot while roosting on the Rockcliffe Marshes, on the English side, by men boating in from the Scottish side, whose shooting limit ought to have been plastic fairground ducks. Last season too, two whooper swans were shot, allegedly by a South African and an Italian living in Britain. Research by the Wildfowl and Wetlands Trust has shown that up to seventeen per cent of whooper swans on its reserve are carrying lead shot; twenty-one per cent of the barnacles have the same problem.

Again last season a Yorkshireman was seen to fire at a shelduck. His excuse was novel: 'What you call shelduck and barnacle geese, we call greylags and Canada geese where I come from, and we can shoot them.' Another group of northerners wounded a pink-footed goose and were trying to make it fly once more so that they could shoot it again, before wildfowling wardens arrived on the scene to intervene. Needless to say the Solway gets tin-can shooters too; those pathetic people who see no geese or ducks at all, protected or unprotected, and so they throw tin-cans into the air and shoot at them instead. Such behaviour anywhere is unacceptable; in somewhere such as the Solway, now an SPA, it seems even worse.

Fortunately the Scottish Solway Wildfowlers' Association, the RSPB, the Wildfowl and Wetlands Trust and the Dumfries and Galloway Constabulary have joined together in trying to stamp out the problem. The foreshore will be patrolled and monitored in an attempt to identify culprits, and offenders will be prosecuted. Already it has had a beneficial effect. John Doherty of the WWT says: 'This partnership is united in its determination to stamp out illegal and irresponsible wildfowling.'

Grahame Young, a policeman, and secretary of the Scottish Solway Wildfowlers, agrees. He was born and bred next to the Solway: 'Wildfowling is traditional here and shooting for nothing along the foreshore is our birthright.' But he is not impressed by what has happened. 'Thirty and forty years ago there were few people here. Now people travel miles to come – it is the Mecca of wildfowling. But they must be taught identification and distances. We will help and advise them, we don't want mistakes made, for then all wildfowlers get tarred by the same brush.' He is not complimentary about the hooligan element, usually from England: 'We must make it quite clear: they are not cowboys, they are irresponsible wildfowlers.' He is right; there is an air of romance about being a cowboy; there is nothing romantic about being a yobbo, shooting and wounding swans, as well as other protected species.

Although barnacle geese numbers are now high, Grahame Young does not want them put back on the quarry list, even for responsible, traditional fowlers: 'They are part of the Solway and they are all right as they are.'

It is right for the Scots to defend their years of free access and shooting. But surely the time has come when Scottish law should not apply to English or foreign daytrippers – particularly in an SPA. All visiting wildfowlers should be members of bona fide wildfowling clubs, affiliated to the British Association for Shooting and Conservation, and like the members of the Scottish Solway Wildfowlers, each should be required to carry a membership card, complete with photograph.

The SPA of the Solway has other problems apart from irresponsible wildfowling. Although the Solway has been declared an SPA, the designation was given before a management plan had been drawn up for the estuary. Such a management plan is a long way off, mainly because of government policy itself. Despite claiming a desire to reduce the number of quangos, the government in fact split the one quango of the Nature Conservancy Council into four separate quangos: English Nature, Welsh Nature, Scottish Natural Heritage and a co-ordinating committee to try to link the three. It did this contrary to all conservation advice and against commonsense as well. Consequently the Solway is now split between English Nature and Scottish Natural Heritage, with both having different priorities and following their own policies.

The absurdity of the dividing line is best shown by the humble cockle. In 1988 the Dutch cockle-fishing industry collapsed because of over-fishing. As a result, commercial cockling boats arrived on the Solway almost immediately, hoovering the cockles from the bottom, and operating so close to the shore that the goose roosts in the Caerlaverock National Nature Reserve were disturbed. By 1991 this unregulated cockling had reduced the cockle population of the Solway by eighty per cent, putting its 33,000 oystercatchers at risk.

After consultation with Scottish Natural Heritage and the local cocklemen, the Scottish Office banned the boat fishing on the Scottish side. On the English side it is still continuing, regardless of the wishes of English Nature, because of the cumbersome bureaucratic process south of the border. Despite the urgency, a ban might be implemented by May or June, if the oystercatchers and local cocklemen are lucky.

English Nature itself has caused problems on the Solway through over-fishing – over-fishing by cormorants. When approached for a grant towards the cost of building cormorant nesting-ledges on an old gunnery range target, for the benefit of a few bird-ringers, English Nature gave permission and paid up. By so doing it failed

27

to take into consideration the other interests of the Solway and has added to English Nature's growing reputation for staggering ineptitude. The cormorant is neither a common breeder on the Solway, nor endangered, but now thanks to English Nature it has become a pest. It is increasing at the staggering rate of eighteen per cent a year and has taken to feeding on the rivers Eden and Esk, both once famous for their salmon, trout, sea trout and grayling. As salmon stocks have fallen, those worried for the long-term future of the rivers running into the Solway now have the added problem of cormorants. One owner on the upper Eden has a bankside tree near his house which regularly contains twenty-six perching and wing-drying birds. If it is assumed that each adult cormorant requires three pounds of fish a day, then stocks of young salmon and trout are taking a real hammering. Scottish Natural Heritage takes the realistic view on its side of the Solway, and issues licences for the control of troublesome cormorants along its salmon rivers. The 'experts' of English Nature have so far refused requests to control its artificially created population explosion.

Black-headed gulls in the area have had a different experience: a population crash. Two years ago 1,000 pairs failed to rear their young: a situation that was repeated last year, with almost complete failure. The behaviour of the birds was very similar to a large black-headed colony that dispersed at Ravenglass, further south along the Cumbrian coast several years ago. The Ravenglass colony was close to the Sellafield nuclear site. The Solway birds are close to the Chapelcross nuclear power station on the Scottish side of the Firth. Unfortunately the incidents raise questions to which no convincing answers are available.

In view of the Solway's new status it is astonishing to report that there are plans for a new nuclear plant at Chapelcross and a

£30 million feasibility study is currently underway. Already permission has been granted to dig holes and pits in the Solway for the study. If the power station goes ahead it will mean a marine off-loading terminal being constructed in the SPA; a shipping channel being dredged out, and then discharges of warm cooling water into the Solway itself. Some of the coolant will contain 'tritium', a substance about which there is very little known, particularly concerning its effects on wildlife.

There are thinking environmentalists who are not against the principle of short-term nuclear energy, to tide us over until more acceptable forms of energy are developed. But a new nuclear plant at Chapelcross, and the changes it could bring about to the Solway, would make a nonsense of the whole principle of SPAs.

Whatever happens to the Solway, the geese depend for their survival on the landowners around the edges. They need salt marsh ('merse' on the Scottish side), and short grazed grass where they can feed. But even the farmers on the Scottish and English sides are treated differently. On the English side, those farmers who encourage salt marsh, and farm in the traditional way, with a few cereals, plus sheep and cattle, can get financial help under the Countryside Commission's Stewardship Scheme. Ninety per cent of the English farmers benefit in this way and it can be seen as compensation for allowing geese on to their land. The RSPB has a reserve on the English side, at Camp Field Marshes, and qualifies for Stewardship money. A near neighbour is satisfied, and is happy with the geese, usually pink-footed. 'The only grumble I've got is about walkers who wander about at all seasons of the year regardless of farm animals or wildlife – they are a bigger pest than the geese.' This was confirmed through my binoculars. On seeing a large flock of waders in flight I looked for the cause of the disturbance; there, a long way out into the marsh were two walkers throwing a Frisbee to one another. How very strange; I wonder if they were members of the Ramblers' Association?

On the Scottish side, where goose numbers are greater, the farmers get no help whatsoever. Jack Graham runs a 180-acre farm; he has forty acres of cereals, the rest is grass and merse. He has a herd of sixty cows, but they depend on the same grass as the geese. Consequently he is a pragmatist: 'I like seeing the geese, but preferably in someone else's field.' Often he has as many as 2,000 barnacles on one field. 'Since their numbers have increased I can no longer winter any sheep. At one time I let my cows out in the beginning of April, now they stay in until the middle. They make my silage late; they make the spring barley late; I have to reseed more often and then when they come back in September it means I run out of grazing earlier. They are costing me between £5,000 and £10,000 a year.'

It does seem unfair that Scottish farmers should have to suffer this burden, particularly when their English neighbours over the estuary get Stewardship payments. It is made even more unfair when it is remembered that farmers on the island of Islay get compensation for barnacle goose damage; the only difference being that the Islay barnacles come from Greenland, not Spitsbergen.

There are yet more oddities too. At the moment pylons are being replaced on the eastern edge of the SPA. Surely it is time for electric cables to be put underground in special places. The National Grid argues that such action is too costly and inefficient, and that the technology is not available. It is strange how the cost, efficiency and technology are all just right to bring electricity from France to England, via the bed of the English Channel.

The threat of a tidal barrage also hangs over the Solway. At present silence reigns on the subject, but regardless of the Solway's wildlife and status, it seems certain that sooner or later the scheme will be resurrected. So, the Solway Firth is a beautiful area at the heart of a bureaucratic and conservation shambles. When I heard the then Secretary of State for the Environment, Mr Michael Howard, announce last year that the Solway had been made an SPA, at a meeting in London hosted by the RSPB, I asked him if being an SPA would give the Solway any greater protection than the 300 Sites of Special Scientific Interest damaged in the last two years. Mr Howard answered by simply saying 'Yes'. From my brief visit to the north the accuracy of Mr Howard's answer already seems in doubt. As for the initials SPA, in the case of the Solway surely they should stand for Shambolic Pantomime Area?

8

Epitaph to the Elm

Whichever way I look out of my cottage windows, I feel a twinge of sadness. I face the sunrise from my study and every cloudless morning the sun streams in. From early spring until late autumn I can have the front door open, so that as I work Bramble dozes in a slowly moving pool of warmth, in the hall, while birdsong filters through the whole house.

In front of the window there are tangles of forsythia and wild roses, silver birches and a farmer's fine ash hedge, behind which is a large field set below a wide lowland sky. It is the great sweep of sky that brings sadness, for until comparatively recently it outlined a spinney of high-standing elms. Now all that remains are a few bare trunks among low hawthorn trees and the occasional ash.

The view from my living room looks into the sunset and is dominated by a half-grown dead elm at the bottom of my garden that I will not cut down. As time passes I seem to miss the living elms even more. The loss was made worse a few days ago when I visited my old friend Gordon Beningfield, the painter, at his Hertfordshire cottage. I enjoy his company. He mixes his rare talent with humour, and his home nestles into an old landscape, complete with country characters.

The village policeman, just retired, rides to hounds, and as I gossiped with Gordon the local baker called. He had not stopped simply to sell bread, but to exchange views and pass on local news. He still bakes his bread in a large brick oven and sometimes uses a horse and cart in preference to the normal delivery van. As the baker left, he managed to sell me a loaf that I did not really want, and placed it next to Gordon's most recent book; it was open at a familiar, yet distant scene: a meadow with a boundary of towering elms.

31

Gordon left school at fifteen, burdened by dyslexia. However, his gift of creation through art is of far more lasting value than a formal education. I was grateful to him for refreshing my memory, for Gordon Beningfield does today with paint and brush what John Clare achieved in the last century with words. They have seen the same things, heard the same sounds, and experienced the same vision.

It is strange that in much country art the elm dominates the landscape, yet in most country writing it is taken for granted. It is mentioned in passing, but rarely described, as if familiarity made description unnecessary. Fortunately John Clare was an exception:

> Hugh Elm thy rifted trunk all notched and scarred
> Like to a warriors destiny – I love
> To stretch me often on shadowed sward
> And hear the sighs of summer leaves above
> Or on thy buttressed roots to sit and lean
> In carless attitude and there reflect . . .

William Barnes also loved the elm:

> Green elm, whose shade, in open light,
> Steals o'er the mead from morn till night,
> As I have known it reach at rest
> O'er rimy grass-blades to the west,
> Or under low-gone suns to lie
> Outlength'ning to the easternsky;
> O let thy shelt'ring shroud, dear tree,
> Yet shed its airy gloom on me . . .

I remember the elm with great affection; in the harvest field on hot days with the smell of corn being cut; the clatter of the binders; the creak of horse and harness; the feel of stubble on bare legs and then tea in the cool shade of the field-edge elms – sitting on sheaves and eating sandwiches to the droning of flies.

It was high up in a hedgerow elm that I saw my first young kestrels – white balls of fluffy down in a hole where an old branch had broken. It was in another elm hole, eight feet from the ground that I found my first wild fox cubs. One, Cassius, I kept as a pet, and the other two the vixen quickly moved to a less conspicuous home. It was elms too that attracted the rooks, and the great spinney rookery has dispersed around the village with the loss of their favourite tree. Even on a cold winter's day, high up among the old nests, rooks would be adjusting a stick here, and rearranging a twig there.

32

Writing about the elm is not just an act of nostalgia, for it is also an expression of anger. It was official incompetence and bureaucratic wrangling that allowed Dutch Elm Disease into the country, and allowed it to take hold. While a government department, local officials and councillors argued over who would pay for its eradication, the disease spread and changed the face of Britain.

With the passing of time many of those concerned with the wrangle will have retired on pensions, with some, no doubt, awarded OBEs for services rendered. They are strange rewards for the destruction of our traditional landscape. It is ironic, too, that the elm should die, for once its wood was used for making coffins.

9

Badger in the Hedge

Further Euro-nonsense continues to flow into my post-box and into my shopping-bag. A reader has spotted more non-Single Market trading in a French market. He saw a French farmer ladling milk from a churn into the assorted plastic containers of his customers, without a single Euro Public Health Inspector in sight.

Last week I bought some Roquefort cheese from my local supermarket. In my view, real Roquefort is virtually the only edible French farm produce available. When I opened the packet the smell was disgusting – goat. Roquefort is supposed to be made from sheep's milk. If that particular cheese had not contained goat's milk, then my name is John Gummer.

I once patted a billy goat's head without thinking. The revolting odour clung to me for weeks. I washed, scrubbed and even plunged my hand into other evil-smelling substances, but it still stayed with me. The only time I would knowingly pat a billy goat today would be if I was due to meet certain members of the present Cabinet, or M. Jacques Delors.

We have just experienced our usual and enjoyable first sign of spring – Badger arrived for hedging and I bought a new chainsaw to celebrate the occasion. I was not sorry to see the back of the old model as it had earlier given me my luckiest farming escape. I was pollarding willows with my father when the chainsaw stalled. I was halfway up a tree, with one foot on a small dead branch. As I pulled the starter, the branch broke, sending me earthwards at great speed, still holding the chainsaw locked on full throttle.

Not wanting to slice myself in two, I threw the chainsaw to one side, but in the process I did not notice the whereabouts of the rapidly approaching ground, and crash-landed with a thud. As I was lying on the ground groaning, with three or four broken ribs, my father, with great consideration went over to check the chainsaw. He inspected it carefully and switched it off. 'That's all right then,' he said with relief. He then walked over to me and asked: 'What did you do that for?' I groaned back and promised myself never to leave the ground with a chainsaw again. That night it took me forty minutes to get from the kneeling position to the lying position in bed – surely almost a record.

A friend did much better on one occasion he performed the old trick of cutting through the branch he was standing on – breaking both ankles. Before he was back at work he was playing football – in goal – for his village second team, standing with the aid of two sticks. Quite unsurprisingly he now walks with a pronounced limp.

The day of Badger's arrival dawned. I don't know what it is about Badger, but after several warm days, with the sap rising and the birds singing, as soon as he appeared on the horizon the wind veered to the north and it felt as if it had been caressing ice. I am sure that if ever Badger visits the Equator, it will snow.

The change in the temperature soon sorted out the fair weather hedge-layers. My nephew phoned to say that he had conveniently contracted a chest infection. My brother John decided that the date clashed with a long-standing meal invitation: I have to confess that from his general shape, malnutrition has never struck me as one of

his problems, and he certainly does not usually require an invitation before he eats. His sin was made worse by the fact that he was eating out with another potential hedge-layer. It is amazing how the promise of one meal can keep people away from a cold hedge for a whole day. What strange priorities.

That left just me and Badger. The wind was so cold that it affected my brain. All day long I kept calling him Bramble. My dog was not amused.

First of all we had to check the pond for frogs; this year Badger appeared before they did. Then my father appeared to check that we were hedge-laying properly; all he saw was me trying to start my new chainsaw. That's right: it wouldn't start, much to their amusement. Finally it burst into life, causing a cloud of smoke so large that all three of us disappeared for half a minute. By this time we were ready for dinner at The Hoops.

We went there to warm up on turkey curry that is so hot that it could also be used as a central-heating device. Earlier in the week John Paley, the artist, had tried it. He started with enthusiasm. After two mouthfuls he began to cough; then his handkerchief came out to blow his nose; finally his glasses came off because his eyes were streaming tears. 'I don't know why I ordered this,' he spluttered, 'but at least it's reminded me why I don't like curry.' After making me so fat in his cartoons – it served him right.

After his hot fill, Badger attacked the hedge with gusto. He must be the best hedge-layer since the Great Hurricane of 1987. Observing this spectacle with admiration, my father only had one comment: 'I wonder when a European directive will insist that we have a vet present for hedge-laying – in case Badger cuts his legs off.'

10

Colours of the Countryside

The predominate colours of a traditional English spring are subtle blends and fusions of delicate greens and yellows beneath an ever-changing sky. They are soothing and easy on the eye and they paint beautiful landscapes on memory. Then comes added scent or sound, the smell of flowers, or the working of bees; we remember them – meadows and cornfields, hedgerows and meandering streams – the gentleness of colour.

It is with colour in poetry that A.E. Housman created an image of spring:

> When green buds hang in the elm like dust
> And sprinkle the lime like rain,
> Forth I wander, forth I must,
> And drink of life again.
> Forth I must by hedgerow bowers
> To look at leaves uncurled,
> And stand in fields where cuckoo-flowers
> Are lying about the world.

His words stir memories, as I can still visualize the springtime haze of green in the old elm spinney that time, and Dutch Elm Disease cannot erase.

The writing of H.E. Bates also produced for me a forgotten landscape when he blended smell with colour: 'Only cowslips have the charm of scent so sweet that it can be tasted, so that a real cowslip-field such as you see often in the flat lands of Huntingdonshire, deep and thick with heavy flowers of almost orange-gold, is still by far the sweetest of the English fields, a joyful and glorious thing, part of the sun.'

It is over twenty-five years since I saw such a field and that too was in the old Huntingdonshire. A small cottage stood at the entrance of an ancient meadow, surrounded by elm, thorn and bramble. Inside the grass was moving in wind-blown waves of yellow and a smiling old country-woman stood at the gate carrying a wicker basket overflowing with flower-heads to make into wine. Then cowslip wine could be drunk with a clear conscience as a basketful made no visible difference to the sweet golden field. Alas, most of those old Huntingdonshire fields have been sprayed away. The field where I met the smiling lady in the heart of the country is now a housing estate, as Huntingdon spreads its bricks and mortar, and there is a high-speed dual carriageway where once the field gate stood.

There have been other colours too, created by wild flowers and changing farming fashions. Saffron fields of buttercups with grazing cattle, and meadows glowing with red clover and pink sainfoin – busy with bees and yielding sweet-scented honey. Yellow again with banks of early primroses, and red where poppies stand above the fields of growing corn; all are tapestries of colour, warm and peaceful, interwoven with birdsong.

Until recently bright colours were the exception rather than the rule, with only the occasional field of linseed, mustard or wild charlock, mellowed by the traditional patterns of the land surrounding them. But gradually the subtleties of colour have disappeared; removed by change. Gone are the cowslips and the clover meadow; they have been replaced by the uniform green of winter wheat, broken only by the brilliant yellow blocks of gaudy oilseed rape.

I find the new patchwork quite attractive – anything to break up the endless acres of mono-green. But I am almost alone, for bee-keepers complain that rape honey is too 'sugary'; hay-fever sufferers claim that its heavy scent gives them headaches, and the general complaint is that the colour is too loud.

Gordon Beningfield dislikes the new yellow fields and they have no part in his landscapes: 'It is alien, it has no place in the English country scene. A vast expanse of colour is not to my taste and the crop has to be sprayed so many times. The English countryside is about the subtlety of colour – a bluebell wood, primroses or even a field of ragwort – not a tract of oilseed rape.'

To some, however, the new farming fashion has not been fully understood. 'They grow a lot mustard now boy,' an old rustic from the next village said as he leant on his garden gate. 'There's a lot more about than in my time.'

'It's not mustard,' I replied, 'it's rape – there's rape all over the place.'

Alas, his hearing is not what it used to be: 'I know boy,' he said, 'we never see a policeman about these days – they should lock them all up.'

Some blame the new acres of oilseed rape for the slugs that now infest arable land, claiming that it allows them to over-winter with plenty of food. We grow no rape, yet we are infested too; indeed without an application of slug bait when the wheat is sown we would get no crop. Sadly it means more poison on the land. My father, after fifty-five years on the land, has one answer. 'When I started, we could only plough an acre a day and the rooks, seagulls, jackdaws and starlings would keep up with us. Now you cover the ground so fast the birds can't keep up and the slugs survive.' He could be right.

I often wonder how the children of today will remember their countryside in forty years' time. Will they write with nostalgia? 'I long for the fields of winter wheat, without a hedge in sight; and the blazing blocks of oilseed rape, where the sprayers fight the blight.' And how will they greet the end of winter? 'The sun is shining on a warm day and I have just seen my first slug of the spring.' What have we done?

11

The Seat of the Matter

I have a serious confession to make: I still have one great ambition to achieve. I would like to ride in a point-to-point race. The only problem is that I have no horse; even when I hire one, I can hardly stay on board, and if I did take part in a race the National Health Service would have to clear a hospital bed in anticipation. Any worm busily minding its own business at the first ditch would also be in for a shock; a nose entering the ground at great speed can be extremely frightening to both worm and man.

I find the whole atmosphere of point-to-points attractive, with country people, in country clothes, doing country things. At the same time, town bookmakers in town clothes also find the atmosphere attractive as they quite legally take large amounts of money from all those nice country people. I stopped choosing horses by form, appearance and fanciful names years ago; I now treat each hard-earned pound as a major investment and back the jockey. Sadly even this system has started to lead me to lose. I think that this year my backing will have to become more sophisticated and scientific; I will back the horse with the prettiest stable-girl. This method has quite a lot of appeal, for it means that if I win, I will also have the satisfaction of knowing that I will have offended all feminists, as well as the politically correct.

The most exciting thing to me about a point-to-point is the first fence. I become tense just watching and my heart misses a beat; it stirs something somewhere as hooves pound, mud flies and bodies fall – there are echoes of a cavalry charge or hounds in full cry; it is elemental with excitement, fear and foreboding. So it is that first jump that lures and challenges; riders trying to take a clear line – the approach, lift-off – what next? Triumph, disaster or even death? I think that many of us still yearn for a whiff of danger and excitement in our increasingly homogenized, safe, easy lives. We want, or at least I want, something that demands an element of courage with a degree of risk. Point-to-pointing provides that challenge in abundance.

Realistically however, I think the adrenaline surge of a fourteen-abreast charge to the first fence will escape me. Anno Domini beckons and when matched with my appalling riding technique it means that I am rapidly running out of time.

I still remember my first ride; I was lifted up on to one of the farm's last two carthorses by my father, when I was a small child, just after the Second World War. It seemed a long way up, and it still does. From the wide swaying back of the carthorse my riding advanced, and descended, to the back of Neddy the donkey. That was a great improvement and much nearer the ground. The only trouble with the donkey was the fact that whenever I wanted to ride, he wanted to stop; whenever I wanted to stop, he would fly off at a very fast, uncontrollable trot; it was like riding over cobblestones on solid tyres.

My next venture into the saddle was many years later. I had started writing for my living and I wanted to study the ethics of country sports, including riding to hounds. So, a local village lass attempted to teach me to ride properly. The first lesson was simple:

how to catch your horse. She would walk into the field with a bucket; the horse would gallop up to her. The second lesson was simple too: how to chase your horse, followed by how to swear at your horse, and then how to hit it with a bucket from twenty yards. Every time I entered the field at one end, the horse would flee to the other. It was something of a humiliation for a sexist bigot like me to have to crawl to the phone, sweating and wheezing, to say: 'Linda can you come and catch the horse please?' She would then appear, with the same bucket, and the horse would gallop over to her like a long lost friend. Why? – that is what I want to know – why would the stupid horse not come to me? Dogs and cats love me.

Once the basics had almost been mastered, i.e., I could hang on, wearing my old donkey jacket, my mother's stretch gardening trousers and cheap plastic boots, I was ready to hunt. My first hunt was with the Cambridgeshire Harriers on a small hired horse-verging-on-pony. The beast was so small that my feet were almost dragging on the ground. I immediately learnt the most important lesson in horsemanship; never ride downwind to a big horse, when you are behind on a small horse. My nose was almost the same height off the ground, or so it seemed, as the enormous posterior of the horse in front. At every stride, for what seemed like thirty strides, the disgusting animal released wind; not silently, surreptitiously or even with dignity, but loudly, never-endingly and at gale-force intensity. There was not an inhibition in sight. The farts were long, loud and disgusting; I gasped for oxygen, which meant that I took down still more of the evil odour. That horse alone must have been responsible for its own huge holes in the ozone layer. Indeed I believe that one horse passed almost as much wind as any two vegetarian members of the League Against Cruel Sports after curried beans. If only all that burnable energy could have been caught – I caught it full in the face, but I mean collected and used for fuel.

My next triumph was a day out with the Fernie Hunt, still in my donkey jacket and my mother's gardening trousers. It was there, in the heart of hunting country, that I experienced my first five jumps at high speed; my score was one fall and three involuntary dismounts. My bent and broken little finger still bears witness to my first double somersault while wearing a donkey jacket and riding boots.

Out with the Cambridge University Drag Hounds, as a visitor, I even nearly managed to jump some point-to-point jumps – nearly. The problem was that at full gallop the horse would suddenly swerve skilfully away to miss every jump, just like a rugby back performing a side-step, flat out. We weaved in and out of a whole line of jumps and with every sudden swerve a delicate part of my anatomy was crushed on the pommel of the saddle. If there is a next time, perhaps I should wear my cricket box, plus a pair of my mother's tights, to go with the gardening trousers. So now my riding career has only one more step to take – a point-to-point.

Soon I shall be with my friends, freezing at one of the local point-to-points. As they try to impress me, showing how easy it is to lose money, even with the help of collective wisdom, I will be gazing at the first jump, secretly saying: 'I want to jump that; I can jump that?' Meanwhile a still, small voice will also be saying: 'Is your Will up to date and have you taken out private health care?'

12

Voles and Holes

On the farm we are attempting to create a 'traditional', wildflower-rich hay meadow in five years. Considering the real thing, in nature (with a little help from early man, the pastoralist), took hundreds, if not thousands of years to develop, it is an interesting and challenging proposition. So far the experiment is working well, with flowers doing better than the old traditional meadow grasses.

This year we have cheated by planting yet another flower – at least the bulbs of another flower. Now we have to wait to see if any flowers of the rare and unusual snake's head fritillary actually show themselves.

Last year I also tried planting a dozen bulbs in the wettest, lowest corner of the meadow, as the flower is usually found in water meadows. Sadly, only one came up. From the neatly excavated little holes that appeared where each bulb had been planted, I assume that the rest were stolen and eaten by voles. If only barn owls would return to fly their nightly vole patrols.

Just as the single survivor was bursting into its snake's head flower, a large foot trod on it, snapping the stem, and so there were no survivors. There was nothing malicious in the destruction; a local man often walks his dogs in the meadow; sadly he was looking at his dogs instead of where to put his feet. Never mind, the flowers are notoriously difficult to grow and so we must hope for better luck this year.

The flowers themselves are beautiful but odd. At one time their local names always seemed to be associated with doom, gloom, death and destruction, hence 'bloody warrior', 'dead men's bells', 'death bell', 'weeping widow', 'widow wail', 'doleful bells of sorrow' and even 'drooping bell of Sodom'.

Yet despite these depressing names the snake's head fritillary is an attractive flower and gives early colour and spring beauty to a few privileged damp meadows. There, the flower does not appear in ones or twos, but in thousands; I sometimes visit one such meadow in Suffolk, Framsden Meadow, that can honestly be described as a floral wonder of the world.

Gerard the herbalist described the flowers with much pleasure: 'Of the faculties of these pleasant flowers there is nothing set downe in the ancient or later writers, but (they) are greatly esteemed for the beautifieng of our gardens, and the bosomes of the beautifull.' In this one sentence Gerard identifies two problems associated with these flowers. The first is the mystery of their origin. There is no record of them growing wild until 1736 and because of their proximity to cities such as London and Oxford some think that they were introduced from Europe, both as garden and wild plants. Those who believe the snake's head fritillary to be a genuinely wild, native plant respond to this by claiming that, where the flower appears, its numbers are so great that it must have been growing since the time when water meadows first evolved.

The beauty identified by Gerard can be another problem, for since people became mobile with the arrival of the motor-car, it has meant that some day-trippers travel long distances to see flowering spring meadows. In the past this sometimes resulted in people returning home with armfuls of flowers and bucketsful of bulbs.

One of the most interesting areas for the flower is in the village of Oaksey in Wiltshire, where it has the name of 'Oaksey Lily'. Elspeth Huxley, the writer, lives in Oaksey and she recalls that once there were six water meadows full of fritillaries, by the local brook, usually flowering the third weekend in April. Alas, during the Second World War five of the fields were ploughed to produce food and now only one flower-filled meadow remains.

Spring meadows invariably turn my thoughts to the onset of cricket. Cricket is one of the sights, sounds and scents of rural England. I say sounds, as the ring of well-struck ball on willow bat, the polite applause of the onlookers, the shouted appeals of the fielders, and swallows twittering overhead are all part of a warm cricketing afternoon. Scent too is important, for cricket also means the smell of linseed oil as I rub it into my beloved bat before the season starts, and then there is the aroma of newly mown grass.

For the spectator it is a marvellous sport. You can watch, sleep, or simply sit in the sun sipping beer; just being there is restful and relaxing, for cricket has an attraction that goes beyond sport; it is part of the very fabric of rural summer life.

Sadly some schools no longer play the game; an omission that denies the pupils both enjoyment and part of their heritage. I shall be playing again this year however; laughing when two fielders collide under the same high ball, and eating tomato sandwiches for tea. I hope to do better than last year; then I started playing again too early after damaging my knees skiing – in the first hour of my skiing holiday. I started playing again with my knees so heavily strapped that I could hardly run. It meant that I was run-out three games running, including a first ball. And how did my team mates show their sympathy? By falling about hysterically of course – that is how sport should be played.

13

Lapwing Lament

I suppose that one of the most difficult questions to answer in the English countryside is when does spring start? When the first flowers appear? When the birds begin to sing? When the leaves of the trees burst from their buds? When Badger arrives for hedge-laying? Or when farmers again start working their land?

The arrival of flowers is not always a good guide, as winter heliotrope, with a beautiful but unusual scent of cherry blended with almond, appears, as its name suggests, in the middle of winter. Aconites, coltsfoot and daffodils are other flowering guides used by many; but often they too become covered with snow as a brief foretaste of spring is plunged back into deep mid-winter.

Similarly birdsong can be very misleading, with robins, thrushes, skylarks and hedge sparrows often in melodious combat long before the feel of ice is out of the air. Even the appearance of the leaves can be deceptive, as I have seen the fresh green of new hawthorn burnt to sudden autumn brown after late frost has replaced early spring. Even the activities of farmers can be no true guide, as in a late year, when cold and wet make landwork difficult, spring sowing can overflow into early summer.

Sadly, one of my favourite signs of spring has disappeared from my parish. In winter we get huge flocks of lapwings settling on both grassland and cultivated fields. They are beautiful birds, with the name 'lapwing' describing perfectly their erratic, flopping flight. Their other common names are also apt; 'peewit' – the onomatopoeic name that matches the bird's attractive two-note call – and 'green plover', because of the plumage, which in sunlight shines with a rich, silken green sheen.

The winter flocks are now almost all northern birds which have moved south away from their summer breeding grounds of moorland and meadow. Not only does the countryman like seeing the lapwing for its own sake, but in darkness the sharp warning cries will often betray the movements of a hunting fox. They are placid, gentle birds: a real part of our winter landscape. At one time I would have called them a permanent part of our winter landscape, but changes and calamities can occur so quickly these days that it is becoming dangerous to take anything for granted.

It was after the large flocks had again moved north, or had split up into pairs to breed locally, that it was once safe to say that spring had arrived. The tumbling display flight and matching, bubbling call of courtship proclaimed that a new season had begun. Grassland and arable fields were the favoured areas for nesting, when spring-sown crops were common. Many times I remember my father spotting their well-camouflaged eggs as he was ploughing or rolling and pushing a stick into the ground nearby to ensure the nest's survival. With early summer the fluffy, mobile chicks were a common sight, as were the hysterical calls of the anxious parents, sometimes feigning injury to lead intruders away.

Lapwings are still breeding reasonably well in northern Britain, but I have not heard their bubbling call or seen their aerobatic display flight over our farm fields in the spring for over ten years. Unfortunately this absence and decline is not a figment of my tired imagination, for according to the Royal Society for the Protection of Birds and the British Trust for Ornithology, lapwing numbers have declined by forty-seven per cent over the last twenty years. The reasons are many: more chemicals are being used on the land; there is more winter corn sown, meaning that by the spring the crops are too long for suitable nesting sites; grassland has disappeared from large areas of southern Britain as land once used for cattle has made way for the plough, and there are fewer gamekeepers. Gamekeepers helping wildlife? The answer is simple: gamekeepers control many of the predators that eat ground-nesting birds. They control them to save the pheasant and the partridge in lowland Britain, and the red grouse in areas of highland and moorland. An offshoot of this is that the lapwing also benefits in keepered areas, because of the smaller number of predators. So, as fewer gamekeepers are now employed in the countryside, there are more predators, and lapwings have suffered as a direct result.

With set-aside there is some hope that the lapwing could return, as more uncultivated land and grassland again break up the rolling acres of winter wheat and rape. On our small farm we are doing our bit; we have plenty of suitable grass and we still grow spring barley. I live in hope that one sunny day I will again stand and watch with pleasure that spectacular tumbling flight. The display call and flight of that lapwing – they to me are the real signs of spring.

The other day I passed a pub called The Peewit. Well, to be honest I failed to pass it – I screeched to a halt and went inside. I was not disappointed as the food and company were both good. Pubs remain a pleasure peculiar to Britain. People travel miles to visit the Royal Oak at the neighbouring village of Barrington, the other side of our only hill. Although the food is excellent, most make the journey to ogle at the make-up of the landlady. It is an astonishing sight, giving her the nickname of 'the painted lady' – also the name of a colourful butterfly. In the unlikely event that she ever fell on hard times she could have a readymade career as a painter and decorator.

According to a friend, at another nearby pub, The Fox, it was not the landlord who was the great attraction, but the landlord's pig. It had been trained to 'sit' and shake hands – sorry trotters – like a dog.

In the same pub, a regular was known to be a restorer of 'old paintings'. One day the landlord greeted him with 'I've got some work for you in the shed'. The restorer was puzzled; on looking into the shed there was not a picture in sight, just a pile of old tins. On his return to the warmth of the saloon bar he said: 'I couldn't see any paintings, just tin-cans.'

'Oh,' replied the disappointed publican, 'I thought you were an old paint-tin restorer.'

14

Wings and White Water

After a quadruple gin and tonic and on with my Sea Bands, I was off to Zimbabwe. I wish I could get over my fear of flying, as each new flight turns the start of what should be an adventure into unremitting terror. I suppose my neurosis has not been helped by one stop in Nairobi where assorted mechanics dismantled an engine, in full view of the departure lounge, and then appeared to have no idea how to put it back together again.

Air Zimbabwe did its stuff without a hitch however: leaving on time and arriving on time, and serving lashings of Zimbabwean wine in between. I first visited Zimbabwe and Harare when it was still Rhodesia and Salisbury. Then, the local wine was absolutely disgusting, only marginally worse than Kenyan wine, which in my humble view is fit only for washing the car.

Zimbabwean wine is now greatly improved: not yet up to South African standards, but almost there. Consequently I could not understand the white Zimbabweans trooping round their local supermarkets buying South African wine at thrice the price of the home produce. I suppose it is similar to the wine snobbery in England which prevents people from buying some of the excellent English wines that are now available.

Zimbabwe's main wine-growing area is an hour and a half from Harare: the Mukuru Winery lies at the end of a dirt road in maize and tobacco country. The industry was started at the peak of the Rhodesian war to overcome sanctions, and it has flourished ever since. The locals certainly must have developed a thirst to risk landmines and things which went bang unexpectedly. When I visited in 1976 and 1979, my main priority was to keep my head down and call all men with guns 'Sir'.

After the images of drought in the media it was good to see

Zimbabwe looking as green as an English spring. Throughout my stay and wherever I went, rain followed; unlike the absurd British weathermen, the Zimbabwean weather forecasters appreciate the links between rainfall, crops and food, and so viewers and listeners are spared the 'and now for the bad news – rain is approaching at the weekend'. Everybody seemed pleased with the rain and a cloudburst in Bulawayo was met with glee.

It was also good to hear criticism that water restrictions had been lifted too early – unlike in Britain, when a hosepipe ban is treated as a major infringement of human rights by some residents of plastic suburbia. Perhaps we need a food shortage, caused by drought here, to teach people the importance of water.

On one farm the cattle looked sleek and fat. The maize was bulging in the cobs and the farmer was optimistic. 'Last year was a disaster; this year we have a good crop; with a little more rain we will have a bumper crop.' Part of Zimbabwe's problem was caused by the government selling off its surplus grain of two years ago and then being confronted by a drought. Before anybody says 'typical Third World behaviour' – Britain is now virtually out of wheat, which means that if we have a bad harvest, then set-aside will make certain politicians look extremely foolish here too.

The Zimbabweans have an excellent sense of humour. During the drought Kariba produced little electricity, and bad management led to breakdowns at the coal-fired power stations. Consequently one joke currently circulating asks: 'What did Zimbabwe have before matches and candles?' Answer – electricity.

Another poses the question: 'What do you call Robert Mugabe and Nelson Mandela having a shower together?' – guerrillas in the mist.

One of the reasons for visiting Zimbabwe was to go to the Zambezi valley, one of the last real wilderness areas in Africa, and now under threat. One threat comes from British overseas aid. The Zambezi has remained wilderness, partly because the tsetse fly has kept people and cattle away. Now, with British aid and work by Bristol University, the tsetse is being eradicated and people and their cattle are moving in. Yet cattle are the last beasts needed in that fragile landscape. Absurdly too, although British farmers are faced with beef quotas, we import Zimbabwean beef. Certainly we should help the Developing World, but not at the expense of British farmers, and certainly not by encouraging them to ruin their last wild places.

Another reason for visiting Zimbabwe was to go white-water rafting down the Batoka Gorge, just below the Victoria Falls. The Falls were even more spectacular than usual, with an immense

51

volume of water thundering over, and I was looking forward to excitement and some giant adrenaline surges. Sadly I arrived in Zimbabwe at a bad time for the Victoria Falls, as the government had just announced an agreement in principle for a new dam which would block off the Batoka Gorge by about the year 2003, for yet another hydro-electricity scheme. So anyone wanting to white-water raft probably has only ten years left. I arrived at the Falls at a bad time too; because of the high water and a recent fatal accident, the season for rafting had just ended; I had missed it by a whisker. Oh dear, that means that I have got to visit Zimbabwe again soon – what an imposition.

Having some time to spare, through having no raft, I walked over the Victoria Falls bridge into Zambia. There the Falls are seen from a different, but still spectacular perspective. So too is the Elephant Hills Hotel. From the Zimbabwean side the hotel appears unobtrusive, blending in well with its surroundings. Sadly the architects, or somebody, only considered half the story, for from the Zambian side it is an intrusive eyesore – like a piece of architectural leprosy. Why, in such an important and beautiful area did the 'experts' only appear to consider the construction from one side? I suppose it was because they were 'experts'; the world population of this strange, arrogant breed is definitely too high.

Walking along the edge of the unfenced path, looking into the awesome cauldron of thundering, foaming water, with the spray falling in torrents like a tropical storm, increased my wonder, not only of the Victoria Falls, but also of those early explorers, and David Livingstone in particular, who 'discovered' the spectacle so far from home.

At the end of a path overlooking the chasm, where the roar and the mist created fear and apprehension were a solitary pair of shoes and a scarf. Inside a shoe was a note – telling somebody the letter was their 'surprise'. It was a suicide note: an African woman had apparently plunged to her death just a few moments before. She had been crossed in love.

It was a strange sensation: I felt immense sorrow for that troubled soul. I could not imagine the depths of despair that could drive somebody coolly to take off their shoes and jump into that. A shiver went up and down my spine; I retreated – I had to move on to Malawi.

15

Cementing Democracy

Malawi was green and lush. It is one of my favourite countries of Africa; it is beautiful, the people are friendly and ordinary things seem to work. Of course an African country that actually works is unacceptable to some sections of the politically pure, and so the West now appears to be trying to make it unstable by withdrawing aid. Apparently Malawi's sin is that it is not 'democratic'. Aid workers are furious; one typical response from an English agricultural adviser was: 'What are Britain and America trying to do? Start a civil war?'

The ex-pat anger has been made worse by the fact that the chief lecturer in democracy has been the former Mrs Lynda Chalker (now Baroness Wallasey). The baroness wants Malawi to have 'one man one vote' and several political parties, with the winner being the one which obtains most votes. It should be remembered that at the last general election Mrs Chalker lost her seat, she did not get the most votes, but she kept her job and went to the House of Lords. The Malawians find this a very strange example of democracy – so do I.

Malawi suffered badly during the drought and had to import food to avoid starvation, making the West's decision to withdraw much aid even stranger. Since my last trip to Malawi in 1985 the population has increased by an estimated fifty per cent; in a small country there are now 9 million people, plus a million refugees from Mozambique.

In 1986 the average land holding in Malawi was not quite 1.4 acres. By the year 2004 it will be down to little more than half an acre. Because of poverty, agriculture is Malawi's main industry; often no fertilizer is used, and because of the growing population, land cannot be left fallow to recover, as it once was. The soil's

53

fertility is declining and as more hillside land comes into cultivation, soil erosion is increasing at an alarming rate. Some believe that, as a consequence, food production will not be sustainable beyond another twenty years. This makes the attitude of the West even more cynical, ignorant and short-sighted. I may be a poverty-striken English peasant whose very livelihood is threatened by the antics of those who are supposed to govern us, but I felt disgustingly rich compared to these real warm-hearted peasants. They need our help, but help linked to a definite nationwide family planning programme – perhaps we should pay for television to be beamed into Malawi.

Lake Malawi is breathtakingly beautiful: it is 365 miles long and 52 miles wide in places. The thought of David Livingstone exploring this malaria-infested land is beyond my comprehension – his achievements will certainly be remembered far longer than those of Baroness Wallasey.

But despite its beauty there are problems at the lake too. Over-fishing has taken place on such a scale that some of the canoe-borne fishermen have even tied mosquito nets to their fishing nets to ensure nothing escapes. Again, hunger will be the only long-term consequence. But in Britain there is over-fishing too. However, Chris Huxley, a technical adviser to the Southern African Development Community, points out the big difference between the over-fishing in Britain and Malawi: 'In Britain we do it through greed and avarice – they do it because they are bloody hungry.'

Astonishingly, the World Bank has added to Malawi's problems. By funding Malawi's mainstream fishing industry, the trawler fleet has increased from two to seventeen trawlers. Now the World Bank is funding a 3-million dollar research programme to study 'over-fishing'. I wonder if the World Bank is advised by MAFF.

I wish MAFF and assorted Environmental Health Officers would visit Malawian butcher's shops; it might make them have twinges of conscience about the ones they have closed down here. At the butchery counter in a Lillongwe supermarket the assistant periodically sprayed the meat with 'Doom' – a most efficient fly-spray. I decided to buy eggs instead.

The drive to the Lake was impressive for reasons beyond the scenery. For many miles the main road is also the border, dividing Malawi from Mozambique. Thanks to the civil war, Mozambique was deserted, apart from the occasional burnt-out house. On the Malawian side there were hundreds of recently built mud huts, full of refugees from across the way. Along that stretch of road there were numerous Africans holding up items for sale: new kettles, paraffin lamps, plates, cooking oil, maize and much more. They were selling off their aid, sometimes still in the bag or box of the donor country. Indeed most of the refugees looked more affluent than the local Malawians. Other things were also for sale, so I was told, although not on open display. It was possible to pick up an AK 47, in good working order for about seven pounds. Having no desire to become involved in any African adventure involving lead flying through the air at great speed, I passed the opportunity by.

The Malawian newspapers are the source of much entertainment and amusement, with headlines such as 'Man Discharged after fierce fight with Monkey', and articles of great educational value, 'Tobacco – A Cure for Every Disease'. One news item quickly caught my eye: 'Former Australian Chancellor on Trial – Former Australian Chancellor, Fred Sinowatz went on trial in Vienna on Wednesday . . .' The mysteries of Malawi become even more complex with stories such as: 'Teacher Killed by Lightning – Party Leader Warns People – After the mysterious death of a teacher by lightning, it is clear from the mysterious circumstances under which the teacher died that whoever was responsible for the lightning, believed to be man-made, intended to disrupt the normal function of the school.' Use of language also gives much food for thought; under 'In Memorium' and the name of a local African I read: 'It is a year since your tragic death. Shall we ever forget? Missed by all niggers.'

There are some interesting names too. For years I have mourned the disappearance from Britain of those wonderful children's books written by Helen Bannerman. They were charming – beautifully illustrated, simply written and loved by most children. They were about coloured children – pure, innocent and entertaining. Then the racism industry got hold of them: they became 'racist', politically

correct shops refused to stock them and they disappeared. As a child, my favourites were *Little Black Sambo* and *Little Black Quibba*. On the farm my second favourite ewe, a black one, is called Quibba – I wonder when I will be reported to the Race Relations Board.

In fact the stories could be quite accurately based. There were many Scottish missionaries in Malawi, and the African names could have become familiar to many of those attending the kirk in Scotland. Even today in Malawi the Minister of Forestry and Natural Resources is Dr Eston Sambo. I suppose if ever he visits Britain his passport will be confiscated and he will be renamed Smith.

Some of Malawi's members of Parliament have wonderful names too – Miss Lonely Mlumbe, Mrs Margaret Perpetual Maimba, Mr Bazaar Nyirenda and Mr Mathew Smoke Chakamba Chilenge. My favourite is definitely Mr Smith Genesis Cement Pengapenga. Cement is an inspiring name. If ever I take the daunting step of wedlock and consider adding to world over-population, I think Silage would make a particularly charming name. To be more environmentally friendly, perhaps Hay-Bale would be better; Reuben Edward Hay-Bale Page has a wonderful rustic ring to it.

In one aspect of farming life Malawi can actually teach us something. Every year the Life President, His Excellency, Ngwazi Dr H. Kamuzu Banda, goes on a 'crop inspection' and meets farmers on their own plots. If only British Ministers of Agriculture would do the same so that farmers could communicate with them about the state of their crops and show them the huge piles of red tape under which their farms are rapidly disappearing.

An inspection by John Major would be even better. Recently a farmer in the Prime Minister's constituency, whose fields are being regularly flooded because of road works, tried to obtain an interview with his MP. 'The Prime Minister no longer sees his constituents,' he was curtly told. Well, what another splendid example of democracy at work. Dr Banda certainly has a lot to learn.

16

Home James

The worst thing about leaving the farm is coming back to a huge pile of newspapers and letters. I always keep the newspapers flowing during my absence, so that I can catch up with all the world's idiocies on my return. The first copy of the *Daily Telegraph* I opened was heartening: there inside was my old friend John Selwyn Gummer telling Parliament how he was fighting EC red tape and bureaucracy.

My joy lasted approximately five minutes, when I discovered that nearly all my letters were varieties of red tape and examples of bureaucracy, all from Mr Gummer's own department. Now Mr Gummer is a good Christian man, or at least so the Pope is soon to be told; I have come to the conclusion therefore that this shining light of British agriculture must speak in 'tongues' and that his words have meanings that we mere mortals simply do not understand.

In my pile of Ministry mail were forms for 'passports' for cattle, issued on 1 April – though apparently not part of an April Fool's joke. Then came a seventy-nine page book, with accompanying forms of many colours; this was the Integrated Administration Control System(IACS). Even solicitors and accountants are refusing to sign these complex Eurospeak documents for their clients, in case they get them wrong. Mr Gummer evidently thinks they are simple; if you speak in 'tongues', then the word 'simple' must mean 'extremely difficult and complex and designed to keep you away from your farm work for at least three days'.

Another interesting aspect of the IACS tome is that although it took MAFF seventy-nine pages to explain the rules, using a strange counting system which features fifteen more than once, it took the French just eight pages to explain, or to ignore, the same rules.

Our hedges are looking beautiful at the moment. The hawthorn is weighed down with 'may' and the wild crab apples are covered with blossom. I mention our hedges as they are such prominent features of the landscape and so important for local wildlife. Yet if we wanted to bulldoze them up we could – we could wreck them tomorrow, as they have absolutely no protection.

Because of this, Peter Ainsworth, Tory MP for Surrey East, recently tried to get his Private Member's Bill on Hedgerow Protection accepted by Parliament. It was modest in its aims and about twenty-five years too late. Yet the Bill was 'talked out' by the manoeuvres of a seemingly eco-unconscious group of Conservative MPs. Some of them did not actually talk against the Bill; they spoke for so long in the preceding debate, that there was no time for Hedgerows. Apparently the subject that caught their imaginations concerned osteopathy. One unflattering observer wondered if their

sudden interest meant that they required massage or manipulation for their brains.

The opponents form a motley crew of agri-farming apologists. Geofrey Clifton-Brown who, although he represents Cirencester, actually farms in East Anglia; Michael Joplin, a former Minister of Agriculture, whose hedgerow-unfriendly views are totally unsurprising; Quentin Davies, MP for Stamford and Spalding, a constituency that could do with more hedgerows, and Sir Nicholas Bonsor. Rather alarmingly Sir Nicholas is Chairman of the British Field Sports Society. With one breath he tells us that hunting, shooting and fishing protect the countryside and its habitats; with the next he is not prepared to support hedgerow protection.

Like Mr Gummer, it often seems to me that some hunters, shooters and fishermen appear not to inhabit the real world. If Sir Nicholas really wanted people to believe in the positive side of field sports, he should have seconded the Hedgerow Protection Bill, not helped to talk it out surreptitiously.

If anyone should have taken an interest in the osteopathy debate it was me, for Cowslip has just had another calf. Cowslip is our Jersey house-cow who supplies us with gallons of unpasteurized, unhomogenized, unsanitized and unGummerized milk, for three quarters of the year. The problem is that just after she has calved, her udder becomes so vast, and my arms are so short, that I can hardly reach her teats. This means that to use the milking machine I have to crawl under her, getting my trousers wet and dirty, or bend double, while at the same time stretching like a contortionist to find the teats at the far corners of her udder.

Forgetting my bad knees I leant over too far on the first morning and slowly toppled underneath her. In theory it should be easy to roll out from underneath a cow; but on this occasion I was face downwards, with her enormous udder on top of me, holding me down. It could have been worse I suppose: I could have been face up!

The only solution was to hitch myself along and creep out from between her back legs, like a rabbit leaving a burrow, hoping and praying that she would not lift her tail. The last thing I wanted in that situation was a pat on the head.

After a struggle I made it to freedom. I hope that no Environmental Health Inspector hears of this fiasco. On current form not only would they prosecute me for being a health hazard, but they would arrest Cowslip as well.

We did well lambing this year, averaging 2.1 lambs per ewe, but I will never understand sheep. The largest, fattest old lady seemed certain to deliver triplets; she managed to produce one feeble little

lamb, yet from her general manner she considered her pathetic effort to be one of the greatest achievements in the history of domestic sheep.

The smallest ewe, on the other hand, managed to surprise me with enormous, healthy triplets. They surprised her too, as she only had one lamb last year; in fact at first she was totally bewildered. During the winter she jumps over the electric fence to greet me as I check all is well. Now the lambs are growing quickly she is jumping out of the old orchard paddock again, simply to get some peace.

We have kept visiting children well away from the paddock this spring. Last year as we bottle-fed two lambs rejected by their mothers, we allowed several small children up close to watch. The normally placid Jacob ewe took great exception to this and with amazing skill put her horns down and charged – skilfully butting one small boy into the middle of a large clump of stinging nettles. It was precision butting at its most spectacular.

The fiercest creatures on the farm continue to be the geese. They have led to our most treasured letter of appreciation from one young visitor:

Dear Mr Page, it was fun at the farm especially when the gander bit the lady. Thankyou for letting me help feed the calf and give the pig a stroke. I liked the donkey best because it nuzzled me. The little rabbit was sweet and Mummy drove into the parking sign and knocked it out. I hope to come again.

17

Curried Salmonella

I hate this particular time of the year; now by MAFF command, we have to test our hens for salmonella. It is a disgusting job and not recommended before meals. We have to stick swabs up the collective orifices of a sample of fifty hens. For any reader not conversant with the anatomy of a hen, this particular orifice is to be found at the opposite extremity to the beak.

It is all nonsense of course, and dates back to the publicity-conscious Edwina Currie in 1988; then the saintly lady appeared to discover salmonella. The media discovered it too and seemed to see all food as a health hazard. Surely the day will come when the great urban majority will demand compulsory feeding through intravenous injections, for the sake of sterile, hygienic food.

The poor egg got the blame for salmonella, and ever since, all laying and breeding flocks have had to be tested. All those birds failing the test are massacred. When the tests were first introduced I phoned MAFF and said: 'We all know this is nonsense; even we have salmonella in our guts, so why test hens and not Mr Gummer and Mrs Currie – I have a plunger almost big enough for them.'

'I know, sir,' the man replied, 'the problem is in the kitchen and the way people fail to cook their food properly.'

'So why test and kill hens if this is known already?' I responded.

For once the MAFF answer was short and to the point. 'Pass,' he said with feeling. The whole charade has decimated the British poultry industry; 5,000 egg producers have been forced out of business; well over 3 million hens have been slaughtered, and the incidence of salmonella in food has increased – well done, Mrs Currie, I can see you had an Oxford education. It does suggest to me that killing hens by the million, which might have salmonella up their bottoms, has little to do with salmonella in the kitchen, or in the mayonnaise bottle that has been left on the sideboard for three days.

But what has happened as a direct result of all this? Why, Britain is no longer self-sufficient in eggs of course, and is having to import from abroad. Yes, you have guessed correctly, none of the hens producing the imported foreign eggs are tested for salmonella; we live in a wonderful world. An old boy explained to me recently how such a system could have been worked out: 'It's simple,' he said. 'Our politicians and their civil servants are like sewage – the solids float to the top.'

From all this I believe that John Gummer and Mrs Currie should have swabs stuck up their orifices to test them for salmonella. If they have it, then Parliament should be closed down as a matter of urgency – and what about all those people put out of business? They should receive the same incomes, expenses and holidays as Mr Gummer and Mrs Currie as compensation.

Now an independent committee, the Advisory Committee on the Microbiological Safety of Food, has recommended scrapping the idiotic tests, except for breeding flocks. I expect Parliament will get round to it one day – after Maastricht.

I wonder how long it will be before MAFF, or Mrs Currie, demand that all migrating wild birds should be rounded up and tested for salmonella? I can just picture the lovely Mrs Currie rushing about with a net, trying to catch birds, as long as there were television cameras present. I was reminded of this hidden threat the other day when watching a great northern diver – surely a bird full of salmonella.

Curried Salmonella

The sighting of the great northern diver demands something of a confession. Alas, there is no privacy in this world, and because of this I was caught doing something shameful in a public place – I was caught 'twitching'.

For years I have mocked, ridiculed, criticized and abused 'twitchers', those strange people who travel miles to 'spot' rare birds. (The name 'twitcher' comes from the fact that when bird-watchers hear or see wings, they 'twitch' in anticipation.) But there I was, surreptitiously twitching by a lake close to the A45 road near Cambridge, when I heard those dreaded words: 'Oh hallo Robin – twitching aye!'

I had been caught red-handed.

Now during this time of year most great northern divers are trying to avoid oil slicks out at sea, particularly those around the Shetlands where the oil tanker *Braer* went down. Evidently this bird was a thinker, or had been blown inland, and had decided to stay. Just before my arrival it had apparently swallowed a large roach and was doing well, thank you very much.

Normally great northern divers inhabit the last great wild places of the Northern Hemisphere. But this one was quite at home on the edge of suburbia with a succession of twitchers and my Daihatsu Fourtrak trundling up close by.

While in a confessional mood I will admit to having twitched once before, when I trekked up to Tiree to see and hear a Corncrake. I have to admit too that I was not disappointed. If ever I go twitching again I think I will wear dark glasses and a handle-bar moustache so that my sin goes undetected.

Talk of twitchers brings to mind a little book I published a few years ago of Rodger McPhail's very funny cartoons entitled: *The Twitcher's Guide to British Birds*. It still rankles that the RSPB refused to stock it, claiming that the drawings of a fulmar, a black grouse and a pair of crested tits represented sexism, racism and vulgarity. The remnants of my Baptist upbringing were not offended in the slightest by Rodger's wit; those people who spend their time searching for hidden 'isms' and political correctness must be amazingly dull company.

Earlier mention of the Shetlands and oil slicks reminds me that, according to the RSPB, the oil disaster off Shetland resulted in the death of about 1,000 birds and one rabbit. How a land mammal could become oiled is a mystery, but as my intellectual vet says: 'At least it brought about the first confirmed sighting of Braer rabbit!'

[Shortly after this chapter first appeared the idiotic salmonella tests

63

were scrapped. Despite this the Government still did not admit that it had been wrong and there were still 5,000 people who had lost jobs and businesses. Meanwhile Mr Gummer and Mrs Currie remained in Parliament, pontificating as usual, and drawing their fat salaries.]

18

A Stroke of Bad Luck

It had been a good day. The sheep were looking well; the meadows were looking well and my old father was looking well. We had been to check the ewes before bringing them home for lambing. We had decided to return the next day – April Fool's Day – to bring them back to the farm in the trailer; soon Tom's enthusiastic work would show itself as newborn lambs.

The brook meadows looked good, too; despite the presence of the sheep they were alive again; the grass was growing, the buds were swelling and you could actually smell the sap rising. Smell sap? It is true, new growth can be smelled, as well as seen. Away from the fields the cows in the yard become restless and impatient in the spring; they can smell their new grazing – they want release and freedom.

On our return to the farm Father was feeling fit; he decided to split some logs with his axe. It is a pleasing pastime and something he has enjoyed doing for years. He claims that Gladstone split logs with an axe to keep mentally and physically fit, until he was over eighty. I was looking forward to the next day as I always enjoyed doing things with Father; there was usually something to laugh about working with him, and often there would be a piece of handed-down wisdom for good measure.

At half-past nine that evening the phone rang. My sister's voice was anxious; would I go down to the farmhouse, Father had had a stroke. He was sitting in an armchair; he looked bemused – he could not stand. One minute he was active; the next he could not get out of his chair. He had felt nothing; my mother had seen nothing and my sister had heard nothing; his body simply stopped.

It is a shocking thing when the unexpected happens. We talk glibly about the transience of life, and suddenly reality enters silently and uninvited; time waiteth for no man. We pretend; we hope; we may even pray, but all too quickly our time passes away; steadily, relentlessly and unseen. It does not wait for logs to be split or sheep to be moved; it simply arrives, unannounced.

My mind was numb. For years my father had been more than a father, he had been my special friend. How do you help a friend in real need? The doctor came and confirmed a stroke. A bed was put up in the living room and there he lay for three days, without the use of his right side. His speech was slurred and his eyes showed fear and frustration. Finally the National Health Service stirred, and my mother, complete with pacemaker, was relieved of the physical burden and Father went into Addenbrooke's Hospital. With service like that, the logo of the NHS ought to be of a hibernating slug.

It is only when somebody is absent that you realize the size of their contribution. Although in his late seventies he had been feeding the ducks, hens, bantams and geese. He had been letting them out first thing every morning and shutting them in at night. In between, he had collected the eggs, washing and weighing them before going to bed.

So my life's pattern changed to take in hens, and hospital visits. Things would never be quite the same again. Since those traumatic days Father has fought and persevered. He has fallen too, but battled on. Slowly movement has returned; first he shuffled with a zimmer frame; then he staggered with a tripod, and now, a year later he can walk carefully with a stick on a good day. He remains happy most of the time, and can walk to his greenhouse, but I miss him around the farm. As time moves on, his company, logging in the winter and shepherding the whole year through, cannot be replaced.

But over the years he has given me something that cannot be taken away; he has given me his example. He is a man who has never drifted with fashion, political or social; in fact his lifestyle explains the old proverb: 'Only dead fish go with the stream.' He has always been a live fish; he has never been greedy or envious of his neighbour and he has seldom ever carried money in his pocket. He has been honest to himself and to his wife and he has been happy and content. Contentment in the modern world: there can be no greater example than that.

The intrusion of a stroke inevitably brings on thoughts of life, death and immortality. It is strange: we live in a society that probes, investigates and reveals, yet seems frightened of death. Death is swept into a dark corner, hidden from view. Meat in the butcher's shop is packaged; it becomes a product. The rare butterflies bulldozed into oblivion for a new housing estate or open-cast mining to 'create jobs for people' become merely an 'issue' raised by anti-social extremists; nobody sees them die. That too explains why so many people want hunting banned; the question of whether it is right or wrong is often not the problem: it is the fact that death occurs out in the open and people see it and are reminded of reality – ban it.

As a Christian, albeit a bad one, I do believe that we continue after death somehow, somewhere. But as for my mortal remains on that day when my pen falls to the floor and is not picked up, what do I want? Certainly not the pollution of the crematorium or the overcrowded churchyard. I want to be taken on the trailer to be buried in the brook meadows; a hole in the ground by the hedge where mayflowers bend the hawthorn branches in early summer and the fieldfares eat the scarlet berries of autumn. I want to become part of the wind and the rhythms of the season and I want Bramble next to me, either before or after.

I am bio-degradable; I want my mortal remains to go back to nature, dust to dust – or in this part of Cambridgeshire, mud to mud. And as for my spirit, I hope it finds that place outside time for those who have tried their best.

But to many this simple wish is a problem of enormous importance. 'A body near a water course? We can't allow that; it is disgusting and against EC regulations. And what is more it would create a precedent – if we allowed one, everybody would want to be buried down there.' All my life I have been a nuisance to the establishment and authority; they do not understand people who say and try to do what they believe. So I suppose, and hope, some earnest Environmental Health Officer will continue to find me a problem after death. He may even have to dig me up again: that, I am afraid, will be his problem. And what hymn do I want singing in those brook meadows so dear to me. My favourite, of course: 'In the bleak mid-winter'. I hope I die in July.

19

Rural Rage

We are now approaching that dreaded season of the year when we open up the farm to visitors. I say dreaded because it is a tremendous tie. We took the diversification step four or five years ago, responding to MAFF's suggestion that farmers should do other things to generate additional money. Since then, I have to confess, I have had a major re-think about the whole principle of diversification: now the whole idea seems to be totally absurd. Farmers should make their livings farming: they should not have to open their farms seven days a week to run tea rooms, supervise paint-ball battles and become agricultural zoo-keepers, in addition to their normal farming jobs.

It has not escaped my notice that Mr Gummer does not open his house at weekends, with fishing in the famous pond as an additional visitor option, in order to make a comfortable living; nor does Mrs Gummer have to sell cakes on the local WI stall to help towards the school fees. Yet it was Mr Gummer who first pushed the idea of 'diversification' for others.

Last week my dentist pulled out one of my wisdom teeth. He too makes sufficient money from his job to live comfortably. He does not have to run a dentistry museum and tea room on Sundays, with a bit of painting and decorating in the evenings, in order to survive. So why are many small farmers expected to do two or three jobs in order to make a living? It seems unfair to me.

The other familiar argument is that this country should buy its food as cheaply as possible on the world market instead of paying farmers a living wage. Incredibly I recently heard Ken Livingstone, a left-wing Labour MP, arguing this strange free-market view. So if people like him hold that position on food, why not on coal? Come to that why not free-market dentists, solicitors and accountants.

They all seem to be doing very well themselves, on fixed prices. Surely it is time for a few plane loads of Matabele and Zulu dentists and accountants to be flown in, to provide a bit of competition at 'world prices'.

What about our MPs being paid on a free-market basis too? Then, at the next election the Conservative candidate for the Suffolk Coastal constituency – yes, Mr Gummer's seat – would be the man or woman agreeing to do it for the least money, with a promise to diversify at weekends. All this is nonsense of course, but it is precisely this nonsense that many small farmers are expected to live with.

Even after deciding to diversify we have had problems. I have mentioned before how Cambridgeshire County Council has stopped us having RAC roadsigns at £150 for twelve, to direct potential visitors to the farm. The County Council wants us to spend hundreds of pounds on its own permanent signs, to comply with its 'tourism policy'. National agricultural policy seems irrelevant.

Another problem stems from the local education department. We get many schools visiting each summer, but the education authority will not let us notify schools of visiting arrangements through its internal mail system. Yet large organizations such as the RSPB use it, despite their £25 million annual turnover. Mail sent internally gets seen by teachers. Mail sent through the post often ends up in the head-teacher's waste-bin.

Again, we tried to contact Cambridgeshire County Council's

Humanities Adviser, to see how the farm could be used as a teaching resource in the secondary schools' curriculum. Sadly my letter was not answered; neither were my telephone calls. I suppose he was too busy advising.

Originally, as part of diversification, had we wanted to have some of our pigs killed locally to sell in the farm shop. But then three local slaughterhouses closed, courtesy of Mr Gummer's silly rules, so we could not get them killed. Even had we managed this, we would still have been stopped, by yet more EC regulations. To have collected the pork for delivery to customers, we would have been required to have a refrigerated van or trailer. The customer, however, could have picked up the meat from the abattoir in his own car, with the heater full on, but unfortunately most customers want a service; they do not want to do all the work themselves.

Some visitors are intrigued by the fact that we grind our own cereals to make our own cow, pig and hen food. Under yet more MAFF regulations we may soon have to stop doing this. To grind our own food we must apparently make our barn and mill 'pollution free'. This in effect means keeping all wild birds out. MAFF claims that this is to prevent unfair competition, as the large millers produce their feed in bird-free premises. It is nonsense, of course, to suggest that we have an advantage over BOCM or Spillers, yet to those bureaucrats living in Cloud Cuckoo land, we represent 'unfair competition'. And what birds fly into our barn to create 'pollution'? Why, our hard-pressed swallows of course. So MAFF wants us to shut our swallows out of the barn. We will not do this, we would prefer to be prosecuted. I suppose, technically, we could be prosecuted for keeping the swallows away from their nests as well – a classic Catch-22 situation.

Perhaps all this means that diversification is not such a bad idea after all. It gives us the chance to make people aware of all the nonsense and red tape that we now have to contend with – with the full approval of our political masters.

20

A Smashing Yarn

May was a dreadful month: at one stage I almost dared not answer the phone. The reason for this British Telecom bonanza was a stream of calls telling me of lapwings, skylarks, partridges, pheasants and mallard ducks being ploughed up under our idiotic set-aside rules.

Inevitably the first call came from my old friend John Humphreys, who had temporarily put down his pen, blackboard chalk, gun, Black Forest gâteaux and trumpet, to pick up the phone. From his part of the Fens he was in a state of eloquent rage. 'It's mayhem out there', he informed me. 'My first reaction to set-aside was – brilliant. There were fields of fallow like the old partridge days. Now it's turned into a nightmare. With the bare land left for carrots and beet, the set-aside land attracted ground-nesting birds like a magnet. As soon as 1 May came the ploughs and cutters came out – it's terrible.'

The next call was a contractor from Northamptonshire who was actually being paid to plough and 'top' (mow) hundreds of acres. 'It was heart-breaking yesterday – skylarks were going spare. I looked for the nest but could not find it – I must have ploughed it in. Lapwing chicks were going everywhere. We've smashed a lot of ducks nests too – we try to save as many eggs as possible, but it's disgusting – criminal. We've had skylarks, pheasants, partridges, lapwings and ducks. The land should have been ploughed earlier, in March, and left until July.'

Then came a slightly better call, from a farmer – name and address supplied – he was going to ignore the rules completely and not touch his set-aside until his young larks, lapwings and partridges were fully mobile.

The sad thing is that I forecast this mayhem many months ago. I get no pleasure in saying 'I told you so'.

Poor old John Gummer and MAFF claim that the ploughing from 1 May is a diktat from Brussels. They are wrong as usual. For a change, Brussels allowed flexibility, and it was wildlife-illiterate MAFF who decided that May was a good month for ploughing and cutting.

But now John Gummer has gone, what will I have to write about? I actually wish him well and am glad that he has gone to the Department of the Environment. For some time I have considered that there should be greater links between the DoE and the Min of Ag. Perhaps with his experience in agriculture there will now be greater cooperation between the two departments and he is an enormous improvement on the dreadful Michael Howard. His first job in the DoE is easy: stop the unbelievably senseless destruction of Twyford Down. If he does not, then it is the environmentalists' turn to become Seldom Glummer.

I think I have discovered why many farmers, particularly young ones, know so little about wildlife and landscape, while being red-hot on cash-flow and cost-benefits. Over the last few weeks, entirely by coincidence, I have met a number of lecturers from agricultural colleges. I have been amazed at what I have heard. Most seem to talk only in agri-jargon; to them farming is not a way of life, it is a business. Value for money and profitability are the twin gods: landscape and wildlife do not seem to be options. As the Prince of Wales says in his excellent book on his Highgrove estate, the 'culture' has been removed from 'agriculture'; to many young farmers fresh from their college brainwashing, it is now 'agri-business' and 'agri-science'. Hence the attitude of: 'It's 1 May, let's plough our set-aside – skylarks, lapwings and partridges – what are they? Do they make money?'

My view of colleges was confirmed by a student from Harper Adams Agricultural College the other day. He has just finished his second year at what is supposed to be one of the best colleges in the country. 'How many lectures have you had on conservation?' I asked. His answer was simple: 'None.'

It was a mistake boasting about our good lambing season recently, as an excellent young ewe died yesterday. She simply went off her feet and died, leaving her twins to steal milk where they can. The vet pumped her full of drugs but all to no avail. I was not happy. The vet understood why: 'If you have up to twenty ewes you love them – if you have more than twenty you hate them.'

Following her death I phoned the kennels of the Trinity Foot Beagles – digging holes for dead farm animals is a long hard job, and for as far back as anybody can remember all our dead animals have gone to the hounds. Another advantage of this system is that when the kennelman cuts up the body, you get a free post-mortem. 'I can't take her, Robin,' he said. 'Sorry. I can only take cows and calves these days – it's EC regulations.'

'Nobody will know,' I urged, giving the new bureaucracy the regard it deserves.

'No, I can't. They inspect me unannounced at least once a month.' So another piece of Euro-nonsense has cost us money and inconvenience. A neighbour's digger was reluctantly hired to dig the hole. For years hunts have been a hidden help to livestock farmers by taking their dead animals – now the Euro-MAFF thought-police have struck again. I wonder if an anti-hunting MAFF official is behind this absurd situation?

One individual with livestock has the answer: 'Do what we do. Take the ear tag out and throw her in the river.' We will never do this, but I can understand why some have been driven to it.

21

The Ghost of Gummer

Oh dear, the ghost of John Seldom Glummer is still haunting the farming community and all of its offshoots. The butcher in the next village waylaid me at cricket last Saturday. He pointed out that one of the final statements made by Mr Gummer as Secretary of State for Agriculture claimed that his new slaughterhouse regulations, allegedly based on EC directives, had only closed down seven slaughterhouses in 1992.

Technically Mr Gummer may have been correct; but what he failed to say was that numerous others had ceased trading, fed up with red tape and harassment. They had also not been prepared to pay the large sums demanded to allow them to meet the new, absurd standards. In fact seventy-two slaughterhouses went out of business in 1992, making Mr Gummer's statement appear to be 1,028 per cent inaccurate – according to the beads on my counting frame. A disgruntled farmer called in the other day for a gossip. He complained that this government has become 'the government of the half truth' – if only its pronouncements were that accurate.

At the beginning of 1990 there were 653 registered slaughter-houses; in 1991 there were 581; in 1992 there were 510, and there are 438 now. Over the last three and a half years Mr Gummer has supervised the destruction of not seven, but 215 – good businesses, large and small, causing needless unemployment, family hardship and trauma, and a decline in animal welfare. The animal welfare problem is simple: as there are fewer slaughterhouses, those animals bought for slaughter are being transported greater distances, with all the accompanying stress and discomfort. So why Mr Gummer seems to have been so creative with the facts over the years I simply do not understand. One to one he does seem a decent individual; the only conclusion that I can come to is that he suffers from the

74

'Yes Minister Syndrome' – he is misdirected by scheming civil servants.

Earlier, I mentioned the skylark holocaust on set-aside, due to MAFF's eco-illiterate rules, insisting that land should be ploughed, sprayed or mown between 1 May and 1 July – again approved by Mr Gummer. The British Trust for Ornithology has now given a conservative estimate of the number of young skylarks and eggs destroyed during this most crucial time of the breeding season: it is 250,000.

The Game Conservancy has also been studying skylarks and in its newly published *Review of 1992*, it reveals: 'Clutch size was significantly greater in nests in set-aside fields ... but when the set-aside was given its obligatory cut, birds were either destroyed, or in one instance, skylark eggs and nestlings in several nests survived the cutting, but were immediately predated by a large flock of rooks which descended on the exposed nests.'

Under the Wildlife and Countryside Act it is illegal to take or smash the eggs of wild birds, with severe penalties for those yobbos who break the law. So what has happened to the man who was in charge of the destruction of at least a quarter of a million young birds? Why, he has been made Secretary of State for the Environment of course. Commenting on his new incarnation, a cynic has commented: 'It can only be a matter of time before Mr Gummer says that the destruction of Twyford Down for the unwanted M3 extension has been of great benefit to wildlife and landscape.' Amazingly, this rather good joke has already been overtaken by events; Mr John MacGregor, Minister of Transport, said almost the same thing, quite seriously, on a recent edition of BBC's *Newsnight*.

But the ghost of Gummer lies over the fishing industry too. Just as British farmers have had quotas imposed on them so that Britain has to import food it could easily produce itself, so our fishermen have had rules imposed on them that seem to benefit virtually everyone except themselves. Again, one of the last schemes argued by Mr Gummer was to cede Scottish mackerel to the Russians, so that German and Humberside vessels could fish for cod in the Barents Sea. With the amount of pollution in that sea some think it would be more efficient to fish with Geiger counters rather than nets. Scottish fishermen only found out about the plan when their Dutch colleagues let the catfish out of the bag. Apparently the Scottish Office had known of the plan but had been sworn to secrecy. Fortunately the whole unfair plan disappeared with Mr Gummer.

One of these days I must invite John Selwyn Gummer out to dinner to chat about his life and times at mad MAFF. I wonder if he usually has cod or haddock?

22

Too Much to Swallow

I have just experienced a well-timed coincidence. Following an earlier chapter in which I mourned not only the loss of a young ewe, but also the arrival of absurd rules which prevented the local kennelman from taking her body, I bumped into one of the country's leading medical/veterinary research scientists, a professor no less. The reason this academic should meet a common or garden peasant is quite simple: when he removes his white coat, he seems to adopt the lifestyle of a peasant, too.

When I told him that the kennelman was no longer allowed to feed sheep to his hounds on the grounds of hygiene and the spread of disease, he burst into laughter: 'How absolutely idiotic – I have not heard so much twaddle in all my life,' he chuckled in disbelief. 'Dogs have been eating domestic sheep for at least 10,000 years and their ancestors before that. We have known of scrapie for 200 years with virtually no evidence of cross-infection, and then who's going to catch it from a hound anyway – you would have to eat it to stand any chance.' I hope this does not start members of The League Against Cruel Sports and the seemingly ridiculous Tony Banks MP eating hounds in an attempt to show that they carry contagious diseases; and what would you eat old foxhound with? Chips or Bonios? Then, of course, the question arises as to how would you recognise a Member of Parliament with scrapie? Would their behaviour during Prime Minister's Question Time be noticeably different from their antics now?

But the professor had not finished: 'It's made even more absurd by the fact that we have been eating sheep's brains for years. Lightly cooked sheep's brains were fed to delicate children, and sheep's heads were a common food for poor people. Some companies have only just stopped using sheep's brains as an emulsifier in baby foods – it's ridiculous.'

From all this nonsense it seems that there could be an EC policy at work, deliberately creating as many absurd rules as possible. The resulting army of officials, inspectors, investigators, advisers, co-ordinators, planners, economists and consultants could add up to a hidden job-creation strategy on a massive scale.

The lawnmower-mender in the next village has it all worked out. With three A-levels to his name he preferred to mend lawnmowers than go to university. His perception is sharper than his lawnmower blades: 'It's all simple, isn't it? Technology means there's less work available and so the government has to come up with a plan to combat unemployment. Well they've done it; for every one of us working at a proper job they've created a platoon of ten inspecting us and snooping on us – it's as simple as that – one working and ten watching.' He's almost certainly right.

London provided some bizarre entertainment the other day. I attended a conference organized by *The Field* on the future of the Scottish Highlands. At the start of the afternoon session a television face sauntered in – it was Alan Clark, ex-MP and author of a now-notorious autobiography. He sat down and almost immediately his head dropped back, his mouth dropped open and he gave the impression of being in a deep, contented sleep. After a quarter of an hour in the Land of Nod, he suddenly woke, shook himself like a labrador leaving a pond, looked around and strolled out. It was all very strange. An eminent observer commented dryly: 'That comes from years of practice in the House of Commons.'

As I write, our first batch of swallows are out of their nest and flying around the barn. This spring our one and only pair arrived early, on 10 April, but no more followed. Recent letters from readers in various far-flung parts of Britain suggest that numbers are down again this year all over the country. My problem is now how to keep the magpies and sparrowhawks away from the new fledglings.

One of the delights of my earlier visit to Zimbabwe was the thousands of European swallows along the Zambezi. Their journey always amazes me: a fortnight after seeing swallows feeding over elephants and hippos, our swallows were flying low over Brynny the donkey and Cowslip.

One sight in Zimbabwe filled me with disgust. As swallows were massing on telegraph wires along a remote country road, ready to migrate, several hundred were actually sitting in the road. A Mercedes, driven at speed by a European blue-rinsed wonder –

mutton dressed as lamb – did not slow. It ploughed straight through them, leaving six dead on the road. On my return, two hours later, a white, overweight farmer in a pick-up truck did exactly the same, leaving a further eleven splattered all over the road – seventeen swallows would not be making the journey back to Europe. In some European circles in Zimbabwe it is said rather patronizingly that 'The Africans do not appreciate or understand their wildlife'. Sadly it applies to many Europeans as well.

Some time ago I mentioned the number of families in my village with bird names. I am not alone, a farmer, Mr A. Mole, informs me that he has a social life involving birds and animals; he married an Eagle, and at a recent farmer's dinner found himself sitting with a Mr Fox and a Mr Badger. Unfortunately Mr and Mrs Rabbits could not attend.

23

For Whom the Bell Tolls

It is strange how death seems to come in threes, whether with people or animals. No sooner had I lost my ewe, than a cow went down for no apparent reason and could not get up again. Inevitably at a time of trauma, it was one of our best cows, with sentimental links to the past that made her more important. She was called Marina, a line going back to when Father first went into farming, which meant that she still had old Shorthorn blood in her. It had been watered down considerably over the years with Friesian and Murray Gray, but she still had markings and features that were distinctly Shorthorn.

It was sad to see her on the ground, unable to stand and it was a total mystery as to how or why it had happened. With the bull still shut in the yard it was nothing to do with him, and all we could think of was that she had come into season; when this happens and there is no bull around, the cow concerned is often mounted, rather pointlessly, by other cows. It is a sign that she is 'bulling' – ready for the bull.

It could have been that she was mounted by a cow, after a shower, slipped and damaged her back. Whatever had happened it was pitiful to see; there was just nothing we could do apart from feed and water her as her worried calf looked on. The vet could offer no help either; he was as baffled as we were – we just had to wait and watch.

When an animal is injured it is the helplessness that is difficult to cope with. What should or could we do as her condition declined? The vet thought that something might happen after a few days, but nothing did, and it was assumed that she had damaged her spinal cord. We were faced with watching Marina fret and fade away or put her down. After a week it was clear that nothing was going to happen and the kennelman was called. There was a bang; her struggle and our anxiety were over. Fortunately the calf was big enough to survive on grass and soon it was simply one of the herd, but all these little incidents of sadness leave an indelible mark.

It was then that more death came, taking the overall total to well over three. A fox removed a wooden slat from a hen coop to take a cochin hen and all eight of her chicks. Those 'experts' who seldom see a fox, but know all about them, are always blaming the farmer for his losses; how can you anticipate a fox that will effectively break-in? Cochins may be rather stupid birds, but they are attractive and make good mothers; I was not happy. Next, they, or it, broke into another henhouse; again the cochins suffered. Three hens vanished, a cockerel died and was not taken, and another was left severely injured. Cochin cockerels are large birds, evidently almost too large for a fox to kill. It squawked, it groaned and its head was drooping almost to the ground, thanks to the fox's unsuccessful attempt to break its neck. Male arrogance has a lot to answer for. Elsewhere on the farm another cock crowed. This was too much for the cochin. He struggled to lift his battered head, a half-hearted crow pronounced his rather reduced manhood and his neck flopped earthwards again, throwing the unfortunate bird into a perfect forward roll. Twice more it rolled in this way; it was the first time I had ever seen a cockerel with an interest in gymnastics.

Still the deaths came thick and fast. The next night wire was pulled out of the deep-litter shed's window and another fifteen hens bit the dust. We hate setting snares in the summer; if we caught a vixen that was obviously suckling young we would be overcome with guilt as the cubs would certainly die through starvation. But with all these losses – none of them our fault – we simply had to protect our hens and a snare was set.

On the first night we caught our fox and the trouble stopped. The villain of the peace was a small, but fully grown vixen. It was the smallest vixen I had ever seen – far smaller than Bramble. She was not suckling young, and her teeth showed that she was quite old, but still able to hunt normally, had she not taken this liking for hens. Why a barren vixen should suddenly create so much havoc is a mystery. Perhaps she was helping another vixen to feed cubs, or perhaps she simply liked killing; I have no idea.

I have to confess that I joined the killing orgy too last week. Every morning, midday and evening, I have to take asthma drugs from inhalers. It is not unpleasant, but I find it annoying as I don't like being dependent on drugs. As usual at breakfast I grabbed an inhaler and squirted. I felt something in my mouth and, assuming it to be a bran flake, I chewed. It was a mistake; the taste was bitter and disgusting – it was not a bran flake, but an earwig. I spat it out in horror. If all insects taste like that, then I am glad I am not a swallow.

The evil beast had evidently crawled into my inhaler during the night and was then shot, at great speed to the back of my throat. It was most unpleasant, for me and for the earwig. That is only one of the drawbacks in using an inhaler; if I have one in my pocket when I am doing dirty work, the case fills up with dust, grit and straw. Then, when I want relief, I shoot this potent mixture into my lungs, causing me minutes of coughing and spluttering. This shows one of the wonders of medical science. I can get an inhaler that will keep me free of asthma; but at the same time it can shoot so much dirt, dust and earwigs into me, that I could die of farmer's lung, or even insect infestation as a direct result. I've heard of cure or kill; this could do both.

24

One Dog and His Man

For years I have bemoaned the fact that British television is overrated and underfunded rubbish. The BBC is good at blowing its own trumpet of course — it could do no other with five radio bands, two television channels and numerous other local radio and television stations under its control. Yet, with all these, it manages to produce few programmes that interest or entertain me. It boasts of free speech, open airways and access for all, but in reality its speech is highly selective; the airways are carefully regulated and access is mainly for those who are politically acceptable and orthodox.

Those living in the country often wonder why there are so few country people on television, people who, in various forms, make up twenty-five per cent of the population. And where are the genuine country programmes, bearing in mind that about eighty per cent of Britain's land mass is countryside — farmed, forested and almost wild? There are a few 'country' programmes, it is true, but usually it is the same old story — rustics and countryside seen through the eyes of urban journalists and high-rise researchers. They see a world in which the peasants are all barbaric buffoons, and a countryside which should be preserved for the benefit of urban man — a gigantic theme park, play area and building site for the masses.

The countryman must stop loving peace, quiet and country pursuits, from quaffing home-made scrumpy to chasing foxes; he must learn to love new roads, accept housing estates, enjoy all-night street lighting and take up playing golf. In addition he or she must start sipping Tesco's Château Yuppie 1983, enjoy giggling at the neighbour's Sunday brunch, and take a holiday in France. Under no circumstances must the words 'urban colonialism' be used and all rural accents must be eradicated. Oh dear, this townie-takeover would make good television itself — but no — it would be too hard to take: viewers would actually be seeing television executives at their weekend homes.

Another reason why true country programmes are seldom seen is that many of them would be 'nice': showing good, straightforward people doing skilful, simple, traditional things in beautiful surroundings. Sadly, many of our media masters don't like 'nice' programmes and 'nice' people. Apart from game shows, they want news and views, confrontation, injustice and outrage, even if they are often contrived.

Once the BBC had a 'nice' programme – *Pebble Mill at One*, with good audience figures for daytime television. It offended no one, it informed and entertained so it was taken off, to be replaced by the *One O'Clock News*, to compete with the news already on ITV – hardly an example of giving viewers choice. Letters flooded in; at first there was an edict to keep them off *Points of View*, a programme of viewers' criticism. It was in the best traditions of Eastern European broadcasting before the Berlin Wall came down. Finally, through the sheer volume of complaint, letters were read out, but the programme was not re-instated, as media managers never admit to making mistakes. The presenters of the programmes, all gifted 'nice' people, virtually disappeared for ever from our screens.

This left just one 'nice' programme, by coincidence, just about the BBC's only real country programme, *One Man and His Dog* – televised sheepdog trials, with genuine country people, attractive dogs, sheep and beautiful surroundings. From its first appearance, it was introduced by Phil Drabble, a do-it-yourself countryman with a twinkle in his eye and a rural burr in his accent. And from its first appearance it was popular and was shown mid-week, mid-evening in mid-winter. The viewing figures were an astonishing 8 million. That was eighteen years ago when programmes were still allowed to be 'nice'.

Since then a new creature has infiltrated the media: Hard-News Man. To these strange beasts television and radio is about more news, more current affairs and more contributions from the confrontation, injustice and outrage brigade. So peak-time viewing disappeared for *One Man and His Dog* and last time around it was on a Sunday night at six-thirty with the evenings still light, when most interested country people were still out, still working or still at church. On the other BBC channel was *Songs of Praise*, hymns sung in churches, often in country settings – in other words, with great skill and flair the BBC programme-planners were managing to get its two channels to compete for the same audience. What an inspired plan – some people are paid very large salaries to achieve this – from our licence fees.

Quite unsurprisingly the viewing figures fell and there were rumours that Hard-news Man was trying to remove the programme altogether; sheep, shepherds and sheepdogs should be replaced by, yes, more confrontation, injustice and outrage – programmes about one-legged disadvantaged lesbians; soya-bean-chewing animal-rights freedom-fighters and unemployable, out-of-work, leather-jacketed victims of society with safety-pins through their eyebrows and rings through their collective noses.

If I was an open-minded television planner I know what I would do. I would show *One Man and His Dog* on one channel with *Panorama* – the BBC's boring – sorry, flagship current affairs programme – on the other. That could provide a really interesting insight into what people really want.

Then came a genuine surprise – a phone call out of the blue. It was my agent (I have to have an agent, to make sure that I am not led up the garden path too often). 'Robin,' she said. 'Did you know that Phil Drabble is retiring, I have mentioned you for *One Man and His Dog*.' I was amazed. Then came a telephone call, I had been short-listed for *One Man and His Dog*, and could the producer, Joy Corbett, come with her video-recorder and do a screen test. I said 'Yes'.

I said yes for two reasons. First, I, like millions of others, love *One Man and His Dog*, but also, like millions more, I am never able to see it, as I am always working, or at church at six-thirty on Sunday evenings, so for me it would actually be one way of seeing the series. The second reason was more obscure: the producer's name was Joy Corbett. I would meet anybody called Corbett, in case they were related to that great traveller, writer, conservationist

and tiger-hunter, Jim Corbett. His famous books on India include *The Man Eaters of Kumaon* and *The Temple Tiger*.

On a recent trip to Kenya I stumbled upon the great man's grave, for after a life of action and travel, he retired to and died in Kenya. I had visited Nyeri to see the grave of Baden-Powell; it was white-washed and well-maintained for tourists, but there, up in the corner, behind the gravestones of young British soldiers killed during Mau-Mau in the fifties, was the forgotten, broken grave of Jim Corbett. One graveyard containing the remains of two great men: one revered and remembered, the other almost forgotten. Death can be as selective as life.

So the day dawned. Joy Corbett and camera arrived. She was not related to Jim Corbett, nevertheless I let her in. But what should I do to appeal to her: have plastic surgery, put on a false beard or, at five foot five, stand on a box? Suddenly, in a flash of inspiration it came to me, introduce her to the good-looking member of the family, Bramble my dog.

Bramble is a beautiful dog, a lurcher, so beautiful that Gordon Beningfield has even painted his portrait. He is like a little deerhound – grey, hairy and streamlined. He has royal antecedents too, as he was bred by Monty Christopher, the retired headkeeper of Sandringham Estate. With a whippet and a Bedlington terrier, Monty had set out to produce a lurcher that would look like a miniature deerhound. He succeeded so well that the first time I walked Bramble up the road, Gypsy Jim offered me twenty-five pounds.

Now eleven years old Bramble can still run like the wind and turn on a sixpence. He has been a pleasure to have – a one-man dog – a friend and a character. Some people say that you should not get sentimental about dogs; I disagree, I would never want to be without one.

So for eleven years Bramble has given me friendship, irritation, consternation and many laughs. He has been knocked over while looking for love, he rides with me on the tractor and in the car, he has chased foxes, run away from Jack Russell terriers and filled the house with fleas. Some of his dietary habits, particularly when in the vicinity of the muck-heap have left much to be desired, but he does like more acceptable morsels, particularly Bonios. He hates water, and dirt, but will chase anything, anywhere even if it means getting soaked and covered with mud. His last chase was perfect. A fox got up out of the hedge fifty yards away and loped across some set-aside. It was confident; it had seen dogs before, and had not been troubled. Bramble was off like a rocket, closing the gap with every bound. The fox trundled on, 'wasn't it a lovely day, its' a pity about this person and dog'. Suddenly Bramble's teeth nipped Reynard's backside and it accelerated away as if it had been hit by 10,000 volts. Bramble's excited yap went up an octave as he chased the fox into a distant hedge. One to one in a hedge, the fox always loses its pursuer very quickly and soon Bramble was back breathing hard and happy.

The meeting of Joy Corbett and Bramble was an instant success; she likes dogs, he likes people (most people), so I was left redundant. We did go to the new hay meadow, with all the flowers in bloom – ox-eye daisies, clover, yellow rattle, bird's foot trefoil and all the rest, and Joy did film me talking to the camera surrounded by this piece of newly created old England. She filmed Bramble too in the long flowers and grasses; I thought she filmed Bramble far longer than she filmed me.

For a few days all was quiet, then Phillip Gilbert, head of the department, phoned. All had been considered and would I like the job? Would I like to take Bramble along too? Answering an invitation like that is not so easy as it sounds, for television could change the simple, happy routine of my life and destroy my privacy. But I said yes – there must be more real country people on television.

So *One Man and His Dog* looms; it should be a privilege and a pleasure. I have a lot to thank Bramble for, however, as I am sure that he got me my new job. But he has not been forgotten and has been one of the first dogs to be included in a BBC contract; his reward – down in black and white – a box of Bonios per programme. Thank you Bramble, you deserve them.

25

Foss

In the last chapter there was an omission. There were not two reasons why I accepted the invitation to present *One Man and His Dog*, but three. I have always been fascinated by the relationship between Man and animals, for as Man has developed from hunter-gatherer to homogenized consumer, from wandering primitive to commuting sophisticate, he has done so with the help and use of animals. Animals have helped Man to hunt, herd and fight; they have carried his burdens, fought his battles and shared his fires. Horses and dogs have been instrumental in this journey: horses for working and riding, farming and fighting, and dogs for hunting, finding, retrieving, hauling, herding and defending.

It has been a close relationship – particularly that between man and dog. There is mutual love, trust and admiration involved. It can be seen between shepherd and dog, huntsman and hound, policeman and alsatian, shooting man and retriever – and pensioner and poodle.

On the farm we have always had dogs – a spaniel, many labradors, a few border collies, the odd mongrel, and Bramble. I have always loved dogs and enjoyed seeing them work. I have watched assorted gundogs, guard dogs and hounds and I have seen sheepdogs, cattle dogs and terriers kept simply for ratting. Out of all these dogs I have long admired sheepdogs. The bond between man and dog, and dog and man is wonderful to see. It is based on trust, dedication and skill. The natural hunting instinct of the dog has been modified to herd, and in the border collie it has been fine-tuned almost to perfection. The dogs love and need work; the shepherds depend on the dogs and it is a system of two-way reliance. It is inevitable that when a skill and a bond have been developed, that men will want to compete. They will want to show others that their dog is superior to those of others. So sheepdog trials developed and I have enjoyed them in Wales, Scotland and the Lake District.

For some years too I have had a cousin sheep-farming in the Pennines. The winters are hard, life is tough and hours are long, but he has loved it. He too has had dogs and worked dogs; he has not trialled them, but he has depended on them as extra labourers to manage his sheep.

When we still had dairy cows, my father always wanted one of Stephen's dogs. He argued that if we could get a border collie to round up the cows, in the same way that they moved sheep, it would save him time and footwear.

The first collie we had was a young female, Plaid, but we were immediately worried by her reactions. It was almost the first time that she had seen a road, and at every opportunity she would crouch in the roadside verge, outside the farm, as if about to round up cars. We called, scolded and even chained her up, but the next time she was released she would again be crouching in the verge. Soon the inevitable happened; she was hit and died instantly. It was a sad waste of a dog.

Next came Foss, a delightful dog, keen to learn and help. She loved work, but was a little too keen to bite heels and tails instead of being satisfied to drive. She loved chasing rabbits and ratting and hated guns and thunder. On hearing either she would run home from the fields and let herself into the farmhouse by jumping up and banging the latch with a paw.

It is strange that all our dogs have hated foxes. It was particularly strange in Foss's case, for at that time I still had Rusty, the last of my pet foxes. She was an attractive vixen, friendly, playful and alert. But however hard I tried I could never house-train her, and however hard she tried, she always attacked the hens whenever she got out. In the summer, when I called 'Rusty, Rusty', Foss would rush up to the run and tear round and round, making a well-worn track. Occasionally I would let her in to play, but I had to be careful as a fox is surprisingly small and delicate, even when compared to a border collie.

Foss had enjoyed the summer, as she was a good swimmer, diving into the brook from the banks after pieces of wood, and each day as Father shouted, 'Come on. Come on', she would cut across the fields to rouse the cows. On seeing her they would immediately head for the farm, and after snapping at the heels of the dawdlers, she would return ahead of them at full speed. She was a brave dog too and, several times, with hooves flying, she would try to drive the bullocks, although in her excitement she would often drive them in the wrong direction. Had she been properly trained, she would have made an excellent cattle dog, but it did not matter, she had heart, character and she was a good companion.

It was because of the wild foxes that we decided to leave her loose at night. Every morning in the early hours we were being woken up by the hens, as a fox tried to break in. At first we left Tinker, the labrador, off her chain, to keep the foxes away, but all she did was raid the local dustbins, and so she was chained up again, as soon as darkness fell. Instead, Foss was left to roam, in the hope that she would discourage the foxes, and save us setting snares which we only do as a last resort. On the first night of her freedom I was awoken at two o'clock; she had been run over. Neighbours had found her whimpering and barking softly in the road, where she had been hit by a car and left. There was no blood, but she could only move her head, and the rest of her body seemed to be completely without life. Father fetched her back to the farmhouse in the wheelbarrow and placed her in front of the Aga to keep warm. It was sad to see, and I had to fight back tears, for we were helpless and her eyes told of shock and fear. Sister Rachael stayed with her, but I could not sleep and after an hour I got up. She cried quietly as I went to her and licked my hand; I stroked her chin and spoke to her, but still she had no movement.

Despite her injuries, her spirit remained, for next morning she growled at a cat which went too near, and she snapped at the lady vet who arrived to inject her. We moved her under the kitchen table and put her carefully on a sack of straw, with a blanket and hot-water bottle for additional comfort. The vet said that movement might return and that we should wait two or three days to see what happened. We gave her tit-bits and glucose in water, and I kept imagining movement and a slight wag of her tail, but there was none. We tried to stay with her all the time, but when she was alone for just a few seconds she would whimper quietly until reassured. She could move her head perfectly, her eyes were bright and alert, and her ears responded normally. When people whom she knew came her excitement showed, as if she wanted fuss, and they had to speak to her and stroke her. It was heart-rending to see, for she showed trust and fear, helplessness and hope, yet there was no real way of consoling her, or of getting her to understand her plight. It was not until the second day that we realized one of her front legs was broken, but she could feel no pain. Tinker too knew that something was wrong, and anxiety showed in her eyes.

The lady vet came again and stuck a pin in various parts of Foss's body, but there was no response. She thought that the spinal cord must have snapped and there was nothing more she could do; she said that the only recommendation she could honestly make was that Foss should be put down, and Father, with grief on his face, reluctantly agreed. I stroked her head and talked to her as the needle went in and almost as soon as blood showed in the syringe, she was dead. I had expected her to tense up, or struggle, but as I comforted her she just stopped breathing; there was no fear and her life had simply been extinguished, like the flame of a candle. It was hard to take, for she had been as one of the family, and I cried like a child, tears streaming down my cheeks.

I carried her out and buried her under the apple trees, close to where she had often rested as I worked in the garden. It is strange how the physical act of digging helps to blunt sorrow. I thought of the ground ivy that would flower beneath the blossom of the trees, and of the bluebells I would plant on her grave. Tinker was visibly concerned, and several times she went slowly and carefully to look into Foss's empty shed. For several days there were deep ripples of sadness on the farm, for familiar things were absent; there was no night-time barking, and the wagging tail, the bounding paws, the self-opening door, and the bright eyes wanting affection were all missing. Another chapter on the farm was over, and so was my real introduction to the border collie. Yes, the memory of Foss was another reason why I was glad for the arrival of *One Man and His Dog*.

26

The Silly Season

The Silly Season in Britain is usually that strange time in high summer when politicians have fled from Parliament and half the country has retreated to Spain, Provence or Greece, for their annual holidays. This leaves the media virtually nothing to write about or film, apart from 'Man Bites Dog' and 'Falling Apple Injures Passing Vicar'.

I have my own Scilly Season however. It is spelt slightly differently and comes fractionally earlier, but every year in May or June, I try to get away for a week or more to the Isles of Scilly.

I discovered them years ago when I was researching a book, *The Wildlife of the Royal Estates*. It has gone the way of all my books which involved blood, sweat, tears and burning the midnight oil: it has gone out of print. But virtually every year since, I have returned to the Scillies.

The islands are Royal land, the most southerly part of the Duchy of Cornwall. They formed a section of the original Duchy way back in 1337 and have been owned by successive Dukes of Cornwall ever since. Now of course they are part of the land owned by the latest Duke of Cornwall, Prince Charles, an enlightened man who looking into the future of the islands has established an Environmental Trust to try to safeguard their wildlife and their beauty.

They lie twenty-eight miles south-west of Land's End, a collection of 145 low-lying islands and exposed rocks, of which only five are inhabited – St Mary's, St Martin's, St Agnes, Bryher and Tresco – famous for its remarkable ornamental gardens. The rocks and islands are separated from each other by shallow sounds and channels and the sea itself is as full of wildlife as the land. In all, the islands comprise a rare concentration of life, on and around a mere 4,085 acres of island and rock, creating a naturalist's paradise.

They are remnants of hard granite, part of the same volcanic chain as Bodmin Moor and Dartmoor, and they are all that is left of land thought to have separated from Cornwall 300,000 years ago. Many islands are simply jagged stumps and pinnacles of bare rock, refuges for sea birds and a danger to those at sea, especially when high Atlantic rollers are crashing around and over them.

The most impressive of these rocks is Men-a-vaur, three close turrets of fissured, sea-battered granite, where kittiwakes, puffins, razorbills and guillemots breed. Others are larger and flatter, the biggest being St Mary's, with 1,554 acres, 1,500 inhabitants and ten miles of road. The total population of all the islands is just under 2,000 – a figure that multiplies several times over during the summer, without altering the essential character of the Scillies.

I go to the islands to relax, reflect and recharge my batteries. It is the closeness of nature that appeals as the whole rhythm and pace of life slows. Each day is dominated by the weather, the sea and the season, and not by the internal combustion engine, the clock and the *Nine O'Clock News*. The locals are governed by day length, moon phase and tide and not by the antics of Parliament.

There are several bulb and flower growers on the larger islands, picking and packing daffodils well before they are flowering on the mainland. The fields look far too small for livings to be made, but one old farmer manages to put things in perspective: 'We've got eight acres of bulbs on our farm. Do you know how many square inches to the acre? Six million. You can't grow a bulb in every square inch, but when you are working out there, it seems like it.' He had a novel explanation for the world's problems too:

'It's all caused by electricity. People should get up when it gets light and go to bed when it gets dark.' His wife had heard it all before and was not impressed: 'That would make you stay in bed rather a long time during the winter, wouldn't it, dear?' she said wryly.

Because the climate is so mild and maritime, exotic flowers once cultivated and now naturalized, Hottentot fig, whistling jacks, three-cornered leeks, the Bermuda buttercup, and many more turn the islands into a botanist's banquet.

Boats take visitors from island to island. Each year I go on a bird-watching boat trip with John Hicks whose family can be traced back on the Scillies for hundreds of years. Like all the boatmen he has a fine wooden boat; their choice of wood is simple: 'If God had meant us to build fibre-glass boats, he would have grown fibre-glass trees.' Last year John Hicks caused a stir across the whole country. He stopped his car on the quay to go to his boat and forgot to put the handbrake on; slowly his pride and joy – an old Mercedes – rolled forwards and toppled over the edge, to nestle comfortably on top of his uncle's fishing boat. It was a most unusual, unpopular and expensive place to park.

Because his ancestors have been on the sea for generations, he knows every rock, cove and current. His trips pass Annet, a wildlife sanctuary; it was ablaze with thrift (sea pink) at the time of my visit. The island glows in the sun when the flowers are out, and, around its cliffs and rocks, puffins, razorbills and guillemots breed. Terns too live up to their other name of 'sea swallow' as they fly over the water with buoyancy and beauty.

In the water, grey seals surface to watch with fascination the people watching them and sometimes huge basking sharks, thirty feet long, drift slowly by. John Hicks entertains and educates as he goes along. He has a simple way of telling a great black-backed gull from a lesser black-backed gull:

> The Greater black-back's back is
> Blacker than a Lesser black-back's back,
> Because a Lesser black-back's back isn't
> As black as a Greater black-back's back –
> It's lighter.

As the sun goes down his boat goes searching for that remarkable wanderer of the sea, the Manx shearwater. As its name suggests, with its long, streamlined wings, it shears through the air just above the wave tops; another good name for it could be the 'maritime skimmer'. Each evening they collect offshore awaiting nightfall. With darkness they return to their underground island nests, hoping to avoid the marauding murderous gulls.

One of the rarest breeding birds on the Scillies is the roseate tern, with just one or two pairs nesting each year. It was thought to be extinct in the islands until 1943; then a young airman, Humfrey Wakefield, decided to take some photographs of a colony of common terns. On developing the films, there in the background were a pair of roseates – he had recorded their return without realizing it. Humfrey has stayed on the island as a potter, creating practical things, yet giving them fine lines and beauty; his craft has become art with a usefulness and purpose.

Now Humfrey has discovered another remarkable return of nature. Until a few years ago the hedgehog was entirely absent from the Scillies; then a captive pair were foolishly released by an islander on St Mary's. Soon it was discovered that hedgehogs have some of the same habits as rabbits, and the hedgehog population increased rapidly. As they colonized the island they discovered Humfrey's henhouse and became extremely partial to his eggs. The resourceful potter was not amused and set a cage trap, catching the offending thief. He released it well away from his house; next morning it was back in the cage in the henhouse. He picked it up; painted it Hammerite Blue for identification and took it two miles away, to Old Town, on the back of a motorbike. The next day the Hammerite Hedgehog was back in the cage. So Humfrey has discovered a new natural history phenomenon – the homing hedgehog; I wonder if it runs or rolls?

Sadly for the Isles of Scilly they have their own 'Silly Season'. Every autumn hundreds of 'twitchers' arrive on the islands searching for rare birds. By a rare quirk of wind, nature and bad navigation, during each migration the Scillies is a resting point for several totally lost little brown birds. Because they are lost they can come from Eastern Europe, Asia or even North America. As they land, tired and bewildered, their confusion immediately increases as they are quickly surrounded by hundreds of camouflaged twitchers with tripods, cameras, huge lenses, telescopes and a strange idea of natural history and communion with nature. All these strange people want to do is claim a sighting of a new bird; the new bird then becomes a 'tick' and another name on their 'life list'.

This searching for the lost, tired and bemused is undertaken with military precision and when a rare bird is located, that island, or quiet peninsula, is invaded at the gallop by the twitching hordes.

The finest day's twitching ever occurred when an American rarity turned up – a rose-breasted grosbeak. As the bird sat there, doing precisely nothing, in front of the assembled throng, a furry paw reached out and the grosbeak disappeared. It was found later as a little heap of feathers – the local cat had claimed its tea; it couldn't have happened to a nicer visitor from America.

27

Meeting, Eating and Competing

What has happened to the traditional agricultural show? At one time the Gransden Show, the Cambridgeshire Show and the Royal Show were eagerly awaited as highlights in my country year. I still go to the Gransden Show, but the Cambridgeshire Show has been devoured and regurgitated as part of a strange summer entertainment called the East of England Show. I still go to the Royal Show too, when invited and given a free entrance ticket, but I attend with reluctance, regarding it now almost as a glorified car boot sale for rural and would-be-rural yuppies.

The first show that I ever attended as a small boy was the Gransden Show. The villages of Little and Great Gransden lie on the border of Cambridgeshire and Bedfordshire. The show is now in its ninety-third year, run by the Gransden Agricultural Society; even before 1901 it was held as an agricultural and horticultural show, judging everything from local rams and jams to beetroot. It was a traditional show run by farming people for farming people – landowner, farmer and agricultural labourer. The days of mixed farming meant that it had crops, implements and livestock. Just after the Second World War when I was taken for the first time, it had pigs, sheep, cows and horses. It had the smells and sounds of farm animals and it attracted the men who worked with them and who knew them. A prod here and a knowing look there revealed shepherds and cowmen who knew their trade; they knew a good beast when they saw one; they compared notes, exchanged stories, laughed and drank beer.

The people reflected the land they worked on. No tractor cabs – or horse cabs – meant wind-burnt, sun-tanned cheeks, and years of walking the land led to a heavy, bowed gait. The legs of those who sheared their sheep by hand developed an even bigger bend:

they could evidently shear a sheep in a pen but not stop a pig in a passage. It is strange too how so many plodded, as if they still had mud on their boots. They were from the land – almost part of the land – but there was something strange about them. Some of them regarded the annual agricultural show as an 'event', a special day, demanding ties, jackets and patent leather shoes. Farmers, cowmen, horsekeepers and tractor-drivers all looked self-conscious and conspicuous, until the tie was loosened and the jacket unbuttoned.

As a family we would watch the judging of the cattle. Father was never impressed and maintained that he had better Dairy Short-horns back home. He would look at the machinery – new drills, a Fordson Major tractor and the Simplex milking machine – and then we would experience the highlight of the show: the company who bought our wheat and sold us binder-twine would have tables set for tea in a wind-blown marquee. There we would scoff cups of tea, sandwiches, swiss-rolls and hand-raised pork pies. Those serving knew us; they remembered our farm, what we grew, what we knew and what Father purchased. Those who worked on the farms met and mixed with those who serviced them and sold their

produce. It was a social event; farming friends would meet farming neighbours, as well as cattle-dealers, barley buyers, blacksmiths, vets and tractor-mechanics. The farmers would compete with each other, too, for the best sheep, cow and mangold-wurzel.

When I was about ten Father suddenly shocked us. Not content with claiming that his cows were better than those at the show, he decided to prove it. We would enter Diana 10th (or was it the 12th?) in the Dairy Shorthorn section. Charlie the cowman (we had a brace of Charlies) was overwhelmed by the opportunity; it meant that he could spend even more time with his beloved cows; he seemed to prefer their company to that of his overweight, battle-axe of a wife.

Diana 10th (or 12th) was shampooed and brushed, her tail was combed, her horns and hooves were polished, her hair was clipped and Charlie led her up and down the road in a halter. Then, the Day of Judgement came; the Gransden Show is still held on the last Saturday in September and Charlie, wearing a white coat and brown trilby, led our pride and joy into the ring. Father was right: the placid red Shorthorn won her class, he had proved his point and she was never entered into a competition again.

The Cambridgeshire Show was bigger and even better than Gransden. There, farmers from all sides of the county would meet, eat and compete. My farming uncles from the neighbouring villages were joined by a variety of great uncles and cousins from the Fens. There were so many companies offering refreshments that it was possible to drink tea and eat sandwiches all day in a great variety of tents.

Twice, even the peripatetic Royal Show visited Cambridge. It was vast; but still those present were essentially farmers and workers who lived on the land, with a visit from a member of the royal family to add meaning to the show's prefix. It was a festival of British agriculture, steeped in pride, tradition, achievement and camaraderie.

I should also say that until just a few years ago I also visited one other show quite regularly, at Cambridge Cattle Market. On the second Monday of December the annual Fatstock Show was held. It was a winter opportunity to talk farming and meet friends, while drinking tea and eating hot pies. Every farmer seemed to be an 'expert', although no one ever admitted to having had a good year. Sadly, it did not pay to be best porker or bullock, or even 'Supreme Champion'. If an animal won, it simply meant that it met the apple sauce or horseradish quicker, as all the top beasts were auctioned off for eating.

They were good days, but they have gone. The Cambridge Cattle

Market is now a business park and the few remaining cattle pens are always empty. Even the old produce auction has closed down, with petty EC directives ensuring that no new one will ever open. The Cambridgeshire Show has vanished and the East of England Show has not been able to recreate its friendliness and its feeling of being an important part of regional farming. With its parachute displays and speedway racing, its clothing stands and videos for sale it is rather like a glorified Sunday market, with a few animal noises and country smells thrown in for good measure. This year the big question will not be about bushel weight or pedigree, but 'Is Mr Blobby going to make a personal appearance?'

The Royal Show is still with us, however, and several years ago its wanderings stopped at Stoneleigh, not far from that sprawling blot on the Midlands' landscape, Birmingham. But is the new static Royal Show the same as the old migratory show, or has it simply become a type of pseudo-rural entertainment, an Agri-Disney?

Agricultural shows started during the great time of agricultural change and advance, inspired by men such as 'Turnip' Townshend, Robert Bakewell, Jethro Tull and Jonas Webb. The farming community, man and boy, wanted to learn the new scientific ways of farming; they wanted to witness new techniques; try out modern implements and see the developing breeds and crops. They wanted to compete too, to see who had the finest turnip, the biggest ox and the strongest horse.

Agricultural societies and their shows sprang up all over the country. The Royal Agricultural Society of England (RASE) was founded in 1838 as the English Agricultural Society. Its first 'country meeting' was held in 1839 at Oxford; the following year it visited Cambridge. As early as 1850 it was realized that a rural location, catering for rural people would lead to financial loss. Consequently, shows were held near urban areas to encourage non-agricultural spectators to visit and swell the coffers. The seed was sown, and over a century later it has grown into the present-day Stoneleigh aberration.

The decline in the number and nature of traditional shows came with more recent agricultural change. Modernization, rationalization, specialization, monoculture and the transformation of a section of the farming community into nothing more than land-managers and growers meant that there were fewer farms, and fewer workers. The mixed farm became a rarity, and the traditions of a whole community became lost in the search for cash-flow and 'efficiency'. In whole regions of the country arable farming usurped rotations and livestock and there was nothing to enter in the local agricultural show except samples of wheat, barley and oats. Such displays would only be of interest to passing groups of grain weevils and so attendances declined, shows lost money and many disappeared altogether.

There are still shows that survive, but many have taken the agri-Disney route to survival. In a cash-flow world, cash-flow decisions have been taken; making money at the gate now seems more important than agricultural traditions and ambitions. The general rule is that the further a show is from a large city, then the more likely it is to be true to its roots. Hence the Royal Cornwall Show, or the Bath and Wells, have more to do with agriculture, as I understand agriculture, than the East of England or the Royal.

Strangely my local little show struggles on and remains one of the best. It still has classes for sheep and grain, although for the first time there was no 'roots' competition last year. Our local agricultural dealers, Collings Brothers, still take their tent for tea and biscuits and I eat as much as possible to reduce their profit margins.

But the East of England Show has changed, as has the Royal. The Royal Show, so we are told, is going from strength to strength, but its links with the real land seem less obvious. The car parks are full, but many of the vehicles are 4×4s which regularly see polish and the car-wash but never mud. Some of the occupants too seem out of place – are they attending a farming festival or a rural fashion show?

It would even be possible to visit the Royal Show without seeing a hen, a sheep or a cow. To some, success seems to be measured purely in terms of the number of clicks at the turnstiles or whether Mrs Shephard has lunch at the President's table.

There are numerous PLCs offering wine and coloured brochures. Their greeting is not 'Hallo, nice to see you again, how are you?', but 'Good morning Sir, do you do business with us?' My local dealers and suppliers can no longer afford the prices for trade-stands, so rather than drinking cheap wine with oleaginous salesmen I do not know, and do not want to know, I queue up for my midday victuals at the hot-dog stand.

It is true that there is an animal section tucked away on one side, and my first ports of call are to the pigs, sheep and cattle to see the Middle Whites, Gloucester Old Spots, Leicester Longwools and those wonderful old long-gone Dairy Shorthorns. After that I have to tiptoe through pavilions promoting Zimbabwean wine and Spanish holidays, double-glazing salesmen and people selling wallpaper. I can buy a roll of Andrex and an Archers' sweat shirt designer jewellery, or a concrete pig for the garden. Why anybody should assume that I would want a concrete pig when I have the real thing is beyond me.

To get to the alternative energy and farming with conservation, I have to pass a physiotherapist, a lady selling dresses and Norfolk County Council. If ever there was a case for 'back to basics', then the Royal Show provides it. Surely the truly successful agricultural show is one that actually concentrates on agriculture. I hope I am in Cornwall at the time of the Royal Cornwall Show this summer.

But what is even more worrying is the fact that some people regard the drift of agricultural shows into the realm of leisure, recreation and car boot as highly successful: so successful that other shows, allegedly linked to agriculture, are springing up all over the place. One gruesome example of this was held a few years ago in London – the Asda Festival of British Food and Farming, in Hyde Park – to celebrate Food and Farming Year. A Food and Farming festival held in London? It was odd from the very beginning.

Despite being in the Black Hole I decided to visit just for the experience. It was an experience I could have done without. On a hot day London was terrible, with its teeming worker-ants peeling off assorted items of clothing in distress, and blatant exhibitionism. From the state and shape of most, I wanted them to put a lot more clothes on.

Their state of semi-nakedness induced many of them to walk along the pavements with a strange narcissistic mince, looking at their own reflections in shop windows. This urban skill is totally beyond me; how these people in various stages of self-love manage to avoid tripping over the kerbstones and banging into lamp-posts is a mystery. As I tripped through the streets of London I passed a redundant church. It had been 'done up', converted into offices, and given the name Spire House; it seemed to sum up well the values and the synthetic nature of the age.

It was a strange 'festival'. As I walked past the stand of the Transport and General Workers' Union, pondering the suitability of their display (images of the Tolpuddle Martyrs), what appeared to be a modern martyr approached and proceeded to tell me of the good work his union was doing for today's farm-worker. 'What are you doing for the small farmer?' I asked him. 'All you have done so far is to make labour too expensive, so that small family farmers like me are the new peasant class of the countryside, with nobody fighting our corner.' He then said something most remarkable. 'We thought about setting up a section for small farmers, so we nearly helped you.' This raises an interesting semantic question. How do you 'nearly' help somebody. A pushy gentleman approached me once and told me: 'I nearly bought one of your books the other day.' How do you nearly buy a book – he hadn't helped me at all.

I don't know if it was the weather, but I seemed to spend the whole day arguing. The RSPCA was the next stop. For years I have thought the RSPCA to be a strange organization. I viewed their video, *The Dark Side of Farming*, with my usual open mind. I happen to be very concerned about many aspects of modern intensive farming, including the way battery hens, pigs and cattle are kept, but the RSPCA seemed to be over the top, appealing to the emotions of a largely ignorant audience, complete with a questionnaire that seemed to be designed to get the answers the RSPCA wanted.

I approached a spokeswoman, hoping that the organization had decided to take an informed and positive line. 'What are you suggesting should replace intensive farming?' I asked hopefully 'low-input farming?' 'What's low-input farming?' she replied brusquely. Trying to get through to her more simply, I continued: 'Well, are you trying to achieve a more positive approach to set-aside by promoting more acceptable, less-intensive farming?' 'What's set-aside?' she asked aggressively.

When both I and a farmer who had been listening expressed surprise that a member of the RSPCA should be attacking modern farming but was apparently unaware of the various alternatives, she became even angrier, as though instead of asking straightforward questions we had been trying to catch her out. In fact she had caught herself out. In my view the RSPCA remains a peculiar organization. After my experience in London I will continue to support Compassion in World Farming, a society that does its homework.

Next I paid a very short visit to a stand proclaiming itself as 'Northamptonshire, Rose of the Shires'. This sad misuse of the English rose, as an advertising gimmick, is becoming very common. I like rural Northamptonshire but was astonished to see one obvious omission from its propaganda; it made no mention of John Clare, the Northamptonshire 'peasant poet'. 'Why have you forgotten John Clare?' I asked. The answer was predictable and, in Hyde Park, clearly contagious: 'Who's he?' came the blank reply; the stooge did not even 'nearly' know of him.

After this I could stand no more; I passed the hot-dog stands, the candy-floss and the stalls selling tea-cloths and special tin-openers – I hurried home.

Last year I went to yet another strange event, advertised as an 'Organic Agricultural Show', in Dorset. Sadly 'The Whole Earth

Show' seemed to have more in common with a New Agers' tea party than an agricultural show. There were numerous jugglers and tattooists and you could get your ears or nose pierced, but real organic farmers were very few and far between. I wonder what jugglers have to do with agricultural shows?

The highlight was a seminar with Jonathon Porritt – a good and sensible man. In tones of great seriousness, Jonathon was asked why the Green movement did not enlist the help of 'extra terrestrials'. The gentleman concerned evidently thought he had goblins living at the bottom of his garden, although he failed to say whether they were red, white or blue. Poor Porritt was almost dumbfounded. At this point it struck me that the questioner, the Minister of Agriculture, the farming establishment and the organizers of agricultural shows all had much in common these days; they all seem to be living in a world of fantasy. I wonder if they are really aliens settling here from a distant galaxy?

28

Town Fox Meets Eco-Man

The urban fox is a strange beast, not because it differs in any great way from its country cousin, but simply because any animal, *Homo sapiens* included, which chooses town life rather than country, must be slightly suspect. Virtually everything about the life of the town fox is disputed, from its diseases to its habit of raiding dustbins, as there are numerous urban fox apologists who view it as a saintly animal living in harmony with its neighbours and their waste-bins.

The urban fox itself is partly responsible for this misinformation, as its rise has helped to create the 'urban-eco-green' – those earnest, bearded individuals inspired to take up 'ecology' and 'environmental studies' from a totally urban background, after seeing their first urban fox. They then try to impose their urban wildlife views and experiences on to the real countryside, often with disastrous results.

Some urban-based ecologists claim that the urban fox was attracted into cities when the cities themselves changed. From the end of the Second World War, they say, the suburbs began to spread more rapidly, with semi-detached suburban Mr James rejecting high density housing, for a house with a garage and a garden. As a result, the urban fox was given acres of trees and gardens to colonize and explore. This theory conveniently forgets that many Victorian suburbs were leafy and green many years ago, but remained fox-free.

The most obvious reason for the rise of the urban fox is simple; rural numbers of foxes rose so quickly from the mid-fifties onwards, that the population explosion spilled over into the towns. Since then London has been completely colonized and a fox has even been seen in Trafalgar Square. Some urban-fox-lovers say that this influx was

104

caused by myxomatosis, with foodless foxes going into towns in search of a meal.

Again this is nonsense. Myxomatosis did deny foxes one source of food – rabbits, but they quickly switched to alternatives. What myxomatosis in fact did was to make rabbit-trapping uneconomic; as the rabbit-trapper vanished, so did his traps, which took a tremendous pressure off the fox. When coupled with a decline in gamekeeping and the disappearance of the backyard hen-run, as it was considered easier to buy eggs at the supermarket, the fox had few human enemies and the population rocketed. As a result suburbia and even town centres were rapidly colonized.

There are a surprising number of places for foxes to occupy in towns. Railway embankments, garden sheds, sports pavilions, waste ground and clumps of brambles all make good places to hide, sleep and breed. Like their country cousins they are not averse to using hollow trees and I have seen one urban earth which is a straightforward hole in the corner of a flowerbed, with no attempt at concealment. It is in a walled garden and the foxes simply jump on to the wall and over, to carry out their nightly task of foraging.

The diet of the urban fox varies substantially from that of the rural fox. Well over three quarters of the rural fox's menu is made up of wild food. Almost half consists of wild mammals, with the remaining wild food consisting of almost equal parts of birds, insects and earthworms. When fruit and vegetables, stolen pets and poultry are added, that leaves just about five per cent of scavenged food, although at lambing time and muck-spreading time that percentage will be higher.

The urban fox is far different, with scavenged food forming about a third of its diet. Chicken bones and scattered chips near fast food shops, greasy papers and boxes, the contents of dustbins and bird tables, and the milk put out for the cat are all accepted gratefully.

Again some urban-fox-lovers seem embarrassed by the fox's love of dustbins, hence Prof. Stephen Harris in his almost excellent book *Urban Foxes* writes: 'Many country dwellers (and particularly the fox-hunting fraternity) refer to "dustbin foxes", which are supposed to be mangy half-starved animals which eke out a miserable existence in our cities: a very common misconception. Urban foxes do not survive by rifling dustbins.' Strangely he then goes on to write of foxes feeding in Bristol: 'The one good time each week was dustbin night, when all the city centre restaurants put out their rubbish.'

In some places dustbins have now been replaced by 'wheely bins' which are fox-proof. As a consequence some country people close to towns are currently reporting seeing even more foxes, almost as if foxes are leaving the towns to search for food in the country.

Although many urban foxes are perfectly healthy, they are more susceptible to otodectic mange (ear canker) and sarcoptic mange than rural foxes. Because of this Prof. Harris urges people not to translocate town foxes to the country, in case they are transporting disease at the same time. Another reason why urban foxes should not be dumped in the country if they become a nuisance in towns is that the released foxes will find themselves in the territories of already established rural foxes and will be subjected to much harassment from their own kind.

Rabies in the urban fox population is a real fear, as it would be extremely difficult to control. The number of stray dogs and cats in some cities could also mean that the disease would be quickly transmitted to other animals, causing a real problem. Another threat from rabies comes from the present climate of animal liberation. Some people believe that it can only be a matter of time before an extremist deliberately introduces an infected animal in the hope that fox-hunting would be stopped.

Although the urban ecologist often criticizes countrymen for killing foxes, and points to an average lifespan of less than two years for rural foxes, the urban fox has a short lifespan too, averaging only eighteen months; half the deaths are from cars.

With the huge amount of death, damage and suffering caused to wildlife by cars, in both town and country, surely it is time for 'The League Against Internal Combustion' and the 'Car Saboteurs' to intervene, with the help of EC grants. The fox would be grateful at such a development, as far more foxes get killed by cars every year than by hounds.

29

Summer Settlers

It is haytime again, one of my favourite times of year. The smell of new-mown hay is sweet, and as the sun dries out the grasses, the scent seems to become sweeter. Even carting the hay is rewarding and as we still use small bales which have to be manhandled, it can be hot heavy work; but at the end of a hard day it is satisfying to know that the cows and sheep have their winter fodder secure and dry.

But haytime gives other pleasure too. Before the mower arrives, I enjoy lying in the long grass, just gazing into a blue sky, watching the swallows and swifts hawking after insects. It is a summer pleasure of which I never tire: the swifts are forever on the wing, even sleeping and mating in mid-air, if the observation of experts is correct; then swooping down in small, screaming packs, flying fast, complete masters of the air. In wind their rate of climb and diving aerobatics can be quite remarkable.

Swallows are smaller and their flight is less frenzied and more

buoyant, but their presence is just as welcome. We still use them as accurate weather aids, for the higher they fly then the better the weather. It is usually an accurate piece of weather lore, although once I saw swallows flying very high after insects in a thunderstorm. If weathermen can get their forecasts wrong with all their scientific aids, then I don't mind the swallows ruining my country weather forecasts now and again.

This year watching the swifts and swallows has been particularly poignant. As I mentioned earlier, a few weeks ago at the end of March I was on the banks of the Zambezi in Zimbabwe. There, European swallows were feeding over that mighty river in their hundreds, sometimes touching the water as they do over an English pond in high summer. It is strange seeing them in such large numbers in such exotic surroundings. It was a small part of England amid bee-eaters, wire-tailed swallows and fish eagles. Higher too were European swifts, still beating the air frantically as they sped after their prey.

Somehow the experience of seeing swifts and swallows thousands of miles away from their summer homes has made their great migration journey seem all the more remarkable. Here they are now, back over an English hay meadow, after a journey covering huge rivers, deserts and mountain ranges. Small fragile bodies journeying against the elements, across half the world; it is both remarkable and wonderful.

Not far from our hay meadow is a small wooden garage; there a swallow with a ring on one leg has returned to nest no fewer than seven times; what distances and what experiences have been faced by that little bird. Air Zimbabwe makes the journey regularly from Africa to England with the help of radar and all the best in modern technology. The swallow has made the journey to the same garage using only its wings and instinct. Nature never fails to astonish and excite me.

I have also encountered another little bird many times in Africa. On my last visit I saw it again – on the banks of the Zambezi, at Fothergill Island in Lake Kariba, and on the shores of Lake Malawi. Again the journey of the common sandpiper is a remarkable one, taking it from the Equator and beyond, to our streams and rivers on moorland, highland and island. Many times I have come across them at their breeding grounds on Speyside, Deeside, the Peak District and numerous other places where the flow of moorland streams can be heard flowing over rocks.

The first sandpipers of summer arrive in Britain in late March, with the main body of birds reaching us in late April and early May. Eggs are laid in May and June and after a twenty-two-day incubation period the young hatch and feed mainly on insects. With the long hours of daylight in northern Britain allowing good feeding, the young birds quickly grow and build themselves up for their long journey southwards in the autumn.

Amazingly some common sandpipers travel so far south that they reach South Africa and even Australia, while some birds are making their long-haul autumn journeys, a few decide that southern England will do, and stay here for the winter. Evidently laziness is catching, as more and more are also spending their whole year in Africa. I prefer those who follow the stars on their traditional migration routes.

While thinking of wings, among the most beautiful at this time of year belong to the white admiral butterfly. Unlike the swallow, the swift and the red admiral butterfly, the white admiral does not migrate, it is happy with its lot among some of the larger woods of southern and eastern England. It is a butterfly of woodland glades and dappled light; in keeping with the season, its flight is leisurely, frequently gliding and alighting on flowers to drink nectar. It is particularly fond of the blossom of blackberries and buckthorn. Its liking for fragrance goes further, as the female lays her eggs on the leaves of wild honeysuckle. Sadly, the one suitable wood near me has no white admirals present; perhaps they should start migrating after all.

30

An Unkempt English Rose

My wild garden would never win a Best-kept Garden competition for, apart from the vegetable patch to supply my kitchen (in theory), and the nettle patch to supply the caterpillars of the peacock and small tortoiseshell butterflies with food, all activity is decided by the wildflowers currently on flower – 'on flower' being Cambridgeshire dialect for what other people describe, quite wrongly, as being 'in flower'.

The cowslips in the front lawn mean that it cannot be cut until they have seeded, and then there are corncockles, violets and lesser celandines as well as the two willowherbs, the 'rosebay' and the 'great hairy'. The back lawn is a proper lawn, full of buttercups and daisies. It is a cause of great sadness that in many gardens the buttercup and daisy are no longer welcomed, and so most of today's children miss out on the old flower games that brought happiness on long, sunny afternoons – daisy chains and looking for the buttercup's reflection to confirm a liking for butter. In the farmhouse garden there are even more wildflowers:

cuckoo flower, primroses, bluebells, wood anemones and marsh marigolds.

But of all the wildflowers, my favourite is the wild rose and in front of my study window the briars form arches of sweet-smelling beauty among the thorns. It is their simplicity that attracts: a combination of fragile flowers and a delicate fragrance. To me the wild rose has far more appeal than the hybrid extravagance and gaudiness of the garden rose. From its mixture of subtlety and simpleness it is possible to understand the feelings of William Wordsworth when he wrote:

> To me the meanest flower that blows can give
> Thoughts that do often lie too deep for tears.

Perhaps today he would experience real tears as many of our wayside flowers slowly disappear.

The wild rose is the traditional flower of rural England and fortunately it is still common. Earlier this century Rupert Brooke appreciated its charm at Grantchester, two miles as the crow flies from where I write:

> Unkempt about those hedges blows
> An English unofficial rose.

The most common of the wild roses is the dog rose, an unfortunate name for the prefix 'dog' usually indicates a flower once thought to be inferior and only fit for dogs. In this case the name probably originates from Greece, where it was once believed that the roots of the plant could cure a person bitten by a mad dog. The other common varieties include the field rose, the downy rose, the burnet rose and the sweet briar, also known as the apple-scented rose. Not only does the sweet briar have fragrant flowers, but it also has sweet-smelling leaves.

The wild rose has other attractions too; its leaves are among the first to show in spring, and during autumn its hips form part of a rich natural harvest. They can be picked and turned into home-made wine, tasting like a good, sweet sherry. Or they can be made into rose-hip jam or syrup. The hips are rich in vitamin C and during the Second World War they were picked in large quantities to provide syrup for children. Children also like them for other reasons, as they can be opened to make itching powder, giving them the local names in some areas of 'ticklers' and 'tickling Tommies'.

Nicholas Culpeper, the old herbalist, claimed that hips had other uses: 'The hips of wild roses, when ripe, are made into a conserve with sugar, of a pleasant taste, it binds the belly, and stays defluxions from the head upon the stomach, and dries up the moisture, and helps digestion.'

According to Gypsy Jim down the road, wild roses can still be used to help check whooping cough. For his coughing treatment he uses robin's pincushions, another attractive feature of the wild rose. They appear as red, moss-like tufts, that grow larger as the summer proceeds, and each year my roses produce several. They are caused by gall wasps which lay their eggs in the unopened leaf buds during May. It is the feeding grubs that cause the strange growth to occur, and they emerge the following May. Gypsy Jim claims that there is no cure for whooping cough, it can only be eased: 'And if it starts in the bud of the year [the spring], it will last til the leaves fall. What you must do is collect those robin's pillows or robin's pincushions, they can be found on any old canker rose [wild rose]. They should be collected and boiled up with a pound of ham sugar [black sugar used for pickling ham]. The children should then drink it and it will help them; it's the best.'

The flower of the wild rose has a much less reliable medicinal use however: if given as a token of love, the condition usually gets worse.

31

In Search of the
Last True Romany Gypsy

Where have all the gypsies gone? I do not mean the assorted scrap-dealers, car-breakers and tarmac layers who live in scruffy encampments up and down the country – in lay-bys, on roadside verges and even on private campsites. Neither do I mean the New Agers, some of whom have taken to horses and trailers. I mean the old-style gypsies, with horses, wagons and lurchers, living the traditional life: working, selling, scrounging and trading their way through Britain.

When I was a boy true Romany families were a common sight, travelling through the parish and occasionally stopping for a few days, camped on a verge or driftway, in the shelter of a large hedge. The women would work the surrounding villages selling pegs and lace, while the men would seek casual farm work, beet-hoeing and fruit-picking, as well as claiming to be expert scissor and lawnmower sharpeners. During the day their running dogs would sleep in the shade beneath the wagons; at night they would work the fields for the benefit of the camp's cooking pot.

When I was small I always feared gypsies. We were told that gypsies 'stole children', a fact confirmed by the swarms of curly-headed gypsy children in and around every caravan. It was only later that it became more obvious why gypsy families were large; it had nothing to do with theft, but a family planning policy approved by the Pope and adopted by most families of rabbits.

Later I got to meet, work with and like several gypsies. Every year a family of Gaskins came to single our sugar beet and I would hoe with them. During school summer holidays I would join them again, picking fruit in the local orchards. At the same time Jim Loveridge and his family would camp near the village. Whereas the Gaskins had moved on to a caravan site in Cambridge, Jim was still free and horse-drawn, sharpening scissors, selling pegs, wheeling and dealing.

But gradually country life and farming methods changed: roads widened, traffic increased, sugar beet husbandry became mechanized and most of the orchards disappeared as did most of the gypsies. Old Jim Loveridge sold his horse and only an occasional scrap-dealer visited the farm; even they have stopped recently, thanks to new legislation and the need for licences.

Jim Loveridge is now permanently parked in the next village on a quarter of an acre. He ceased travelling six or seven years ago; he sold his last traditional caravan ten years ago: 'I was broke and I wanted the money', and he got rid of his last horse about five years ago. Now he lives in a small touring caravan, with the vans of his sons and daughter in the other corners of the little meadow, which he keeps mown, clean and tidy.

He enjoyed the old days: 'But there's too much traffic today; it's dangerous to travel along the roads with a horse. We've not forgotten the way to make a livin' travellin'. I still sometimes call on homes sharpening scissors, knives and lawnmowers, but I don't pedal the ol' grinder – it's driven by an engine now – technology!' He looks like a gypsy, talks like a gypsy, but his traditional life has gone. 'I'm a true Romany – I was born in a trailer at Chatteris Turf Fen. I've travelled all over the country: Hampshire, hop-picking in Kent, fruit-picking in Wisbech, beet-singling and chopping. We did a lot of hard work and got sweet Fanny Adams for it – I'm telling the truth. We had hardly any trouble, only when people didn't know us. I can still make pegs and paper flowers. They were bloody good days. You could walk into a boozer with a shillin' in yer pocket and have three pints of beer – now look what you have to pay.' He still goes into the local 'boozer'. When the peak of his cap is to the front, he's sober; when it's to the side he's happy and when it's to the back, he's crawling home.

Sadly, Gypsy Jim, as he is affectionately known, does not know anybody who is still living and travelling in the traditional way: 'I've got two sisters in houses in Biggleswade and nearly all my relations are in houses now – if you want horses and wagons you'll have to go to Appleby Horse Fair.'

Appleby Horse Fair is the largest gypsy gathering in Britain. The actual day of the fair is the second Wednesday in June, but the travellers arrive the week before, with trading in horses, heather and fortunes starting immediately. I have been to the fair several times and this year there seemed to be even more people and horses than ever. Eight hundred and sixty caravans were on Fair Hill just outside the town, with as many again in smaller encampments in the surrounding countryside.

In the Appleby tea shop, famous for its cheeses and cream cakes, a gypsy family was having breakfast – happily and unselfconsciously dunking bread rolls in steaming hot soup. No, they were not 'horse-drawn', they lived on a site in Sunderland and regarded Appleby Horse Fair as their annual holiday.

A dark gypsy-looking man and his peroxide wife sat at my table – I was having a cream cake for breakfast. No, they were not travellers, but day-trippers. He was a gypsy and she was Irish, but they ran a small bed and breakfast hotel in Blackpool, with Brian also running a 'tarmacking business'. 'Oh yes,' I said with scepticism. 'How thick do you lay your tarmac?'

'No I am genuine – I do a lot of council work under contract,' he assured me. 'There are a lot who give us a bad name, but I'm not one of them. The worst case I heard of was of a gang who agreed to do a drive, complete with white chippings. They hadn't got any chippings so they rolled ten packets of crushed Polo mints into the tarmac. Another lot charged an old lady fifty pounds to spray the new drive with weedkiller. They told her to put the cat inside the house and then sprayed the drive with milk – which looked just like weedkiller. But these crooks are in a minority and most of us do a proper job.'

Again he knew nobody living the traditional life: 'You must remember that there are some very rich gypsies these days with interests in businesses, such as carpets and property. They know more about accountancy and investment than making clothes pegs and cooking hedgehogs.'

At the River Eden horses were being swum and washed in the traditional way, but again the owners were a mixture of horse-dealers and one-time travellers, all of whom lived in houses or on permanent caravan sites, with large chromium-plated caravans, pulled by pick-up trucks and smart 4×4s, rather than by horses. It was an old traditional scene, evocative of a pastoral past; but in reality it was again modern-day non-travelling 'travellers', playing at being traditional gypsies during their annual holiday.

Many of those travellers visiting Appleby only 'travel' for three weeks a year: a week to get to Appleby with their horses and wagons; a week in Appleby, and a week to get back home. Many more have no actual link with gypsies, travellers, or even New Age travellers. One man who looked just like a gypsy was in fact a butcher from Blackpool, who had turned Appleby into one of his annual holidays: 'There are a lot of gypsies in and around Blackpool and I just like to come with them here; my other holiday's in France.' His friend, also gypsy-looking was in fact a farm-worker, James Brooks from Bower, near Caithness: 'It's my first visit here – it's great. It's my holiday after lambing. I used to be a keeper and would like to go back to it, but all the big estates are cutting back and I can't get a keepering job – I wish I could. I'm really enjoying Appleby – it's a lot better than the Royal Show.'

Johnny Eagle is from genuine Romany stock and has been visiting Appleby ever since he can remember. He is a showman and on a grassy slope at the side of Fair Hill he bends iron bars, lies on nails, swallows chains and encourages people to try to hang him. He survives almost intact, although he did break a leg last year while escaping from a strait-jacket at the Tower of London. He has performed all over the country from small horse fairs to the Royal Albert Hall. He is a genuine gypsy who for years lived in a horse-drawn caravan. Sadly I was again too late: 'I live in a pensioner's flat in Lancashire now. I had a horse and caravan until last year, but I can't read or write see – I was getting on bloody motorways and everything, so I packed it in.'

He claimed that many travellers still keep horses: 'But you never see anybody working horses any more, do you? To me they keep them as bloody ornaments. The fair is not a horse-dealer's fair any more, they come here to show who's got the best – the best tackle

and the most money.' According to Johnny, when deals are done some of the prices are astonishing. Ordinary gypsy piebalds go for £1,500 – cash of course – and one stallion owner was said to have refused £55,000: counting that out in cash would have been a sight well worth seeing.

One woman was in a 'vardo', a traditional gypsy caravan, but as a 'palmist and character reader': Madam Smith was using it more as an office than a home. 'I was born in a van and I've travelled all over the country in a van.' But her current van is simply her place of summer work: 'The road isn't made for 'osses these days. Most of the year I'm in a bungalow. I don't like it – it's four walls – like a prison. When you lock the doors you are locked in like a prison.' Her comments were typical; although many gypsies now live in comfortable houses they claim a loathing for them, almost as a sign of 'Romany correctness'.

Outside one luxury van Beryl Price was looking attractive, middle-aged and decidedly middle class. 'I'm a gypsy,' she said. 'My childhood was spent in a horse-drawn caravan and my cradle was a horse's collar with a blanket over it. I remember the horses, the caravans, country roads, trees and wood fires. It was a lovely life, but sometimes we would be moved on and in bad weather it was a hard life.' Her family has moved from buying and selling horses to buying and selling land. She has just sold her house to move back into a mobile home: 'I can't live in a house for more than a year at a time.' She has travelled the world, and gave birth to her daughter in Australia, where her husband was working, painting and tarmacking. The multi-national menfolk are currently working in Germany. Far from being traditional gypsies they appeared to be affluent citizens who had managed to miss out on the recession. Away from Appleby their gypsy ancestry would have passed unrecognized.

As Beryl took me with her daughter and new granddaughter to see the old caravan of her childhood, which is now owned by another family, a strange noise came from her daughter's bag – it was her mobile phone.

There was only one thing left to do in my search for an authentic gypsy: visit the comfortable modern caravan of Billy Welch, Romany, Appleby Fair troubleshooter and gypsy historian. Many of his neighbours had expensive new Mercedes outside their vans and one even boasted a satellite dish.

Billy Welch had many facts and figures at his fingertips. The Fair was started by Royal Charter granted by James II in 1685, but it actually dated back to the thirteenth century when the English were fighting the Scots and needed to buy horses. Today he reckons that up to half the people at Appleby Fair are from genuine gypsy stock. 'The gypsy race is doing well. There are four Romany tribes, the Sinti, the Manouche, Rom and Kalderish.'

He separates New Agers from real Romanies: 'I view them with scorn. They do us a lot of harm as some people cannot tell the difference. The fact that we wash and are clean and we don't have tattoos and earrings seems to escape them. A few years ago inter-marriage was unheard of, but now it's more common. Non-gypsies take to it like ducks to water – but the gypsy identity will never disappear.'

Billy Welch himself has a caravan site for gypsies in Doncaster with room for up to 100 mobile homes – all pulled by internal combustion. He is affluent and looks more like a squadron leader in the RAF than a Romany gypsy. His sons are currently laying tarmac in Germany for Mercedes – like good Europeans. But although his knowledge of gypsy life is impressive, he does not know anybody living the whole year in the old way: 'There may be a few, but I know of nobody. They will be very few and far between.'

'And would you ever go back to a horse-drawn caravan?' I asked.

'Not really. I've got double-glazing, air-conditioning, central heating, electricity and gas.' 'Romany Rides' has evidently become 'Romany Rides in Luxury'.

Driving back to Cambridgeshire it seemed sad that gypsy numbers appeared to be flourishing, but the romanticism of the traditional gypsy had died. On reaching home I spoke to Stewart Coulden, travellers' liaison officer for Cambridgeshire. Despite the popularity of Appleby Horse Fair, he confirmed that Cambridgeshire is still the gypsy capital of Britain with 858 caravans, 270 of which are in my area of South Cambridgeshire, with all but thirteen being on approved council and private sites. Then came a surprise: 'We also have one family still living the traditional life with horses and wagons.' It was a family in a small field, squeezed in between the busy A45 road and Cambridge City, whom I had assumed to be New Agers. I was amazed; I needn't have trekked up to Appleby after all.

Patrick Knox and his wife have been travelling horse-drawn since 1978 and their four small children have all been born 'on the road'. 'I'm not just saying it, but it's a better life isn't it, more peaceful and less trouble.' Despite the nearby road, the small field with its grass and trees made the perfect setting for the two vans, five horses, traditional lurcher and one terrier, for keeping rats away from the camp.

He does fruit-picking, buying and selling and whatever comes his way: 'I've been here for three years and will be going to Norfolk next year. I'm not the last gypsy living like this – there are a few of us about – but I don't move all the time as it's harder to find camps. A lot of the grass verges have been planted with trees and ditches have been dug to prevent us getting on commons. The New Agers have made it more difficult with their mess and convoys – everybody thinks we are them.'

He has noticed a change in villages too: 'At one time ordinary villagers knew us and accepted us. But now people are frit of you at the door. Years ago when you went to a village, people knew you, but now the villages are being taken over by people out of the town. They are becoming very hostile.'

Although illiteracy is still a problem with gypsies, Patrick Knox can read: 'I am a great believer in it: it ain't a crime to be ignorant, but it's a crime to stay ignorant.' He gets little trouble from the police although he did get a visit from one ignorant constable: 'He tried to do me for bald tyres. Of course they are bald – one of my wagons has steel tyres. I don't know what's the matter with the world: everybody spends their time chasing money. Nobody does anything for the future, they do it for the present.'

I was pleased to have found one of the last traditional travelling gypsies in East Anglia, but unfortunately his future is already under threat: Not from roads, hostile villagers or silly policemen looking for bald tyres on horse-drawn wagons, but from Parliament itself. Under its proposals to reform the 1968 Caravan Sites Act the government intends to make camping off approved sites a criminal offence and powers will also be available to obtain exclusion orders to prevent people from returning to a given area. It seems that the proposed legislation is aimed at dealing with the New Age traveller problem. Sadly, unless it is amended, it could also force the last few genuine gypsies off the road. That ought to be unacceptable in a country that boasts of its proud traditions of tolerance and freedom; sadly in Britain today real tolerance and real freedom are becoming almost as hard to find as real gypsies.

32

Kicking the Pigs

I have just come second in a brand-new sport; it is called kicking
the pig. As I went into the pig-sty the other day, for some reason
known only to themselves, eight large porkers decided to rush out
– to the left of me, to the right of me and through my legs – proving
what some people have thought for some time, that I could never
stop a pig in a passage.

With a rattle of the food bucket most of the beasts quickly
returned to their trough, except one who decided to eat a substance
that the average European directive and environmental health
officer would find unacceptable. The pig, however, was obviously
a great believer in subsidiarity.

I sneaked to the back of him, but he would not be driven, and as he
burst past me again I launched an enthusiastic kick in his direction.
It was about as effective as the average tackle made by the current
England football team, with about the same result. Porky ran on,
completely unaffected and unhurt; I was left writhing about in the
mud holding my right knee (yes, my dodgy knee ligaments had again
done their immitation of elastic that has lost its stretch). With the
help of two dogs, one sister, one mother, a wildflower-grower and
a stick, the pig was returned to its sty and given a stern reminder
of the main use of apple sauce.

Last time I mentioned the state of my knees, readers were very
helpful. Then, I had been to the Artificial Limbs and Appliances
Clinic at Addenbrooke's hospital on the outskirts of Cambridge,
limping, and clutching a note from my doctor asking for a pair of
knee braces. The idea was to hold my legs together to enable me
to cart the hay in reasonable comfort. Unfortunately the hospital
technician was not impressed and turned me away, saying that
knee braces were impossible to prescribe without a note from a

consultant, and that there was a two-year waiting-list to see a consultant. Fortunately, numerous kind readers sent me brochures about knee braces, to help me overcome my problem.

I wrote to one company, Remmedi. An astonishing letter then arrived telling me to see their 'onthologist' at where? Yes, that's right – Addenbrooke's hospital. So bearing my Remmedi letter I again attended the Artificial Limbs and Appliances Clinic. There, the same technician who had turned me away greeted me like a long-lost friend and ushered me in. My knees were measured and he recommended a pair of knee braces. 'Sign here,' he said. 'You need to pay for them to avoid VAT.' A fortnight later my knee braces arrived.

So, attending Addenbrooke's hospital with a note from a doctor who had actually examined my knees meant that I was turned away. Arriving with a letter from a commercial company, that had not examined my knees, meant that I was ushered in straight away and treated. What a very odd way for a hospital to run.

Due to the lethargy of the NHS I have since been examined privately to be told that I have ruptured ligaments in both knees. This means another haytime and harvest of heavy work carried out carefully with my knees held together by elastic. But there is a happy ending to this little medical saga. I have now received my NHS appointment to see the consultant. I damaged my knees in March 1992; I am to see the consultant – if I am still alive – on the 22 April 1994.

My earlier mention of my pigs with their snouts in the trough

121

reminds me that I have just paid an exciting visit to the European Parliament in Strasbourg. Strasbourg is a very beautiful city, apart from its lack of cricket and the fact that the Palais de L'Europe seems to have been spawned by an architect who only had one Lego set when he was a boy. The taxi-driver who delivered me to the Palais was not impressed. On telling him of my destination he spat the words out again in disgust and exhaled so much garlic that I had to open a window. He then drove like a maniac. I have only ever experienced one more-suicidal driver and that was in Lusaka, with a hole in the floor on the passenger's side. His steering was rather like that of my pig: we passed on the inside. We passed on the outside and when he could not go straight on he leant on his horn. There is obviously no European directive on traffic regulations – or, at least, no such directive that applies to France.

My purpose in Strasbourg was to talk to assorted Euro MPs on the threats to the countryside, wildlife and country people, throughout Europe. There were some very impressive Euro MPs – a French Green, a German Liberal and a Spanish Socialist, who seemed to understand the problems far better than most of the present Tory clones at Westminster. I found that rather worrying.

Some French diehards were different – defending the indefensible. They were arguing the virtues of shooting migrating turtle doves in the spring as being 'tradition'. I am a traditionalist, and we have no traditional turtle doves on the farm this year – possibly for the first time ever: the French seem to be supporting extinction rather than tradition, and of course extinction is final.

After the meeting I went to watch the European Parliament in action. The MEPs were discussing Angola and Venezuela. Quite what those countries have to do with Europe I did not understand. As I left I asked an official just how important the European Parliament was. 'Oh,' he said. 'It's totally unimportant and almost a complete waste of time.' I passed Mrs Kinnock in the foyer; she hopes to become a member of this waste of time at the next European election. She obviously wants to keep the family's political tradition going.

33

Raptors on the Rampage

The 1960s were bad years for Britain's wildlife and country-side. Agricultural change and the increasingly enthusiastic use of agro-chemicals, particularly those containing DDT, threatened to transform our traditional landscape and the wildlife within it, beyond recognition. The great rush into arable monoculture meant the ripping-out of countless hedgerows, spinneys and water meadows, as short-term profit became more important than long-term responsibility, sustainability and sanity. It was a stampede encouraged and paid for by successive governments.

As a result, habitats which had been available to wildlife for generations disappeared almost overnight. With physical change came technological and chemical change as the great agricultural revolution gained pace. Toxic sprays and dips spread over the land, seeping into it, and settling into the food chain. Seeds, crops and weeds became poisoned, as did the animals and birds which fed upon them, and the predators beyond; Britain's wildlife began to die. The cold winter of 1962–63 finished the work that the poisons had started. From my own parish otters, sparrowhawks, kestrels, barn owls, kingfishers and green woodpeckers disappeared. Elsewhere the most noticeable casualty was the peregrine falcon, with numbers falling to only about 360 pairs.

This catastrophe coincided with Rachel Carson's book *Silent Spring*, warning of impending doom. As a scientist she reported accurately and objectively what country people had been saying from their hearts: they had seen their heritage dying around them. At last the politicians heard and action was taken – just in time. The prairification of much of Eastern England continued, but the use of organochlorine pesticides was banned.

When added to the effects of an earlier age of persecution, Britain was left with a landscape almost devoid of hawks, falcons and eagles. As a result many people began to hold an over-romantic view of raptors, coloured by the birds' primeval beauty and grace, as well as by their rarity. The fact that raptors were, and are, ruthless killers was not an issue; the closest the average citizen came to a bird of prey was sitting in front of his or her television screen, where the reality portrayed was of a magnificent parent bird feeding its fluffy, down-covered young. The flowing blood and the shattered bones of a kill were rarely shown; the tele-viewing, 'semi-detached, suburban Mr James' watched in peace. In the conservation movement the view of raptors was slightly more refined; they were seen as rare birds that must be protected at all costs.

Gradually, and fortunately, the status of birds of prey has improved. Most toxic chemicals have gone from the land and greater enlightenment has meant that most old-style persecution has disappeared. This improvement can be seen on our small farm where kestrels quickly made a welcome return and they are again common. Four or five years ago I saw the return of the first occasional sparrowhawk; now sparrowhawks are already common and again breeding in the area.

The comeback of the sparrowhawk is countrywide. In the early 1960s there were so few that they could hardly be counted. Now recovery is virtually complete with over 25,000 pairs and 30,000 non-breeders.

The kestrel too has made a complete recovery with about 70,000 pairs; it is thought to be at its capacity level.

Strangely, although in the media the peregrine is still referred to as 'endangered', and some conservation bodies use its attractive image for emotive fund-raising appeals, many conservationists believe the bird to be more numerous than for hundreds of years. Officially there are said to be about 900 pairs. Unofficially the number is thought to be about 2,000; indeed it is so high in some areas that it is now breeding on high buildings in towns and cities. Raptor-lovers are turning a blind eye to many of the occupied eyries to avoid the wrath of pigeon-fanciers and grouse-moor owners.

For many years hen harriers were badly affected, not by poison, but by persecution. On sporting estates this magnificent bird was simply not tolerated and its numbers declined to just a few pairs breeding in the Orkneys and the Outer Hebrides. With afforestation on the mainland it has gradually re-established itself and is steadily moving south. In 1968 the British population was thought to be between 300 and 400 pairs. By 1973 it was estimated at about 500 pairs. In 1988/89 there were over 500 pairs in Scotland alone.

Golden eagles are also on the increase, from 300 pairs in 1969 to

424 pairs, plus 87 single birds in 1982. Thirty years ago the goshawk was thought to be virtually extinct; now, with a possible mixture of a few wild birds and birds released by falconers, it is back and its population is rising rapidly. Quite how many of them there are is a mystery, as conservationists are coy about releasing numbers, to protect it from egg-collectors and guns. There is no doubt that the goshawk is a beautiful bird, but it is also a powerful ruthless killer. Gamebirds, protected birds and even magpies form its diet; it is either loved or hated. In Finland numbers of goshawks are so high that the government controls them to protect more vulnerable species, such as blackcock and young capercaillie.

This raises the whole question of the status of birds of prey. When numbers are low and the birds are at risk it is right to protect them. But what should be done when raptor numbers are so high that some of the birds they prey on might be put at risk? In Britain this question is becoming particularly relevant. Before their numbers decreased through poisoning, there were huge quantities of songbirds in field and garden. Now, sparrowhawks and peregrines are back in force, but they have returned to a countryside in which their habitat has shrunk and wild bird numbers have plummeted. So now it is the raptors themselves which are causing alarm in many areas.

Around our small farm this alarm has been felt. Owls and kestrels cause us no concern, neither did the buzzard which arrived one autumn, but the sparrowhawks are worrying. It has been estimated that a pair of sparrowhawks need the equivalent of 110 woodpigeons a year to survive and rear their young. Translated into other bird species this is 600 blackbirds, 2,200 house sparrows or 5,000 blue-tits. Of course the diet will be mixed, as sparrowhawks do not specialize in one variety of prey, but it does mean that a large number of birds in any one area will have to die.

When I was a boy the farm supported fourteen pairs of swallows in the summer. Last summer just one pair returned; so our farm population could not tolerate depletion by sparrowhawks. Yet as soon as each brood fledged, a sparrowhawk appeared as if aware of the young birds. Several times I shouted and waved at it to make it fly off. With the third brood, one of the adults disappeared, and it seemed to me that the sparrowhawk could have been responsible.

Phil Drabble, who has devoted his whole life to conservation, has also had troubles with sparrowhawks. They have actually been inside his outbuildings after swallows and house martins, and they have taken almost all his beloved ornamental ptarmigan pigeons. Around his house there are many feeding places for an assortment of tits, nuthatches and even great-spotted woodpeckers. On occasions he has seen as many as ten blue-tits taken in a day.

125

At a wood in Norfolk, famous for its flowers and birds, sparrow-hawks have cleared out all the woodpeckers. In Holland a hawk was even seen taking young birds directly from the nest hole. Some people believe that the drastic decline in the numbers of once-common garden birds, such as song thrushes and robins, could be linked to the return of the sparrowhawk.

But other scarce and endangered birds are being taken. In Wales there are reports of peregrines taking merlins, while in Scotland forest merlins have been preyed on by goshawks.

Terns can be particularly vulnerable. In Norfolk, near Great Yarmouth, little terns have suffered extremely badly. The colony contains ten per cent of the British population, yet in 1991 wardens actually saw three pairs of kestrels take 143 chicks from 227 pairs. Only twelve young fledged that year, a fledging rate of 0.04 per pair. Last year RSPB wardens tried to distract the kestrels with dead mice. They were partially successful and 176 chicks fledged, at a fledging rate of 0.71. This was still poor however, as the fledge rate should be about 1.7, with little predation.

Roseate terns have suffered even more drastically. In 1970 over 600 pairs were breeding in Britain. For many years the main colony was on a small island off the coast of Anglesey where between 100 and 200 pairs bred. In 1990 the number dropped to between 30 and 40. For the last two years the site was deserted with only a handful of birds breeding in Britain. Their decline was begun by foxes, and finished by peregrines. The remnant birds have since tried to breed on the Irish coast. This is a case of a truly endangered bird being put at risk by a now plentiful but still 'protected' bird, as 'conservationists' stood by and watched. Nichola Crockford, species

management officer of the RSPB believes that the problems created by birds of prey should be overcome with mice, as at Norfolk. Is it really practical to litter mice around all the tern colonies and grouse moors of Britain? Soon the Animal Liberation Front will have another readymade grievance.

It is also odd that despite the boom in raptor numbers the RSPB still makes much of the few birds of prey found poisoned every year. No doubt it is good for publicity and helps generate income, but with raptor numbers at their current high levels, poisoning is absolutely no threat. Gamekeepers inevitably get the blame, but it can be argued that it is shoot management, and the habitat created by shoots, that have helped birds of prey to return to their current high numbers. This is not to excuse poisoning, but in 1990 there were only thirty-six cases and in 1991 twenty-eight. Each year far more birds are killed on the roads, so why not have a high-profile RSPB campaign demanding wildlife speed limits? Presumably it is not so emotive and the car lobby is too strong.

Oddly enough, whereas some conservationists are good at esti-mating the number of birds of prey killed or poisoned each year, they are less enthusiastic at estimating the number of dotterel, roseate terns or golden plovers killed by birds of prey annually. Parts of this mystery may soon be uncovered in a five-year study of raptor predation on red grouse populations being carried out by the Game Conservancy's Upland Research Group in conjunction with the Institute of Terrestrial Ecology.

There are conservationists, however, who believe that the time is approaching when the whole question of raptor management must be discussed. Habitat management is accepted as an established conservation tool, so why not population management? Ian Mercer is a forthright and practical conservationist of many years' standing. He is also chief executive of the Countryside Council for Wales. He says: 'The peregrine is so successful that it does appear to be competing with other species now and I have heard that goshawks are becoming a real problem in some areas. The logic is that if we want to keep maximum diversity in bird populations, then we have to take responsibility for controlling the top of the triangle. It may be unpalatable logic, but it is something that has to be threshed out for our long-term objectives into the next century.'

Phil Drabble agrees: 'Raptors were quite rightly given maximum protection. But now they are back in such numbers there are problems, and I believe that sparrowhawks should be removed from the protected list. I am not talking about an open season, but proper control under licence.'

Even Dr Ian Newton, author of the classic natural history

book *The Sparrowhawk* is not opposed to population control. He believes that much of the alarm at the activities of sparrowhawks is unfounded as predator numbers closely reflect the numbers of prey species. But as a population biologist he says: 'At the moment I think predators are making little impact. However, my feelings would change if predation by a successful predator endangered a genuinely endangered species. Each case would have to be judged on its merits and the control carried out selectively.'

In the 1981 Wildlife and Countryside Act there is provision for the control of predators under licence. It has never been used and English Nature says: 'No one here can imagine an occasion when they would have to control birds of prey.' The RSPB, through Nichola Crockford, holds a similar view: 'We are opposed to any form of control for birds of prey as they are particularly sensitive birds. We believe it would be the thin end of the wedge.' Perhaps the roseate terns of Anglesey would disagree. Surely the time has arrived for a complete review of the problems posed by the rampaging raptors? An honest and open discussion is called for without delay.

34

The Return of the Otter

Somehow, the great agricultural revolution of the 1960s almost passed us by. We still had hedges, grass meadows and wetland, and twice a day our dairy cows continued to slow down the traffic on the main road outside the farm, but the land and farms around us changed. Meadows which had been grass for as long as anyone could remember were ploughed; hedges which had been planted at the time of the Enclosures, and before, were bulldozed away, and farm animals left the land. The great age of arable monoculture had arrived.

We were happy in our backward isolation: cowslips still grew in the meadows by the brook; larks sang and our farming methods followed a pattern and a rotation that farmers of earlier generations would have recognized and understood. Indeed our dairy cattle became so rare for East Anglia that they almost became known as an endangered species.

But even here some things eventually began to change. Men in smart cars started to call, telling us of wonderful sprays and fertilizers that would control pests, cure disease and increase yield. As their products were spread and sprayed, so our poppies, cornflowers and cowslips disappeared with the 'weeds'. More ominously other things vanished too, slowly and silently as the poisons spread – the barn owl, otter, green-woodpecker and yes, the sparrowhawk were lost as the new chemistry and technology killed far more than pests.

Yet as the landscape changed around us, one part of traditional England remained the same – the brook – a meandering ribbon of water meadows, flowers, deep pools and running shallows which continued almost untouched and untamed. It was an unofficial nature reserve, where herons fed, willow warblers nested and large pike basked in the summer sun. Each winter

129

it flooded several times and the water meadows lived up to their name.

Then, in 1971, the brook changed too. Unwanted and uninvited scoops and draglines suddenly moved in; the brook was 'cleaned out' and the meadows drained. Many bankside trees were felled; the beautiful flowering rush rotted beneath piles of spoil and the old otter holt beneath an overhanging hawthorn tree was gouged away. Quite why this was done nobody seemed to know, and my protests were met with mild official amusement. To me it seemed obvious that the resulting lowered water table would lead to land being brought into production, at a time when more cereals were not really wanted. Such a view was regarded as eccentric. As sure as night follows day, so the plough followed drainage and most of the water meadows became yet more fields of cereals. I have since had the last laugh and now many of those same fields have been taken back out of cereal production as set-aside – with the unamused tax-payer paying on both occasions.

Then another change came. A Ministry man asked if we would consider going out of cows. Apparently there was a European butter mountain and milk lake and would we take an inducement to get out of cows? What the officials failed to say was that the over-production was elsewhere in Europe and that British milk production was to be deliberately reduced to below self-sufficiency, to allow in French imports. So the cows went too and we were unhappy. We had not wanted to change – but it had simply arrived and engulfed us.

Our fields and hedges remained, but much of the wildlife had gone; our livestock was going and the brook had become a ditch. Even one of our small grass fields had dried out so much that we ploughed its seven acres; wheat was sown and I felt guilty.

We had a choice. We could remove all our hedges, like many others, and become yet another block of 'efficient' East Anglian monoculture, or we could try to restore what had been damaged and attempt to farm in an environmentally friendly way. We chose the latter; our dairy herd became beef cattle and it became my personal aim to try to restore the land to the richness that it had held during my childhood; I wanted otters back and barn owls too, as well as cowslips in the water meadows.

The loss of the otter was particularly tragic. As a boy I remember crying in bed as I read Henry Williamson's *Tarka the Otter* and there were numerous stories of otters being seen along the entire length of our little brook. Their demise through pesticide poisoning was made worse when it was followed by the destruction of their habitat. It was a sad pattern, repeated over much of lowland England; many experts thought that the otter had gone for good.

I have seen otters several times since, but many miles away, on the islands of Rhum and Tiree, as well as in the Shetlands. But the opportunity to see wildlife should not be limited to a distant place, nor should its presence be seen as an unusual agricultural option; it should not be an option but a responsibility and available in and beyond every garden.

I imagined that it would be an immense task to restore a damaged landscape. Almost immediately the draglines departed, we began replanting the banks of the brook; but then each year the old Anglian Water Authority would come and cut down all new growth. After several years of persuasion, invective and abuse, they eventually stopped their annual ritual and the National Rivers Authority (the current river-watching quango) has so far left the banks almost alone.

The brook has been virtually untouched for nearly ten years. Willows are growing; water mint, hemp agrimony and marsh woundwort have returned. Water lilies too are back after an absence of nineteen years. Unfortunately the flowering rush remains absent, but we have planted yellow iris, marsh marigold and purple loosestrife, to help nature in its task of restoration. Tench are absent, but dace, chub, perch and pike are back, and if the water level were slightly higher then it would again be a perfect place for otters. At last the brook is beginning to behave like a brook, instead of a drainage channel, and in winter it has started to flood again.

Since the autumn of 1989 we have carried out more work by the brook. Through sponsorship given by the Country Gentlemen's Association, we have put our seven-acre meadow back into grass, but not ordinary grass. With help from the remarkable Miriam Rothschild, we planted her traditional hay meadow mixture – over seventy species of grasses and wildflowers. I was naïve, expecting a miracle in the form of an instant hay meadow; drought came, nothing much grew and frustration followed.

But slowly flowers and grasses have come and are still coming, but for some reason cowslips stayed away. Last summer I phoned Miriam to check whether the mixture had included cowslips. It had and she expressed sorrow at their absence; I was resigned to partial failure.

At the beginning of April this year my brother said casually: 'Have you seen the cowslips?'

'Where?'

'In the hay meadow.'

131

I was astonished; suddenly well over 1,000 cowslips had appeared. It was a sight that I presumed had gone for ever.

A phone-call the same week was even more remarkable. It was from the Cambridgeshire Wildlife Trust and simply said: 'Did you know you've got otters.' A map from a recent survey was produced to show the otter sprainting sites – a 'spraint' is an extremely polite word for an otter dropping. Downstream, where the brook's banks are open and unaccountably mown, the droppings were few and far between. On reaching our restored wilderness the spraints came thick and fast.

With Sharon Hearle, a member of the otter survey team, I checked along the brook: yes, we did have one of Cambridgeshire's rarest animals on our land. It was remarkable; it made twenty years of fighting bureaucracy and agricultural fashion seem worth while.

Where the otters came from is a mystery. It is thought that they could be two of three otters released in 1991 on the River Stort and that they have moved into the catchment area of the Cam. On finding our little backwater they liked it and lingered. In all probability they will not stay during the summer as the water level still falls too low, because of the needless drainage done in 1971. But it is likely that they will stay in the general area.

Cowslips, otters, and even the return of the sparrowhawk have convinced me that the wildlife and landscapes of the general countryside can be restored if presented with the opportunity. It has reinforced my view too that wildlife and farming can co-exist, given the chance.

Sadly there is much of Britain still to be restored, but in our small way we have shown what can be done. Because of this I have been speaking to several friends to see if there is any way in which we can encourage countryside restoration on a larger scale. In an attempt to achieve this we have formed the Countryside Restoration Trust. My fellow trustees include Elspeth Huxley, Jill Barklem, Jane Wallace, Gordon Beningfield, Jonathon Porritt and Sir Laurens van der Post. In addition we have received much encouragement from others such as Lord Deedes and Christopher Booker.

Our long-term hope is to buy over-intensively farmed land and to restore it; replant trees and hedgerows; restore water meadows, and farm sympathetically with wildlife. We want to show that commercial farming can co-exist with conservation and we want to allow controlled public access, so that people can get back to the land, to look, learn, admire and enjoy. Other important elements will be to explore new avenues of diversification, to consider multiple land use and to co-operate with other landowners to increase options and to encourage a greater diversity of wildlife and habitats.

There are, of course, charities who already have excellent wildlife reserves; there are organizations which advise farmers, and there are even Environmentally Sensitive Areas where a degree of wildlife-friendly farming is encouraged. Indeed the RSPB hopes that the government will have thirty per cent of Britain covered with ESAs by the year 2000. But what about the other seventy per cent?

We do not wish to advise; we want to show by example. We don't want island conservation, with wildlife restricted to nature reserves, we want it back in the general countryside where we can all enjoy it, and we want people to return to work in and experience the countryside.

As a first step we want to acquire forty acres of land close to where the otters have reappeared in Cambridgeshire. We hope to restore the land that has become cereal monoculture back to the water meadows they once were, with hedges and traditional flower-rich grassland for hay and grazing. Its purchase will enable us to manipulate water levels too, in the hope of giving the otters a firm foothold from which to breed and colonize.

From its position, a properly monitored barn owl reintroduction would be possible and the speckled wood butterfly is another possibility.

It is hoped that this initial project will show on a small scale what could later be undertaken on a large scale, with the purchase of complete farms – a 'prairie farm' in East Anglia would be a high priority, to show that the general British countryside can be rehabilitated and restored.

It is an exciting project that could show the way forward for farming and for wildlife. If we do not attempt it, who will? Our politicians seem to have forgotten that there is a countryside; indeed, most of them would find it difficult to tell the difference between a scarecrow and a blue-tit.

Because otters are shy and easily disturbed, readers are asked not to go looking for the Cambridgeshire otters. Once they have become firmly re-established, then their numbers will grow and their range will expand. With countryside restoration too, further reintroductions could be undertaken when habitat has been re-created, so speeding up the otter's return to areas that are considered suitable.

35

Pre-Harvest Havoc

I like this time of the year. After the surge and urgency of spring and early summer, wildlife appears to rest. Growth slows and birdsong quietens, almost as if nature itself has decided to wait for the grain to ripen. The countryside seems at peace; thistle heads turn to down that drifts on the breeze; bees and butterflies take nectar from the teasle flowers and the young partridges ruffle their feathers in dust.

The other morning the air was almost still and, after checking the sheep, I walked along the old grass meadows of a neighbour – also given over to sheep. I chose his meadows as they seem to miss the noise of the nearby main road; unfortunately the prevailing wind, even when faint, pushes the sound of infernal combustion all over the farm. Traffic noise is one of the worst, untamed pollutants in the countryside today, yet most MPs seem unaware of it and certainly have made no effort to legislate against it.

It is therapeutic to sit in silence with only the odd bleat of a lamb to break the mood. A solitary skylark briefly sang and a yellowhammer made a short musical mark on the day – then silence again. Damselflies took in heat on the reeds, uninterested in flight. Beyond, the fields of wheat burned in the sun, drying and ripening. Next week, if the weather holds, the pre-harvest pause will be over; suddenly all will be noise and dust as the combine rolls: harvest will start in earnest.

Last week the launch of the Countryside Restoration Trust went quite literally with a bang. A public meeting was held in a neighbouring village and Phil Drabble and Gordon Beningfield came to speak to the assembled throng. In front of a packed hall it fell to me to introduce the speakers. After I had listed Phil

Drabble's impressive pedigree, including his recent OBE, the great man walked over to the lectern and microphone. As he stepped forward, I stepped back, inadvertently leaning on the large screen behind me, ready for Beningfield's illustrated talk. As I leant, the screen bent, I staggered, wavered, and then with amazing elegance and beauty, pirouetted on one leg, before falling headlong into the screen, which collapsed around me.

Quite rightly, with this additional free entertainment, the audience hooted with laughter, with several of its members in danger of falling off their chairs, before bursting into rapturous applause. Poor Phil Drabble was totally bemused. After years of public speaking, and without the advantage of eyes in the back of his head, he had never been greeted with howls of laughter before. He looked down to ensure that he had remembered to put his trousers on, and checked his flies. All was well and once he had begun, I crawled off: exit, stage right.

A few days later, a lady phoned to congratulate me, urging me to apply for a role in *Swan Lake*. She says that she has now given up counting sheep when she can't sleep; she thinks of me gracefully collapsing into the screen, and actually falls asleep laughing.

A few weeks ago, following my thoughts on sparrowhawks, I received a deluge of letters, nearly all agreeing with me: yes, there are too many sparrowhawks and as a result, songbirds such as song thrushes have suffered. Many correspondents also mentioned the other old enemy, the magpie, and several also raised the question of slug pellets. Slug pellets are now widely used over farm fields and private gardens, and it seems to many, me included, that their increased use and the decline of the thrush cannot be coincidental. The last thing the survivors want is to be confronted by marauding magpies and sparrowhawks.

Last year my brother found a sparrowhawk in excellent condition; it was dead and had flown into his conservatory window. He promptly put it in his deep-freeze – no doubt contravening numerous EC regulations and the Wildlife and Countryside Act.

Earlier in the summer another sparrowhawk did almost as well at the local pub. It flew at a starling, killed it, but kept going at speed, right through the closed French windows of The Hoops. Diners jumped in shock as glass showered over their dinner plates and the bird landed next to a plate of sausage and chips. Amazingly, it was not the table next to the window, but a table in the centre of the room, ten feet from the hole in the glass. The velocity of impact must have been amazing. Even more astonishing was the fact that the bird was not dead, only dazed. I would have banged

135

it on the head and sent it to the kitchen to meet some chipolatas and parsley and thyme stuffing – I've never tasted roast sparrowhawk. Fortunately for its future, the bird fell by the plate of a sympathetic RSPB member, who wrapped it up and took it to a bird hospital for treatment. I hope it didn't eat any of the other patients.

Shortly afterwards, I had an unfortunate birthday and my brother gave me a surprise present: it was his deep-frozen sparrowhawk, in a glass case, stuffed, with its talons embedded in – that's right – a song thrush. If the local sparrowhawks continue to upset our swallows, I think I will take my stuffed friend to the bottom of the garden and shoot it.

36

Nostalgia Revisited

Summer, and particularly harvest-time, always makes me feel nostalgic. I was born aproximately fifteen feet away from where I am writing this memoir, in the summer of 1943. It was next-door, in the farm cottage, where my parents already had two small children. I tried to enter the world sideways and have not been happy with the accepted pattern of things ever since.

My grandparents lived in the large thatched farmhouse up the road. I cannot remember my grandfather; it is one of my few regrets that I never knew him. He left school at the age of eleven to become a shepherd boy, before moving on to Cambridge to take up a butcher's apprenticeship. He took to business like a duck to water and finished with a chain of local butcher's shops and a reputation for making some of the best pork sausages in East Anglia. Page's pork sausages were served at many of the university's breakfast and dinner tables and occasionally we still make sausages using the old recipe.

My father was not happy as a butcher and wanted to farm, a wish aided and abetted by my mother, a farmer's daughter. They fell in love when he was thirteen and she was twelve; after fifty-seven years of marriage they are still in love today.

Unfortunately my grandfather did not take my father's wishes seriously, and so in the 1920s, instead of buying a large farm when land prices were low, which his successful sausages could have allowed, he bought a small farm. My father ran it for him, and we still work it now, despite the forces of 'rationalization' and 'efficiency' that want to force small farmers away from the land.

It was a traditional mixed farm in a traditional mixed landscape of rural England, before the advent of the motorway, the superstore and over-intensive prairie farming. Sentinel elms stood at the bottom of the garden and along the hedgerows; there were water meadows,

137

hay fields and areas of standing corn. We had pigs, free-range hens, a dairy herd and the two carthorses, Dolly and Diamond, stood in the stable, ready to work alongside the new Fordson Major tractor that would soon make them redundant.

Early summer was my favourite season: a time of growth, scents, sounds and colours – dripping greens, the smell of lilac, honeysuckle and wild roses. Larks sang, swallows hawked after insects and as the evening mist hung over the brook, the white owls would quarter the water meadows for mice and voles. An old fisherman talked of otters too, in a holt of tangled hawthorn roots on the bank of the brook.

The brook was a special place of play and observation; dams, wet feet and homemade rafts mingled with flowering rushes, marsh marigolds and the fleeting azure blur of a kingfisher in rapid flight. Nature was not taught and learnt, it was around us as part of life.

Harvest was a special time. The greens dulled, the grasses browned and nature seemed to pause, bathed in a haze of summer heat. The Flower Show came, where bunches of wildflowers – now weeds – competed for first prize: poppies, field scabious, campion, cornflower and chicory.

Slowly the standing corn changed from green to golden ripeness. Out came the Fordson Major with Jim the one-eyed First World War veteran at the wheel; he would hitch it to the binder; the grease-gun and oil-can would do the rounds and harvest would begin. My father sat on the binder, raising and lowering the sails and cutter-bar and after every few feet a sheaf of tied corn would be automatically thrown out with a clatter.

As the area of standing corn became smaller, so the rabbits would bolt and run for cover. Both Jim and Father would stop and blaze away; Jim with his ancient single-barrel shotgun and Father with his double-barrelled twelve bore. Rabbit pie and jugged hare were part of the kitchen's smells of harvest, along with plum-treacle, blackberry and apple pie and cider. Mother's was a seasonal kitchen and I would still choose her country cooking in preference to overpriced cordon-bleu cookery in London.

As soon as bindering was finished the sheaves were stood up in shocks to allow the ears of grain to dry. A pair of sheaves was leant against each other and there would be anything from six to sixteen sheaves in a shock. In some areas, even just a few miles away, they were called stooks and ricks, but in our part of Cambridgeshire they were shocks and stacks. Oats needed the most drying in the shock, with Father needing to hear three lots of church bells between cutting and carting.

Carting was a happy time. Dolly and Diamond pulling the carts;

138

Judy the labrador and Peter the spaniel hunting for rabbits and Father, Jim and anyone else who was available pitching the sheaves on to enormous loads. Under one sheaf was a tiny, newborn leveret, so small that it could fit into my child's hand. Father left the sheaf with the small hare beneath it so that its mother could find it and carry it to safety later.

It was exciting climbing up the cart rope to ride back to the farm on top of the load. With each easy stride of Diamond, the sheaves would sway and the rope creak, and only once did the rope fail to hold us. Children and sheaves were spilled over the farm track but there was no harm done. Today, officers of Health and Safety, Child Welfare and assorted EC directives would all be following in a procession of nonsensical rules, regulations, red tape and bureaucracy. We rode on the loads for enjoyment; in the same way that countless generations of children had done so before us.

It was hard work for the men, and we would join them as they stopped for dinner and a picnic tea in the deep shade of the wide elms. After a long day Father would not have a bath; instead the whole family would clamber into the Hillman Minx for a cooling, evening swim in the river Cam at Grantchester. Then the water was clear, pure and free of sewage disposal and agro-chemicals; swimming there did not require courage and the threat of a stomach pump.

Gradually the stacks grew towards harvest home. A sigh of relief went up when the last sheaf was pitched and the stacks were finished and thatched. They were thatched to protect the corn

from rain, until the threshing tackle and its gang of men arrived in the autumn. Then there was only one thing left to do: sing 'All is safely gathered in' with relief, thankfulness and sincerity at the chapel's annual Harvest Festival.

Thinking of my childhood harvests, it seems like yesterday. Reading of my childhood harvests, it seems like history.

37

A Wet Harvest Pause

Harvest has stopped again and the combine is silent, with rain falling from a heavy sky. The soil takes in yet more water and a blackbird bathes in a roadside pool. But in the wood it is strangely refreshing; raindrops fall on the canopy of leaves, and it is wet and humid with the soothing sound of dripping.

My hair is soaked and water runs over my cheeks: it is a welcome relief after a break in a hot, dusty continent. I did not realize it was possible to miss an English summer so much, even a wet one. Long grasses hang down through the weight of liquid light and the flowering heads of meadowsweet are bent on slender stems. Despite the rain, insects fly in the still-warm air and a warbler flies daintily after them to feed its brood. High up in an old oak a family of great-tits flit among the leaves and, hidden by foliage, comes the muffled sound of a working woodpecker, pecking and probing into the bark. Woodpigeons coo, their calls magnified and clarified in the natural cloisters and chancels of the trees.

Without warning, along a ride, comes a small deer, a muntjac, its coat steaming in the dampness. It browses quietly, unaware of my presence, completely at peace. A pheasant calls and showers leaf-held droplets as it flies to roost. The deer looks up and walks slowly through an archway of meadowsweet and bramble leaves; a low summer world of abundance and fragrance.

The air holds a heavy blend of scents, clear, yet wafting and dissolving in the first stirrings of a breeze. The leaves of aspen seem to tremble as a sigh passes through them. The flowers of the woodland ride have created a wild, flowering border, confirming the words of Henry Williamson: 'Oh yes, flowers do talk, to the spirit, even as the notes of wild birds fall upon the hearing.' There is purple loosestrife, water mint, meadowsweet, wild angelica, enchanter's

141

nightshade and willowherb; dripping, swaying gently and smelling sweet. A ripe dewberry gives me my first wild fruit of the year.

The English names of flowers and plants can be so accurate and descriptive; 'dewberries' do appear to have been touched by dew, and the old name of purple loosestrife – 'long purples' – is exactly right. Meadowsweet really does sweeten any meadow and enchanter's nightshade is enchanting, with small flowers that in dampness shine like petals of moist white silk, angelica too, tall and white with a hint of pink, is an attractive plant, but often overlooked in the abundant growth of late summer.

Underfoot there are smaller flowers: selfheal and the trailing stems of creeping jenny with petals of vivid yellow. Creeping jenny also has an appropriate country name – 'herb tuppence' – because of its rounded leaves growing in pairs. Botanists with their narrow gaze have a lot to answer for, hiding the beauty of wild flowers with science and lists of long and tedious Latin names.

Near a pond, covered in duck-weed, thick mud is caught by a shaft of weak sunlight, reminding me of the squelching lines of Edward Thomas:

> The rain of a night and a day and a night
> Stops at the light
> Of this pale choked day. The peering sun
> Sees what has to be done.

In a clearing the long wet grasses soak my legs, but there is no discomfort for it is pleasant to walk out in summer rain. Where the wood is darker, pigeons fly in alarm and an owl calls:

> Suddenly, silhouetted in the trees,
> The presence of deer.
> Gentle and beautiful with eyes
> That look on the present,
> But go deep into the past;
> The deer are wild,
> Fragile, uncertain and living in fear.

Hooves run, the ancient woodland floor padding the sound. Only breaking twigs betray the direction of flight.

Light creeps into the woodland edge where trees and leaves give way to a farmer's field and an instinctive feeling tells me I am being watched. A fallow buck is standing in the corn with only his head and neck rising above the close-ranked ears of ripening wheat. Profiled against the grey sky and harvest gold, he is a fine sight, with his antlers covered in velvet. All of a sudden he runs – bounding through the standing stems to leave only his image locked in memory.

The rain falls harder, pattering on hazel leaves and many nuts, showing that they, at least, have thrived in the damp of the year and the path shows more clear signs of deer. Two heads appear close by, just above the corn. Fallow does with doleful eyes and working ears, hearing only the rain and the birth of a new wind. One licks at the small rivulets of water running down the other's neck, before they walk slowly by.

The rain stops and the dripping slows; in the west the sky opens to a vivid red glow of a dying day. Perhaps tomorrow evening we can resume harvest.

38

Plum Crazy

Last year was a plum year; I cannot ever remember seeing so much fruit. Indeed the Victorias were weighed down so heavily that several branches snapped and the rest were bent almost double. Few country people complained, for plum treacle, plum pie, plum pudding, plum crumble and stewed plums followed in abundance. In addition plums galore went into the freezer and there are many people who still bottle plums, ensuring that the supply of home-produced fruit stretched on into autumn, winter and spring.

The only people to miss out were those unfortunates living in towns and cities, for despite the bumper crop many of the supermarkets continued to stock only plums from Italy, Spain and France. Now their warmer climes can produce excellent peaches and apricots, but I have to say, compared to an English plum, the plums of Southern Europe are quite disgusting – soggy, tasteless and insipid; I would rather eat cotton-wool dipped in fruit juice.

No, the plum is best grown under a temperate sun and I have yet to eat anything that can compare with an English Early River. Because of my liking for good, natural plums, I watch their progress through the year; plum blossom sets off the spring and then I wait anxiously until the middle of May, hoping that the frosts stay away. Frost and blossom do not go well together and if the skies clear and late ice comes, the young fruit is 'cut' and finished. Over several recent years we have had no plums whatsoever because of late frosts; my worst remembered wipe-out was on 11 May, although an old great uncle who once grew fruit in the Fens had his entire crop ruined by frost and snow one June.

Gradually, if the frost stays away, the fruit swells, and in July the Early River slowly ripens, turning a deep, dark purple with a bloom that collects the perfect fingerprints of the picker. Its taste is exactly right for the season, turning summer rain into a sweet syrupy juice, touched with an apricot tartness. My favourite Early Rivers are eaten raw; next comes my mother's plum treacle; an ordinary treacle tart, covered in plums (halved to check for maggots) and cooked together.

Somehow the plums always seem to taste better if you pick them yourself. It is a satisfying and fulfilling pastime that turns a task into a pleasure and echoes our hunter/gatherer past. I always pick my plums into a handwoven wicker basket – somehow that seems more appropriate than plastic.

This year the blossom was not so abundant, as if the trees exhausted themselves last year; but there is a reasonable 'bait' – enough for a few tarts, pies and bottles. The most abundant fruit on my old trees this year are greengages, my second favourite plum. They are notoriously inconsistent croppers. What luxury to have greengages two years running!

This year we have reasonable numbers of plums, apples and pears after last year's glut, and these follow good crops of gooseberries, blackcurrants, redcurrants, strawberries and raspberries (I feel hungry as I write). It is truly a privilege to live in the country and eat all this fruit freshly picked, instead of buying stale fruit from a supermarket, all nicely sealed in cellophane.

Old orchards are good for more than fruit and blossom. Birds love them and each year we get nests of goldfinches, greenfinches and linnets. A great-spotted woodpecker regularly inspects the bark for signs of insects and eggs, and when the surplus apples fall, starlings, thrushes, blackbirds, fieldfares and redwings feast on the free harvest.

Strangely, the orchard is even important in deep midwinter, as logs from fallen branches of plum and apple burn warm and smell sweet. There is farming lore too linked to the orchard in winter:

> Sun through the apple trees on Christmas Day,
> Means a fine crop of apples is on the way.

Animals also benefit from the orchard. Our old Jacob sheep and her lamb graze the grass between the trees, and fallen plums are an added bonus. Even foxes visit the orchard and eat the ripe fallen plums, with damsons being their particular pleasure. And how do I know that foxes eat plums? It is simple; fox droppings tell you what the foxes have been eating. I am a great prodder of fox droppings; it sounds unpleasant but in fact it is most interesting. At this time of year they are usually full of plum stones and beetles' wings. A few weeks ago feathers from our hens featured rather too prominently for our liking; at that time the cubs were still at the earth and eagerly waiting for food.

It is a dilemma; we don't want to lose our hens, but we don't like killing foxes either. This year in late May I almost trod on four young cubs sunbathing on a pile of sand outside their earth. They are beautiful animals; on seeing me they quickly disappeared underground. I wish they would become vegetarians and leave our hens alone.

39

One Man and His Dog

The day of Bramble's imminent fame dawned. We were to travel up to the Lake District to film. It was a shock for me: for the first time in my life I was taking luggage, bags of it. All the clothing options possible to please the producer, the director and the camera. Normally, even in the middle of Africa, I travel light, but a simple journey to the Lake District was demanding jackets, ties and shirts. I had almost forgotten what a jacket was like, but I managed to dig out my old ones and I bought two new ones from John Brocklehurst, the 'Countryman's Outfitter' – a good man with country values, from Bakewell. Jackets were bad enough, but the BBC also wanted ties, eight different ones: one for each programme. In my humble opinion the most obvious use for a tie is to keep your trousers up; it is a most odd piece of wearing apparel. Ties and jackets, my local street credibility – or, more accurately, my field credibility – was going to be seriously compromised.

Then there was the problem of how to get Bramble to the Lakes, and to stardom, as normally, after eight miles in a car, he gets dreadful travel sickness. Well he is not actually sick: his mouth opens, he pants, dribbles and looks as if he is about to depart this life. What would he be like after 260 miles?

Fortunately help came for Bramble, and the inside of my car. A friend had tried homoeopathic travel sickness pills for his dog and they had worked. Previously Bramble's only homoeopathic treatment had been administered by himself; eating grass in the garden. He was duly doped up; his mouth stayed shut; his dribble remained hidden and he went to sleep. The journey was not a problem.

The Lake District looked beautiful with its lakes and valleys. But Bramble was singularly unimpressed. He went off his food, including Bonios, he looked at the Herdwick sheep with disdain, and he was not amused when, in the middle of an interview, a competing collie cocked its leg all over him.

A lurcher, by its nature, is thin; without food it quickly becomes even thinner. It takes a small army to make *One Man and His Dog*. With countless cables, way out in the back of the beyond, there is a host of electricians, engineers and camera crew, who all get hungry; consequently there is a canteen, the sort that cooks at television spectaculars and film sets. This came to Bramble's rescue, for with Bonios off his menu, he decided to specialize in liver, prime-cut beef or chicken on his own plate. With this special status his interest and appetite quickly returned – a star was born.

Making the series was pure, unadulterated pleasure; shepherds, dog-handlers and the country people who watch them are unassuming, unpretentious, real people; I even stopped locking my car. They came from Ireland, Scotland, England and Wales. They had skill, sympathy, humour and humility. Perhaps the solution to Britain's problems would be to organize a role reversal. A start could be made by putting the *One Man and His Dog* competitors, their friends and

relations into Parliament, while clearing out our present bunch of MPs and sending them out to various remote farms. There they could work a full day for little reward; dip sheep, clip hooves and keep their mouths shut.

There were several locals on the site too, helping and advising on the course, and the sheep. Being a novice shepherd I spent much time picking brains and seeking advice. At home I always find it difficult to know when to get rid of my ewes. I have so few that I know them all as individuals and like them. I try to reward their lamb rearing, in ones, twos and triplets, with loyalty. 'How long can I keep a good ewe?' I asked Chris, a man who has spent his life working with sheep in the Lakes. 'Oh that's a difficult question, Robin,' he replied. 'I'm not really experienced enough to know.' And how many ewes did he have? – over 800. In reality he found the question difficult, as he also became sentimental about his old ewes.

The Herdwicks used for the trials are the traditional sheep of the Lake District. They are attractive animals, at times looking more like cuddly toys than farm animals. One story suggests that their ancestors swam from a Spanish galleon which sank off the north-west coast of England. Another says that when God made the Lake District with its hills, valleys, streams, lakes, colours and seasons, there was still something missing – so he made the Herdwick to complete the picture. Both are stories that I could easily believe.

There were two real highlights in the series for me. After a long day filming near the shores of Buttermere, I decided to walk up to the head of the valley with Bramble, at dusk. It was still and beautiful up there: the curves of the valley, the lake tinged with pink, then more water and lowland beyond. We could see ridges and hills, rock and pasture, almost from the top of the world, or at least the top of the Lake District's world. I sat and simply admired the view. Bramble stopped and sat too, looking at the hills and valleys almost in wonder. For a dog which had only previously seen our lowland fields his expression almost said: 'Isn't it astonishing.'

The area was wonderful for wildlife with wildflowers, red squirrels and swallows flying so low in the warm rain that they looked as if they were actually plucking insects off the grass. The locals also spoke of another part of the Lake District's wildlife – foxes.

As I drove to the site one morning, a fox hunt was already in full progress. The Lake District has many of its own traditions and fox hunting on foot is one of them. The foot followers were halfway up the valley side, with the hounds strung out in full cry running through the bracken. I stopped to watch where a group of locals were looking knowledgeable. By now hounds were running out on to grass and rock. One old boy had obviously lived and breathed hunting for years. 'The fox will have gone up into the scree,' he said. 'They will have to follow it up and then over into the corrie.' He certainly knew the way of the fox. By now the hounds were distant specks. But what was happening? Instead of going over 'into the corrie', they appeared to have stopped.

There was a commotion fifty yards to our left and a fox, tongue hanging out – THE FOX – was trotting through a flock of sheep, crossing the valley floor towards a plantation, not climbing 'into the corrie'. Suddenly I looked at the old boy in a new light; he took one look at the fox and fell silent. I drove off to the first semi-final, chuckling.

It was a happy series; the whole crowd were delightful, from the locals who released the sheep to the experts who twiddled and pushed the bewildering array of knobs and buttons in the large lorries. Once away from the cut and thrust of the policy-makers, the BBC does have plenty of pleasant, able people, doing highly skilled work very well. What a pity so many of them are disappearing with redundancy and early retirement. Perhaps a role reversal is wanted in the BBC too, with the Chairman and the Director General pushing the tea trollies and some of the programme-makers actually deciding what programmes should be made. There would certainly be more 'nice' programmes as a direct result.

One Man and His Dog

At the end of the filming it seemed as if another 'nice' series of *One Man and His Dog* would result, with me, and the other new-boy, Gus Dermody, being eased, helped and encouraged into our new, unfamiliar roles. And as for Bramble, how has stardom affected his everyday life? The answer is simple: it hasn't, he was almost edited out of the series. Never mind, he did get his eight large boxes of Bonios.

40

Summer Gold

It has been a strange harvest; yields and quality have been down; weeds, oddities and ergot have been up. Ergot is a peculiar dark fungus that grows out of the ears of wheat and this year one of our fields was full of it. It comes and it goes, and its presence is very difficult to forecast. Next year the same field will probably be completely ergot free, for no obvious reason. In years gone by the whole of a wheat crop was ground into flour for bread-making. Wheat, ergot and assorted weed seeds all went into the bread. This was unfortunate, as ergot can cause gangrene as well as various psychotic disorders.

During the 'good old days' it was always a matter of speculation why there were so many village idiots living in the Fens for those of us living in my part of Cambridgeshire – we are at least twenty-five feet higher than them. Some blamed it on in-breeding; others blamed it on ergot. My father blamed it on both.

Before any wild-eyed food-faddist starts a campaign to ban bread for the benefit of the nation's mental health, they should be reassured that the ergot is now removed before the grain arrives at the millers and so all is well. Even the mental health of the Fenmen seems to have improved as a result, although some cynics claim that the arrival of television must be given the main credit.

A friend believes that although the effects of ergot have generally disappeared, MAFF officials are still eating ergot-infected bread in large quantities. The reason for her theory is that at a time when ragwort seems to be rampant in the countryside, there are some members of the MAFFIA who are anxious to repeal the Weeds Act of 1959. This requires owners of land to control 'five species of pernicious weeds' – spear thistle, creeping thistle, two types of dock and ragwort.

Of these the worst is undoubtedly ragwort and it is one of the few weeds that can never be called a wildflower, well almost never. It is toxic: cows and horses dislike it; it ruins grazing; it spoils hay and the only creature which eats it with relish is the yellow and black striped caterpillar of the cinnabar moth. It is for this reason that I suppose it can be tolerated on a nature reserve. I have to admit that on the RSPB's famous reserve of Minsmere, in Suffolk (where there are no horses, cows, or sheep), it can look attractive in sunlight. John Clare once wrote:

> Ragwort thou humble flower with tattered leaves
> I love to see thee come and litter gold.

I don't mind it littering gold, as long as it does not litter our fields of hay and grazing.

This year ragwort has appeared out of control, growing in grassfields; infesting set-aside and invading roadsides and motorway verges. Indeed, instead of scrapping the Act, the Ministry should have been rushing around, reminding landowners of their responsibility to control ragwort. As some of the worst offenders are local authorities and the Department of Transport it seems that there could be more to this foolish retreat than meets the eye.

To get some background into MAFF's unusual thought processes I recently phoned its Head of Land Use and Tenure Division. I asked the gentleman why the Ministry wanted the Bill scrapped when there was more ragwort around than for many years. 'We think the Bill has been completely successful,' he said, 'and so there is no more use for it.'

'How many prosecutions has it led to?' I asked.

'None,' came the peculiar reply, 'which confirms its success and that it is no longer required.'

'How many people do you have visiting landowners to enforce it?' I queried naïvely.

'Oh we don't send officers out to enforce it,' he replied. 'We rely on neighbours to sort out their own problems.' I found all this astonishing and could contain myself no longer: 'Well, no members of the public asked you to visit small slaughterhouses and butchers' shops – but MAFF wasted no time in descending on them and closing them down right, left and centre. What's the difference?'

Quite unsurprisingly my phone went silent for several seconds. I suspect that if the Weeds Act had been part of an EC directive there would have been more MAFF officials roaming the countryside than there are stems of ragwort, but it is not, and so the Ministry boasts that it is anxious to 'deregulate'.

To sum up: MAFF considers the Weeds Act 1959 to be a great success, even though it is not implemented and it has no officers to enforce it. If any readers have a ragwort problem I suggest that they immediately write to the Ministry, with a duplicate copy going to the Secretary of State, Mrs Shephard, who is apparently still giving the impression that she is inhabiting the real world.

In the West Country I have discovered a farmer who has solved his ragwort problem. He has been picking it in the highways and byways and selling it in his farm shop as 'Summer Gold'. He is very pleased with the results: 'The tourists love it. Can you imagine visiting a flat in Birmingham and seeing a tasteful vase of ragwort on the sideboard – bought here at a very reasonable price.' He certainly deserves a special diversification award: what next I wonder? 'Summer Gold Honey' and 'Dried Summer Gold to brighten up your winter days.'

For me the real pleasure of this harvest has been the ban on stubble-burning. Usually, every year as I am out carting bales I suddenly become engulfed as neighbours burn their stubble – quite regardless of wind direction – and the whole village disappears from view. This year it has been a real pleasure to be working outside, smoke free. I became a supporter of the ban after hearing criticisms on the radio, several years ago, of the Third World burning its forests, on the same day that the whole of First World Cambridgeshire appeared to be going up in smoke. As usual the big farmers and most of the farming organizations were dragged kicking and screaming up to the ban. Roll on the day when the NFU actually leads on environmental issues instead of follows. Then, even I would rejoin, but I suspect that my subscription fee is perfectly safe.

41

A Sight to Behold

The great ragwort saga rolls on. A few days ago I simply gave the official view about our toxic yellow friend, ragwort, as dictated to me by a senior MAFF official. MAFF claims that the Weeds Act 1959 should be scrapped as it has never had to be used to prosecute anybody for failing to control ragwort. The gentleman, if that is the right description, also suggested that his Ministry had received no complaints from members of the public.

It must be extremely pleasant being a senior civil servant living away from reality, on a high salary, with good pension rights. His fantasies have brought a deluge of correspondence and phone calls from members of the public who have contacted MAFF, only to be fobbed off with a mixture of apathy and indifference. Not only have I simply had letters, but copies of whole correspondence showing that the information given to me in the first place was totally untrue.

The favourite ploy of MAFF is to claim that implementing the Weeds Act is the function of local authorities. But as the senior planning officer for the County of Avon has pointed out to one correspondent, the responsibility for implementation clearly falls on MAFF, and he quoted chapter and verse of the Weeds Act for good measure.

One elderly widow near Bristol has taken her problem as far as Earl Howe, the junior minister of MAFF. His advice was entirely in keeping with his department; he told her that she ought to take civil action. Her solicitors told her that such a course would cost her anything from £100 to several thousand pounds. It is possible that a legal bill would be of no consequence to Earl Howe; to the widow it was out of the question.

A retired police superintendent in the Fens has had MAFF men

155

out to visit him on three occasions to view the summer gold. In his view the law is clear, as was the attitude of the Ministry officials: 'They were not interested.' He simply does not understand their attitude.

Yesterday the great mystery of MAFF's inactivity was solved. I was contacted by the Redwings Horse Sanctuary, near Norwich. They have the problem of a forty-acre field nearby which is almost eighty-five per cent ragwort. Even the RSPCA has made representations to MAFF, still without inducing action. Now the sanctuary has been informed by the ministry that it will not issue an enforcement order to prosecute on the grounds that the Minister (Gillian Shephard) will not authorize such action as the costs of prosecution will exceed the maximum fine of £75. Once again MAFF puts costs before principle and in so doing Mrs Shephard's halo is beginning to slip. The answer is simple: increase the fine.

With such a circus in operation it confirms my view that the letters MAFF stand for Ministry of Agriculture, Fisheries and Farce.

One correspondent, however, has come up with a place where ragwort is loved. In the Isle of Mann it is the national flower and known as 'Cushag' – not the 'Summer Gold' of Somerset, but 'Manx Gold'. It even features on the Manx ha'penny – there is no accounting for taste. I suppose if MAFF is successful in its ploy to scrap the Weeds Act, the next set of wildflower stamps produced by the GPO could feature the dock, the creeping thistle, couch grass and of course a beautiful clump of Summer Gold. This series could be followed by another, featuring animals just as welcome: a slug, a rat, a mink, and, worst of all, a politician.

It has been disappointing to see the number of mowers out again since the end of harvest. It is now the accepted fashion to flail-mow hedges and ditches in late August and September. More and more, not satisfied with just smashing the hedge itself, are now cutting everything beneath the hedge as well. It is not simply farmers, but local authorities too have joined the ranks of the eco-illiterate hedge-bashers. I am often asked to estimate the percentage of farmers who care for the countryside. My formula is to subtract those farmers who cut their hedges straight after harvest – together with those who have no hedges at all – from those who leave their hedges until all the berries have been eaten by the birds.

Sadly, in some areas, this produces a very high figure of eco-illiterates. Some cut their hedges early out of genuine ignorance and a desire to be tidy, while others simply could not care less. These are not farmers, but land-managers; they do not run farms but factories.

A Sight to Behold

One big farmer in Suffolk who never cuts his hedges before the end of January is quite clear on the subject: 'They just don't think. I would rather see a hedge full of fieldfares and redwings in January than a bald apology for a hedge in September. My pheasants like the berries too; I do not understand this stupid fashion of early cutting and mowing.'

Hedges are not the only things to suffer. I have noticed more sick trees this year than ever before. It is a problem that seems countrywide: sick oaks, ashes, field maples and even hawthorns. Again the official view is odd: 'It is a coincidence; there are always dying trees in the natural cycle.' I have been watching the natural cycle for years. The present state of dead and dying trees seems totally unnatural to me. A farmer on the Cambridgeshire/Essex border, with trees making up over ten per cent of his farm, noticed many of his trees dying after the National Rivers Authority had approved a new bore hole. Needless to say the official view is simple, it is our old friend: 'There is no connection – there are always dying trees in the natural cycle.'

I am beginning to believe that somewhere in the depths of Whitehall there is an actual Ministry of Silly Excuses. I can think of many candidates for Minister – I wonder if Mr Gummer has any spare time?

42

Great Oaks from Little Acorns Grow

It is now just over four months ago that I first wrote about the launch of the Countryside Restoration Trust. The response has been astonishing. There has hardly been a single day since, that I have not received letters for the Trust, including still, first-time enquiries quoting that original article: some people have strange reading habits. In all there have been over 800 enquiries; we now have 500 'Friends of the Countryside' and have received the staggering sum of £63,000 in donations, with another £15,000 promised in interest-free loans, should we want them.

Consequently we now need just another £17,000 for the completion of the first stage of our plans to purchase meadows alongside a small tributary of the River Cam, where otters have recently returned, and to restore them back to water meadows. Just this week we have purchased the initial twenty-two acres, with another eighteen acres to follow next year. It is a chain of events that has given us hope and restored some of my faith in the human condition.

I suppose the seeds of the Trust were sown as far back as 1979, just before the Wildlife and Countryside Act came on to the statute book. Gordon Beningfield joined me in concern over the emphasis in the Act on special areas for conservation – Sites of Special Scientific Interest. It seemed to promote the concept of 'island conservation'; but we didn't want wildlife restricted to 'islands', neither did we want to be forced into our cars to drive to nature reserves every time we wanted to see kingfishers, otters or English partridges. We wanted to see them where they had traditionally been – over the hedge and by the stream in our own parishes, in the 'general countryside', where they had once survived easily and in harmony with farming and sympathetic husbandry.

158

Years ago, at Gordon's suggestion, we even went to The Lodge, at Sandy, to urge the then Director of the RSPB to argue for a broader view, which would give protection to our dwindling number of water meadows, hedgerows and country streams. We wanted this protection in addition to reserves for specialities and rarities. I can still see the look of astonishment on the Director's face as Gordon banged the table in urgency and anger. Alas! our views were met with little enthusiasm; now, fourteen years on, the RSPB shares our earlier sympathies – we have moved on. With wildlife still in rapid retreat it became clear to us that a new Trust was needed to buy land – not special land – but intensively farmed land, to restore it, to show farmers, and the general public, that wildlife, landscape and profitable farming can still co-exist, given the chance.

We began setting up the Trust in 1989, before the recession began to bite. At that time a landowner who was selling much of his land, promised to sell us the forty acres by the small brook. There we hoped we would soon show on a small scale what we later wanted to achieve on a large scale. By the time the Trust was properly set up in 1992, however, the country was in deep recession; promises of business donations had disappeared and we had no money to buy the land. Max Hastings, the Editor of the *Daily Telegraph*, agreed that I could write an article on the Trust, to coincide with our public launch; but even on into 1993 the signs were bad. Indeed a professional fund-raising adviser told us that we were not ready to launch, and if we did we would raise only £2,000.

The return of otters to the brook forced our hand. Their new holt was actually in a pile of wood on the land wanted by the Trust.

Gone to the Dogs

I decided that we could not risk the landowner's impatience any more; to ensure the security of the otters we had to 'launch' in a do-or-die effort. The article appeared on 24 July.

The result was remarkable. In the first post, the following Monday morning, a cheque for £1,000 arrived from the Midlands. There followed cheques great and small, as well as loose change. The highest has been £10,000 from a lovely elderly lady near Stoke, with old Cambridgeshire and rural connections. The lowest, and equally welcome, was a one pound coin stuck to a postcard with Sellotape, placed in an envelope and posted anonymously.

Now, with over half the land purchased, arrangements are being made to plant a new 400-yard-long hawthorn hedge, complete with the saplings of oak, ash, field maple, blackthorn, spindle, crab apple and wild pear. In the spring Miriam Rothschild's special traditional hay meadow seed mix will be sown. We have a Management Committee set up of Trustees and co-opted experts and enthusiasts, with ages ranging from twenty-three to eighty-seven. Other charitable trusts have approached us, and given us help – including the Prince's Charities Trust and we are talking to a number of other organizations including the Royal Society for the Protection of Birds, the Campaign for the Protection of Rural England, Wildlife Trusts and the Game Conservancy; we do not wish to compete with them, but to co-operate with and compliment their work. We are now even more convinced that there is an enormous need for what we are doing in the general countryside.

To make the story even better, the otters are still present and from their fresh tracks, they use their woodpile holt every day. Philip Wayre of The Otter Trust believes that they are part of a movement westwards by otters originating from his successful re-introductions in East Anglia. He thinks that the cubs, and grand-cubs of re-introductions on the Rivers Blackbourne and Thet, in 1983 and '84, have moved down the Little Ouse and into the Cam system. We hope that, with their current security, 'our' otters will breed successfully to help the flow westwards, eventually joining with otters from Wales and the West Country which are already gradually moving east.

So far, the day-to-day running of the Trust has been done by me, the Treasurer, a Jacobs biscuit representative, and the Secretary – his wife, a school secretary. In addition too my part-time secretary Margaret has pitched in during evenings and days off. It has been a very satisfying task, but with livings to earn, it has also been difficult. Now, to keep the momentum going we need to raise the remaining £17,000 for the water meadows, before seeking funding for a professional director and secretary, so that correspondence, newsletters, sponsorship and land-purchase can all be carried out quickly and efficiently.

I have tried desperately to be efficient, but with cows to feed, articles to write, the next *One Man and His Dog* to finish, the duties of a councillor to perform, plus the Trust to run, life has not been hectic, it has been chaotic, and inefficiencies have crept in. Some hastily scribbled addresses have disappeared completely and I hope a Welsh farmer with meadows and otters will phone again.

But it has been a remarkable four months. From our beginning, we now hope that within a year we will have the whole forty acres; the otters will have bred; a director will be in place and the next aim will be to buy a complete prairie farm, to restore it for the sake of wildlife, landscape and farming itself. I am a great believer in the old saying 'Great oaks from little acorns grow'. We want to ensure that those acorns so recently planted will grow, and then of course we want to plant some more.

43

Anti-Hunting, Anti-Green?

I do not hunt, shoot or fish. The reasons are simple. I do not have either the time, money, or inclination to spend whole days galloping across the countryside, blasting lead shot at foolish pheasants, or sitting by a river drowning maggots. Despite this, I have to say that if ever hunting was due to be banned I would immediately join my local hunt – The Cambridgeshire – as a show of solidarity, and I would urge people to keep hunting.

My life is spent farming, writing and travelling, with football-watching in winter, now that my playing days are over, and rustic cricket in the summer, for added pleasures. Yet each year I seem to return to writing in defence of hunting. It would be far easier to keep my pen in its holder on my desk; it would probably be more profitable too, as the media fashion is to be anti-hunting, and so a strongly anti-hunting stance, coupled with my normal 'green' views would certainly make me flavour-of-the-month for many publications and programme-makers.

The only problem is that for years, too, I have been wri-ting about conservation; indeed I was writing about the great green issues of the countryside before they came to be regarded as 'green'. But during that time I came to accept that hunt-ing was, and is, a genuinely 'green' activity, for hunting really does help to preserve the traditional English scene. Following this argument to its logical conclusion is interesting too, for it means that those who are opposed to hunting are therefore anti-green, anti-conservation and anti-countryside. Can that be true?

The problem is that Britain is becoming an entirely urban-dominated society. Most people have never seen a fox, or smelt a fox, yet it is an attractive animal and so they identify with it

162

emotionally; consequently anyone who chooses to chase a fox across a field is considered to be beyond the pale.

Regrettably, this view is also gradually being reflected in Parliament itself. Alarmingly, only sixty out of 651 MPs list Agriculture/ Rural Affairs as a 'Special Interest' – just 9.2 per cent. When added to the twelve farmers in the Commons, it gives the figure of eleven per cent interested in rural affairs. No wonder we get motorways across Twyford Down; traditional slaughterhouses and butcher's shops closed down and, yes, attempts to ban hunting. If eighty-nine per cent of those who govern us appear to have little interest or knowledge in the ways of the countryside, perhaps it shows that field sportsmen and women ought to be more active in their local political hierarchies.

I went to my first 'meet' when I attended the local village junior school. Every time the Cambridgeshire Hunt met outside the pub we would troop out of school to watch. Imagine a modern-day schoolteacher leading her pupils out to look at the hunt: there would be uproar. Later I saw my first fox moving through a thick, bramble-covered hedge, next to the brook. Apart from the area around our henhouses, I began to associate foxes with hedges, woods and unkempt meadows. Since then I have watched a fox hunting for voles in a sunlit water meadow; I have had a fox actually bump into me as it ran out from a sprawling hedge – I don't know who was startled the most – and I have even found a litter of fox cubs up a tree, at least eight feet from the ground, in the trunk of an ancient elm.

The problem in my part of Britain has been that all the beautiful places which I once associated with foxes have gradually disappeared. The beloved Cambridgeshire landscape of my childhood has been transformed. The agricultural revolution has meant that thousands of miles of hedgerows have vanished; woods and spinneys have been ripped out and water meadows have been drained and ploughed. In just one generation, the present generation has been denied part of its country heritage. In my own parish, barn owls and nightingales are now all restricted to memory and several other birds, flowers and butterflies are in steep decline.

Only our small farm hedges and meadows remain; we are a fifties time-warp – a conservation island in a sea of intensive and over-efficient farming. But fortunately we are not entirely alone, for there are other islands too, large and small, where woods, hedgerows and grass fields remain. The reason for their preservation is both obvious and simple – they are farms and estates where the owners and tenants shoot or hunt or fish, and where the habitat left for the fox and the pheasant remains the traditional rural scene of

England. So the landscape becomes a map of farming methods, attitudes and interests. The land of Farmer Bloggs is hedgeless and grassless; it is also flowerless, butterflyless and badgerless. Bloggs himself is humourless, despite having three BMWs and taking a January holiday in the Canaries. On the other hand, the land of hunting Farmer Furlong has hedges, meadows and streams, as well as Fox Copse and Badger Wood; he has foxes, but he also has white admiral butterflies, orchids and barn owls too. He is a happy, contented man.

To country people and honest, practical conservationists, the link between country sports and conservation is obvious; the habitat preserved or created for the fox is also vital for a host of other wildlife from bugs, beetles and butterflies to deer and birds of prey. Indeed it is even fair to say that attractive, varied land, where hunting and shooting give an abundance of habitat for wildlife, creates a far greater acreage for wildlife than the various nature reserves dotted around the countryside.

Consequently those who threaten to ban hunting also threaten to deliver a huge blow to what is left of Britain's wildlife. Sadly the threat goes further still, for country people themselves, their traditions, culture and heritage are also threatened by those who want to stop hunting. Many countrymen have been hunting, or following the hunt, as a normal part of their lives for as long as they can remember. They know the ways of the fox; they enjoy the hunt and to them hunting is as much part of the country scene as morris dancing, cricket and singing carols at Christmas. Some stop earths; others follow the hunt by bike; and a few simply want to sample the stirrup cup; but whether they ride, follow, or lean on gates, it is their chosen way; they do not want an ignorant urban majority deciding what they can do and what they cannot do.

Sadly a ban on hunting would not only threaten our wildlife and landscapes, it would also threaten us too – aristocrat and country bumpkin alike: we are all endangered species now.

44

Bottoms Up

I had to go to North Wales the other day. It is beautiful at any time of the year, but in October, with the leaves turning and the roads almost empty, it is particularly appealing. For me, both Scotland and Wales are at their most exciting and beautiful in the autumn, just when the tourist season has almost ended. I never have understood the taste of the great British tourist.

Fortunately there were still two holidaymakers in the principality. As I stopped in a lay-by, admiring the view across a valley, a husband and wife tourist team arrived noisily in second gear. On surveying the scene the woman became visibly agitated. She was gazing over a flock of sheep, their rear ends blue, showing that the ram had done his autumnal duty by marking each delightful ewe with colour as he said 'Good morning' to them.

'Isn't that disgraceful,' the lady said with anger. 'Why do these stupid farmers paint their poor sheep like that?' I was speechless, having visions of Welsh farmers chasing their sheep around the fields, paint-brushes in hand.

Fortunately her husband came to the rescue: 'Oh they have to dear. It's so they can count them more easily, especially when it snows.' What a wonderful addition to my shepherding education. I hope nobody tells the Ministry of Agriculture this new revelation, otherwise painting sheep could become official government policy to help MAFF's sheep-subsidy checkers.

The way the ewes are marked is simple; the ram wears a harness, holding a coloured pad – a raddle – during the breeding season. Each time he does his duty, the coloured pad marks his progress. An old gamekeeper came up with a new use for a raddle the other day: 'I think MPs should wear them, the trouble is the way they've been carrying on lately there wouldn't be enough colours. And then there's the question of where would they wear them – David Mellor would want one on his big toe.'

Three chapters ago I evidently made a mistake. Mrs Shephard's halo has not started to slip on the question of ragwort. The Ministry has now decided to retain the Weeds Act and Mrs Shephard has never instructed her officers to take no action. In addition the maximum fine for allowing ragwort to grow unchecked is not £75 but £1,000. One mystery remains, however: why was a letter sent by MAFF's Cambridge office containing these inaccuracies? Sadly, there appear to be several MAFF officials up and down the country who seem to operate on an independent freelance basis.

Although Mrs Shephard's halo is still in place on the subject of ragwort, it has slipped on the Meat Hygiene regulations. Recently she was defending them on television and several people have sent me copies of strange and misleading letters they have received from officials and politicians after they had protested about the closure of their local slaughterhouses and butcher's shops.

One set of regulations concerns wood. It has been banned from slaughterhouses and cutting-rooms; wooden benches and wooden handles are all outlawed as being unhygienic; plastic and metal are the accepted surfaces now, thanks to the bureaucrats and Eurocrats. Yet someone from Derbyshire has sent me a report from Wisconsin University. There, experiments have been held on the spread of harmful bacteria such as salmonella and listeria. After leaving the bugs overnight at room temperature, they found that the bacteria on the plastic surfaces had multiplied, while the wooden board was clear. Researchers believe that the porous wood soaks up and destroys the bacteria with anti-microbal chemicals that trees use to protect themselves. It seems that even when a tree is dead its wood can still attack micro-organisms.

I like disgusting cheese which is usually overflowing with flavour-filled micro-organisms. I will not look at blue cheese until it is at least one month past its sell-by date and has begun to grow fur. Indeed the whole notion of having a sell-by date on cheese seems totally absurd. Certainly the average supermarket cheese, eaten within its sell-by date, is so bland that it is virtually inedible.

On my trip to Strasbourg earlier in the year a Spanish Euro MP told me that Spain still manages to boast some of Europe's most disgusting cheeses. One is apparently so bad that it makes my ancient bacteria-oozing Stilton seem quite ordinary. Its manufacture breaks virtually every EC hygiene rule possible, and the Spaniards love it, and buy it in large quantities. They are allowed the luxury of this revolting cheese as long as it is not exported. Why, therefore, was Britain not allowed to keep all its traditional slaughterhouses and butcher's shops under the same condition; that no meat be exported? What is good enough for Spanish cheese ought to be good enough for the British mutton chop.

45

Vermin Ermine

The stoat is one of the commonest, but least-known animals in Britain. The usual view of this small carnivore is a rufus-brown streak, as it rushes across a road or path. Such a fleeting vision usually leads to the question: 'Was that a stoat or a weasel?' Whenever I asked that as a boy an old countryman who often visited the farm would say: 'You should know that: The weasel is weasily distinguished because the stoat is stoatally different.' His other stock answer to 'What's the difference between a stoat and a weasel?' was: 'The spelling.'

Fortunately there are several differences. The stoat is longer; its body length is about eleven inches, plus a four-inch tail. The weasel is only eight inches long with a three-inch tail. The tail of the stoat is also something of a give-away, as it has a distinctive black tip.

At high speed across a road, it is difficult to measure miniature carnivores in full flight, but both the stoat and weasel are very inquisitive little animals and it is often possible to 'call them up' for a second opinion. An old gamekeeper's trick is to suck the bottom lip, or the back of the hand loudly – it sounds like a frightened rabbit. I have called a weasel up to within three feet using this method, and it has also gained me several excellent views of stoats from ten feet to ten yards. At such distances the size differences and the stoat's black-tipped tail can readily be seen.

In winter the problem of identification can be easier to solve as the stoat sometimes turns pure white, to match its background – except for the conspicuous black tip to its tail. In the north of Britain the white winter stoat is common, the further south the rarer it becomes. I have only seen one in its 'ermine' form and the poor beast was most conspicuous, as there was no snow. It was shot in a pile of wood – thought to be a ferret, escaped and gone wild. It was given

168

to my father to skin and it was then that we discovered its close relationship to the polecat: the smell was terrible. Other members of the 'weasel' family are polecats, martens, badgers and otters.

For years stoat skins in their ermine form have been highly prized and made into robes and capes for the aristocracy. When in my early teens, this process inspired me into verse:

> An animal I know is very forlorn,
> It's cursed by all gamekeepers as being base born.
> They trap it and shoot it and say it is vermin,
> Then flog it to Royalty who wear it as ermine.

Unfortunately for the stoat it looks extremely attractive when worn as ermine.

On farms and wildlife reserves stoats can be unwelcome guests as they are quite ruthless killers of animals and birds much larger than themselves. On one occasion I saw a stoat (weighing about one pound), easily dragging a large rabbit (weighing approximately four pounds). They also sometimes indulge in 'surplus killing', which means that they will kill far more than they need. One day on the farm we lost an entire clutch of three-day-old chicks from a henhouse, in broad daylight. We suspected a stoat, as they are active day or night.

With ground-nesting birds such as terns, stone curlews, pheasants

and partridges, stoats can cause problems; hence they are not welcomed by gamekeepers or wildlife wardens. However, they are not totally harmful as they eat many rabbits, rats and mice. The hunting stoat will often pursue just one rabbit remorselessly, sometimes causing the terrified animal to freeze with fear. The scream of a frightened rabbit can be quite unnerving. The death blow comes from a bite at the back of the neck. Often the stoat will then lick the blood away from the wound, giving rise to the old country belief that 'stoats suck the blood from their victims'.

One of the most fascinating methods of hunting is for the stoat to 'dance'. They have been seen to jump and roll, frisk and frolic, before suddenly striking out and seizing the over-inquisitive bird or beast. There are also stories of stoats hunting in 'packs', probably family parties, and due to their inquisitive natures and comparative fearlessness, there are stories of them attacking people. Such incidents are extremely rare and border on the verge of mythology.

The stoat's breeding behaviour is unusual. Like its relative the badger, the female experiences 'delayed implantation'. The male is fertile between March and August, yet when the female becomes pregnant the embryo remains in suspension in the womb and does not grow. In the spring it 'implants' and a normal pregnancy follows with five to six young (kittens) born in March or April.

The den of a stoat is usually in a hole in a bank, tree, or stone wall. The average life expectancy of a wild stoat is only one and a half years, with the oldest recorded wild animal living to the age of seven. The stoat's most dangerous predator is Man, followed by hawks, owls, foxes and dogs – hence the white camouflage during winter to give it some extra protection. It is ironic that this 'protection' actually makes it attractive to Man, especially when trapped, skinned and wrapped around the shoulders of a duke. If there are any deep-thinking rabbits out there, I'm sure that they are all hoping even more stoats than usual will be turning white this winter.

46

A Hole in One

There are times when I wonder which planet several of my fellow Earth dwellers actually come from. It happened again the other day when I was approached by a complete stranger who asked: 'How are your beavers getting on?' There may be beavers in America and several parts of Europe, but in Britain the beaver is as common as the dinosaur – the pterodactyl and the dodo. In other words it is extinct, long gone from these sceptred isles. So why did this visitor from outer space enquire after the health of my 'beavers'?

The poor demented soul meant 'otters', although how and why anybody living in Britain should get the two muddled is beyond me. Once on a visit to Kenya an American state senator told me that she was looking forward to seeing the 'lions and tigers'. I have nothing against Americans (I'm being polite) but somehow you expect that sort of in-depth knowledge from a state senator – tigers in Africa. But beavers in Britain? I am left speechless, sorry, inkless.

I would never want to see a tiger in Africa, but the incident does raise the question of the extinct large mammals of Britain: the wolf, the bear, the boar and the beaver. Apparently we expect Indian peasants to live alongside tigers, and African tribesmen to cope, next door to a multitude of hazards from elephants downwards. But at the slightest sign of trouble in the past, our large animals were hunted into history.

It so happens that our otters are still doing very well; but surely it is time that some of our extinct animals were reintroduced to join them. At the moment the beaver would find things rather difficult, due to the absence of woods along the banks of our rivers and streams. Beavers gnaw down trees to create their own highly efficient dams; that habit could be a problem, although a huge dam in the mouth of the Thames would help to turn one of Britain's largest eyesores into a marina. Who needs or wants London anyway?

The ideal animal for reintroduction is the wild boar. Friends of mine already keep them in the Highlands of Scotland. They bought them to get them to turn over land with their snouts. It was hoped that with pig ploughing in an enclosure, seed germination would be triggered and natural forest regeneration would begin. The wild boar are quite fascinating, and when covered with apple sauce, delicious!

Tilly and Alan also keep Scotland's only herd of reindeer, another once extinct British animal. They think it is time to release their wild boar, but such action is currently illegal: 'They are beautiful animals and should be part of our woodlands and forests again.' They are only dangerous when threatened, surprised or surrounded, and so it is surely time for the return of the wild boar.

Extinction was caused through persecution, after damage to crops, but if compensation was paid, there would be no problem. In France there are wild boars living within a few miles of the centre of Paris, at Versailles, so why not in Britain? (Just in case any American state senators are reading this, there are no wild lions and tigers living in France.) If the wild boar is ever successfully reintroduced to Britain, then perhaps we can start on the beaver, or even the nice, friendly, cuddly wolf.

I am suffering from an extremely traumatic condition at the moment; it is known as *golf*. I have not adopted this silly game by choice; but my knees have finally announced – quite independently of my brain – that my footballing days are over. Consequently, in an attempt to fill the void, I have taken up golf. The choice was not very difficult, for all over Britain a golf revolution is taking place and new golf courses are sprouting up all over the county, putting the game of golf within the range and pocket of all sorts of people, including peasants like me.

A cousin is one of those farmers who now grow putting greens and golf balls instead of sugar beet and wheat. It pays him much better too, especially as nearly all the work of golf-course creation was done with local labour, without the advice of overpaid 'experts'. The finished result is excellent, but I have to confess that I find the game totally boring; it really does spoil a good walk. It would be much better if you had to chase the ball and hit it while it was still moving. I have come to the conclusion that golf is taken up by people whose coordination is so bad that any other sport would be beyond them.

Then of course there is the club house. The golf club bar-proppers give a new dimension to the word 'boredom'. Do people really want to hear about the slice at the fourth and the putt at the fourteenth for three and a half hours non-stop. I don't; usually I can't even remember where the fourth and fourteenth are anyway.

Sadly, many new courses have lost a great opportunity for conservation – they cut their 'rough', the grassland on either side of the 'fairway'. If the 'rough' really was rough, the long and tangled grasses would provide perfect habitat for birds, small mammals and butterflies. More balls would be lost, but think of all the extra employment created in golf-ball factories.

Real rough could also make an interesting new game. Each golfer would be required to play in partnership with a dog. Once in the rough the dog would have to respond to whistles and commands to find the ball within two minutes and place it in the middle of the fairway. Failure to achieve this would bring one penalty stroke. An uncle has already taught his labrador to find golf balls and he has bags full of the things. Dog golf, that could be exciting and spectacular – I think I will start training Bramble tomorrow; it would be almost as exciting as *One Man and His Dog*.

My cousin married an all-round sportsman, that is, he is much too 'round' to play sport, and so he talks it. Indeed the only sporting competition I can imagine him winning would be for secret eating. Even when my cousin insists that he goes on a diet he will suddenly appear at my back door looking forlorn, obviously wanting a coffee and a heap of chocolate biscuits.

Whenever a sport is mentioned, the reaction is always the same: 'I used to play that': 'I won cups at that': 'I could have played for Luton Town you know': 'I've done it – I was good at it – why wasn't I picked for England'. It is just strange that somebody who is younger than me has given up everything before me; and from his shape and general fitness I cannot even see him having enough stamina for tiddlywinks.

The inevitable happened on the question of golf. 'I've started to play golf Malcolm,' I told him late one night. I should have known better. Malcolm immediately replied: 'I used to play golf,' and then came a list of mighty golfing achievements.

I decided to call his bluff: 'Come off it Malcolm,' I foolishly said, 'you've never played golf in your life.'

'Oh yes I have,' came the instant response. 'I'll get my clubs.' Sure enough he returned almost immediately with a posh set of clubs, complete with leather bag.

'I was quite good at putting,' he said, as he putted across the lounge carpet; Malcolm's golfing master-class had begun.

'I liked using the sand-wedge,' he informed me. The putter went into the bag; the sand-wedge came out of the bag, and he proceeded to chip the ball expertly from the hearth rug into an armchair.

'My favourite club was the driver,' he announced with a triumphant grin. The sand-wedge went into the bag and his gleaming driver, club of clubs, came out of the bag. 'I could hit the ball a long way,' he said, as he set himself for the hitting position, in the middle of the room, directly beneath the light. It was a beautiful light, a hanging light with a wooden frame from which came three brass stems, each bearing a beautiful glass shade and bulb.

I could not believe my eyes; he wasn't going to was he? He did. Malcolm swung his club back; down it came and up in a perfect arc. There was a tremendous crash, glass showered over the whole room, the lights went out and the shattered chandelier was swinging violently from side to side. It was the best drive I have ever seen played in my life; the lounge door burst open and my cousin Margaret stood, wild-eyed in her nightdress. I then created a new sporting record of my own. I sprinted the thirty yards out of the house, down the drive and into my car in 2.76 seconds precisely.

47

A Ring of Bright Water

I am sorry, I simply have to write about otters again as their return is such an exciting and unexpected development. The advance of the otter into Cambridgeshire took me completely by surprise, as did the occupied holt along the brook. It is a sight that I did not expect to see in my lifetime, unless a reintroduction programme took place. Ironically the new natural holt is just twenty yards away from an artificial holt prepared by the local Wildlife Trust several years ago. The otters knew best, however, and their chosen home is a large pile of wood in the corner of a field, close to where a small stream flows musically into the brook. They arrived when the field was in set-aside; now much of the land is in production again, but the landowner has left the area immediately around the holt undisturbed. Soon the Countryside Restoration Trust is to buy the field and so the future of the otters, and the land surrounding them, seems secure.

Although the local Wildlife Trust 'found' the otters, in fact my brother and a friend, Marcus, may have stumbled across them unknowingly several months earlier, while out rough-shooting. Rinty our labrador, and Denza, Marcus's Chesapeake Bay retriever, would not come away from the wood-pile holt for well over half an hour. They were allowed to hunt so long as they were expected to flush out a rabbit or a fox, but nothing appeared; we now presume they had scented the otters. This year the dogs will be kept well away from that important pile of wood.

My interest in otters began as a boy. My uncles remembered seeing otters, and hearing stories about them along the brook, in their childhoods, and in the fifties an old fisherman, standing on the bank in one of our farm fields, regularly saw otter cubs playing around the tangled roots of their hawthorn tree holt.

At about the same time the old Eastern Counties Otterhounds killed a dog otter close to where the brook flows into the Cam. It was the last time that particular attractive rag-tag collection of hounds found any scent of otters at the confluence of river and brook. By then, too, the hawthorn tree holt was empty; it was a pattern that was repeated in many parts of the country.

With otters so scarce, I did not approve of otter hunting, a view reinforced when I read Henry Williamson's wonderful novel *Tarka the Otter*. As a teenager I recall reading the last two traumatic paragraphs in bed and crying like a child, quite unashamedly. Recently, talking about my favourite books on the radio, I read those last two paragraphs again, bringing a real lump to my throat once more:

'Deadlock saw the small brown head, and bayed in triumph as he jumped down the bank. He bit into the head, lifted the otter high, flung him about and fell into the water with him. They saw the broken head look up beside Deadlock, heard the cry of Ic-yang! as Tarka bit into his throat, and then the hound was sinking with the otter into the deep water. Oak-leaves, black and rotting in the mud of the unseen bed, arose and swirled and sank again. And the tide slowed still, and began to move back, and they waited and watched, until the body of Deadlock arose, drowned and heavy, and floated away amidst the froth on the waters.

'They pulled the body out of the river and carried it to the bank, laying it on the grass, and looking down at the dead hound in sad wonder. And while they stood there silently, a great bubble rose out of the depths, and broke, and as they watched, another bubble shook to the surface, and broke; and there was a third bubble in the sea-going waters, and nothing more.'

Strangely, it was otter hunters who first warned of the disaster that was overtaking the otter. Rivers on which they had found otters for generations were becoming otterless. Hunting days were being cut and the huntsmen and followers were becoming concerned. Their concern was first put into writing by Jack Ivester Lloyd in 1962. Slowly the fears became facts, as naturalists and scientists confirmed the continuing tragedy, with pollution getting the blame: poisoning by organochlorine pesticides, DDT, dieldrin, aldrin and heptachlor.

Otters were not the only creatures affected. Birds of prey were particularly hard hit; the peregrine, the sparrowhawk and the barn owl all but disappeared. During the seventies, although bans were put on most of the toxins, otter numbers continued to fall. In 1975 while writing *The Hunter and the Hunted*, a book investigating the ethics of 'blood sports', I had a day's hunting with both the

Dartmoor Otterhounds and the Eastern Counties Otterhounds, to see for myself what went on. On the edge of Dartmoor nothing was found; in Suffolk coypu were flushed in large numbers; both hunts confirmed that to find an otter was a rarity. I thoroughly enjoyed the two alcoholic romps through the reed beds – possibly because we did not actually pursue an otter; I could even see why the hunters enjoyed their sport, but I could see no justification in hunting an animal that had become so rare. In 1977 I wrote: 'Even so, the sport [otter hunting] cannot be defended, particularly in the slow flowing rivers of lowland England where the otter is scarce. The Ministry of Agriculture does not consider it to be a pest in any part of the British Isles, nor do most fishermen, who see the protected heron as a far greater nuisance. Consequently otter hunting should not be banned as such, the otter should simply become a protected animal'; in 1978 the otter received complete protection.

Sadly, there was no protection for some of the otter hunters, who were real characters in the best traditions of country life. Indeed the biggest problem I encountered on the two hunts I attended was to get the hunters out of the pub in order to start, and then no sooner had they started than they were back inside the pub for 'dinner'. With the water of the River Lydd in spate, the old Master of the Dartmoor Otterhounds explained, 'It is so important to get the level on the inside, the same as that on the outside.' That was said shortly before he fell slowly and gracefully into the swirling brown water. When I commented on the fumes of alcohol that seemed to follow us all day long he observed warmly: 'It's a good thing. The smell has the same effect on huntsmen as dangling a carrot in front of a donkey.'

During 1978–79 the Vincent Wildlife Trust carried out the first national otter survey. It confirmed that the plight of the otter was desperate. Out of 3,200 sites visited, only six per cent were occupied by otters and the otter's range had contracted to just the south and west of England and central Wales and Scotland – where the population remained strong. The centre of England was an otter wasteland, although there was a small remnant population in East Anglia.

It was during this time that much unsung, but important work started in an attempt to secure a future for the otter. The Hon. Vincent Weir founded the Vincent Wildlife Trust and walked miles along our river banks looking for otter droppings ('spraints'), to provide a picture of otter survival. He funded similar monitoring in Scotland carried out by Jim and Rosemary Green, and he also began the work of creating 'otter havens', to provide areas of quiet overgrown islands and river banks for otters, sometimes with artificial holts, to give otters areas of security, free from disturbance.

Angela Potter and Angela King – the 'two Angelas' – undertook much of the otter haven leg-work, including the task of talking to landowners. In the early eighties I had the pleasure of walking with them along the bank of a 'haven' on the River Piddle, in Dorset, where otters were still present – just.

At that time too Vincent Weir himself showed me the spraints of almost the last otters in Norfolk. He also explained the difference between otter droppings and those of mink. An otter spraint smells like bloater paste – very fishy; a mink dropping smells exactly what it is – a dropping – it cannot be recommended.

One day when Vincent Weir was picking up and sniffing assorted droppings at Blakeney, an old lady began watching him intently. After yet another smelling session she approached him and said angrily, 'You disgusting man.' He paid no attention and continued his noble 'research'.

Others too were undertaking invaluable work at that time. Dr Don Jefferies at the old Nature Conservancy Council, who later spent hours radio-tracking released otters. Philip Wayre founded the successful Otter Trust, now a vital breeding centre of captive otters for reintroduction, and Dr Paul Chanin studied the habits and habitat of otters in the West Country, where a reasonable population lingered on. Even in the West Country however, some populations retreated. In 1981 otters had even retreated from the River Otter in South Devon. As I walked from the village of Otterton to Budleigh Salterton, hoping to see my first wild otter, all I saw was my first wild mink.

In 1985–86 the Vincent Wildlife Trust sponsored another national survey. The same 3,200 sites were visited, revealing a slight improvement. Twelve per cent of the sites showed signs of otter occupation, although the otter population in East Anglia had continued to contract and had almost vanished. The pressures in East Anglia were probably caused by continuing pollution problems and loss of habitat through agricultural 'improvement'.

Much of this 'improvement' was undertaken by the now discredited Anglian Water Authority. It seemed to have an obsession with 'improvement' and 'efficiency'; to achieve these dubious aims, bankside vegetation was removed; trees and bushes were felled; the water table was lowered and the general habitat degraded. What the Third World does now out of ignorance, the Anglian Water Authority did out of 'expertise'. This legalized vandalism turned numerous living rivers, brooks and streams into dead drainage channels and ditches; fish died, plants vanished, water levels dropped and farmers ploughed to the very edge of their river banks, allowing fertilizers and chemical sprays to be leeched away quickly in rainwater run-off. It meant that disaster continued for the otter in East Anglia; it was sacrificed to the false god of agricultural 'efficiency' and 'progress'.

'Improvement' was forced on to our little brook in 1971; even the old hawthorn tree holt was removed. The otters only returned after a twenty-three-year-long battle to turn the brook back into a wildlife haven and a living part of the landscape. Most people with feelings for wildlife breathed a sigh of relief in 1989 when the water authorities were replaced by the National Rivers Authority – an organization with obligations to promote wildlife and conservation. But, even so, some of the old attitudes and engineers passed from one quango to the next, and in some instances it has taken the NRA a long time to change.

Since 1986 a transformation has occurred, not only in the otter population, but also in the thinking surrounding river management. The current 1993–94 Otter Survey is being carried out by Rob Strachan, again for the Vincent Wildlife Trust. This seven-year otter-itch is taking him to all the 3,200 sites once more and he will have walked along 1,500 miles of river bank. Already it seems likely that the report will reveal that twenty-five per cent of the sites are now occupied and the otter population has increased and advanced in many areas. It should be said that each occupied site does not represent one otter, as the territory of an otter can cover several miles and more than one monitoring point.

Rob Strachan is excited at the improvement: 'We still have to be cautious as the recovery is slower than for the peregrine and sparrowhawk, but there is evidence that the Scottish population is expanding southwards to Cumbria and Northumberland. The Welsh one is advancing eastwards and the otters from the south-west are also spilling out into new areas. (They have also spilled back to the River Otter). In East Anglia the remnants of the wild population have been joined by successful reintroductions from the Otter Trust and that population is now expanding westwards.'

With this pincer movement in progress Don Jefferies believes that the whole of Britain should be occupied again by otters within fifteen years. Evidence of this occurring was confirmed recently when an otter was killed on the M4 near Reading, an area previously thought to be empty of otters.

The reasons for the otter's successful comeback are numerous. Laws outlawing the DDT-derived chemicals have been effective and Philp Wayre's reintroductions, starting in Suffolk in 1983, have been extremely successful. In addition there are now numerous otter

179

projects all over the country, co-ordinated by the Royal Society for Nature Conservation, involving the improvement of riverside habitat and the creation of otter havens. These include the Tarka Project, The Wessex Otter Conservation Project, the Hampshire and South-East Otter Project, the Surrey Otter Project, the Upper Thames Otter Habitat Project, the Hertfordshire Otter Project, the North Norfolk Otter Project, the River Avon Otter Project, the Otter Project Wales, the Lancashire Otters and Rivers Project, the Cumbria Otters and Rivers Project, the Yorkshire Otters and Rivers Project, and the Northumberland Otters and Rivers Project.

In the creation of rough quiet areas, the much maligned set-aside has been important – by accident rather than design. It is becoming increasingly obvious that MAFF must be made aware of the habitats that set-aside is creating, and it is vital that agricultural opportunities for wildlife should not be withdrawn as quickly as they appear.

The attitude of the National Rivers Authority (NRA) has also been vital. The NRA is the statutory body with obligations covering pollution control, water resources, flood defence, fish, recreation, conservation and navigation. These responsibilities relate to all inland and coastal waters and to the land associated with them in England and Wales. The NRA's conservation responsibilities also cover wildlife, landscape and natural beauty and so their positive response to these duties (in most cases – but not all) has been important.

The management of bankside vegetation is one of the keys for the return of the otter, and undoubtedly the best bankside management for otters is no management at all. The old water authorities were obsessive bank-mowers, tree-fellers and scrub-clearers; the NRA is now responding more sympathetically to landowners who want to leave trees, scrub and undergrowth, providing shelter, cover and protection not only for the otter, but for a wide range of game and wildlife. To help with this process the NRA published *Otters and River management* in October 1993 as another sign of a change of heart and direction.

Dr Tony Mitchell-Jones, mammal ecologist of English Nature (he is not 'senior' or 'junior' – he is the only one) is pleased with the changes: 'Because of the improved quality of water and the better bankside management things are looking very optimistic. Consequently the rate otters are spreading is extremely encouraging.'

But he is also careful to emphasize that we must not become over-optimistic or complacent: 'There are still difficulties that have to be overcome; pollution still occurs and there are real problems with fyke nets (The traditional nets used to catch eels) and road mortality.'

The main pollution threat is now thought to come from PCBs – polychlorinated biphenyls, used in such items as capacitors – when they leak into river systems from landfill sites, or from the factories where they are produced. The consequences can be deadly and long term. Unfortunately they can become absorbed into the fat of eels, the otters' favourite food. A build-up of PCBs in the otter is thought to affect reproduction capability.

Another continuing pollution problem is that of phosphates released by sewage treatment works. Although much effort has been spent on the study and control of nitrates in water, phosphates can also pose a threat to much wildlife in our river systems, and consequently the otters that depend on them. Phosphates can be removed from sewage quite easily, but the process is an additional expense; as a result most water companies seem reluctant to take action, despite the huge profits they are making, and the large salaries and share options they are paying themselves.

The pollution of disturbance is another growing menace that must be closely monitored and controlled. More leisure time means bankside access and navigation increase pressures; so the creation of otter havens and artificial holts must be a continuing process.

Dr Jefferies has studied the problems of fyke nets and road casualties for several years and confirms that they are a growing threat. There have been several hundred otter road-deaths in the last ten years and he is about to begin a paper on the subject. Sadly, with the government's announced road programme, the problem is likely to become worse, particularly in overpopulated, car-dependent, southern England. Where new roads cross rivers and water-sheds at traditional otter crossing-points, there can be real problems. Wildlife reflectors and otter-underpasses are the usual solutions, although an enforced wildlife speed-limit would probably be more effective. An even better solution would be to stop the madness of compulsive road building.

Fyke nets cause the death by drowning of numerous otters each year. Again Dr Jefferies has studied the problem and found that if otter guards are attached to the mouth of the nets, otters cannot enter as they try to get at their favourite food. With otters spreading rapidly through Eastern England, where much eel-fishing takes place, isn't it surely time for the regional NRA's to pass by-laws insisting on the fitting of otter guards to all fyke nets?

I have to confess that the return of the otter has also highlighted another subject of much controversy – the relationship between otters and mink. On many subjects I am an unashamed bigot, and I believed that otters were reluctant to recolonize where mink had filled the carnivorous bankside vacuum. I believed that otters did not like their aggressive, smelly neighbours, and were reluctant to move in to new areas. The advance of the otter has, I am glad to say, proved me totally wrong. Indeed Dr Mitchell-Jones believes that the return of the otter could actually suppress the mink population. The otter certainly has a large weight advantage; the average male otter weighs about twenty-two pounds, while the male mink weighs in at two and a half pounds. The female otter is fifteen and a half pounds, with the female mink being one pound. However, this does not alter my belief that the mink is totally unwanted; it should be exterminated as it is doing untold damage to our indigenous wildlife.

But all this still does not tell us where our otters actually came from. The answer is almost certainly from reintroductions carried out by the Otter Trust. The Otter Trust was founded in 1972 by Philip Wayre. His wife Jeanne is now Director. Philip first became concerned at the otter's decline in 1960, at which time they were not protected. He was making a programme on the Norfolk Broads for Anglia Television and he wanted some captive otters to film. Surprisingly he received no reply to his advertisements and it suddenly dawned on him that something drastic must have happened to the Broadland otter population. He eventually used Canadian otters for filming.

Shortly afterwards an intensive trapping campaign was started to eradicate coypu and he heard that a few otters were being caught quite unharmed, that is until the trappers shot them to sell their pelts for five pounds. The Ministry of Agriculture at Norwich then allowed him to pay ten pounds each for every live otter, and over the next five to ten years he saved up to twenty animals. Some he released, but some he kept back for his captive breeding programme, which is still going strong, and many of the descendants of those first otters are still at the Trust.

It is a difficult task getting otters to breed in captivity and it was the first time they had been successfully bred away from the wild since 1884. By 1994 he was still the only person breeding them on a large scale and his otters are producing between fifteen to twenty cubs a year. But even so things are far from simple. As Philip Wayre says: 'We had to build up numbers at the Trust. It is more difficult than it sounds, breeding for release. If you assume that a bitch only lives eight years and perhaps has four litters, she is only going to produce eight cubs. They then have to replace her and her mate, leaving only six, then one or two are going to die, and so you've got to have a lot of otters to have fifteen to twenty to spare.'

The first release took place on the Blackbourne River in Suffolk, where it passed through the land of John Wilson. Because he has a shoot of wild pheasants (not reared in pens and released), he has much good habitat, including untouched, overgrown river banks, ideal for otters. In 1984 another release took place on the River Thet. Prophets of doom forecast that the otters would not live; but they did and breeding started almost immediately. There have been cubs on both rivers almost every year since then.

In all, over sixty otters have been released in Norfolk, Suffolk, Hertfordshire, Dorset, Wiltshire and Hampshire and the releases are continuing. Philip Wayre believes that our brook otters will be the great-grandcubs (possibly with a few more greats) of his early releases. In his view the population spread from the Thet and the Blackbourne into the Little Ouse and then the Cam, where, at Byron's Pool, near the village of Grantchester, a right turn has taken them into the Bourn Brook. There the overgrown banks, after a mile of swimming, give cover, and an old pile of tree trunks has provided an ideal natural 'holt'. From here it is hoped that breeding will take place so that the westward movement and re-colonization continues.

Philip Wayre warns of over-optimism, however: 'We must not be complacent and we must keep on our guard. Something could easily happen to knock them out again – we've got to be very careful.' On our stretch of brook we intend to be very careful.

So the return of the otter is a happy, encouraging story. Certainly the day that I was wading through the gravelly shallows of the brook, close to the musical little stream, simply to see what fish or damselflies were about, is a day that I will cherish always. I paused by bare earth at the water's edge, unthinking. Suddenly it dawned on me: there was not one clear, fresh footprint in the mud, but a whole set of them, leading to a well-worn track towards the bankside woodpile. The otters were back and in residence. I was so pleased I literally jumped for joy, and I hope that over the next fifteen years many more people will feel the exhilaration of that experience.

We almost lost our otters through ignorance and stupidity, but the loss was accidental. If, despite our accumulated knowledge and experience, we lose them again, it will be through greed and expediency – it will be criminal.

183

48

Where Has Winter Gone?

Whatever has happened to winter, those cold days when the wind veered round to the east and the frost set in? For days, even weeks, the landscape went white as the frost of early morning was still with us by evening, when the stars announced another night of arctic weather. Then wisps of cloud and a watery sun announced that snow was on its way: not sleet, or a light covering of slushy flakes that sends today's transport system into chaos, but real snow, snow on snow, deep and crisp and even. With more frost the snow would hang around for weeks, and even with the thaw a snow line would linger along the hedgerows, almost into spring.

Of course there is always a great danger in writing about the weather: talk of drought and it will rain; complain of the cold and a heatwave will become unbearable; talk of global warming and the kitchen taps will freeze solid. Despite this danger I do intend to complain of the winters getting warmer and if this brings on the coldest winter this century I will be genuinely delighted.

That is part of my problem; I love cold weather and ice, frost and snow are welcome parts of my winter life in the country. On the farm we can cope and when the cold locks the rivers, streams and water meadows of my native Cambridgeshire with ice, it means only one thing – skating. Not the namby-pamby skating of the ice-rink and Torvill and Dean, but real skating – Fen skating – which in today's terminology means 'speed skating', although to enjoy it you do not necessarily have to skate at speed. Indeed during the rare cold winter today, old Fenmen still seem to skate all day, effortlessly and easily, with their hands behind their backs and their skates rhythmically cutting patterns into the ice.

Cold winters were a regular part of our past. Skating itself must have started as an answer to the cold, yet today's winters seem to be just murky extensions of autumn. Stories of the cold becoming so intense that rivers, including the Thames, froze over now seem so remote that youngsters could be excused for regarding them as fiction.

Yet during my childhood almost every winter saw snowball fights, sliding on the village pond and skating on the brook. Today, a few frosts may bring ice, but then the temperature rises and the ice returns to water and my skates go back into the cupboard. Last year the temperature fell to about freezing point and lingered for several days. We had just one day's skating before a slight thaw put paid to our hopes. Some people claim that my mind is playing up and that memory only retains the highlights of childhood, turning the exceptional into the normal. I disagree.

Winters were colder; every family owned skates and newcomers to the area could buy them over the counter at a number of shops in Cambridge; the folklore and weatherlore of cold came from familiarity not rarity, and the old carol writers were portraying the seasons people recognized, that is why they have remained popular for so long.

Every autumn day after the first frost I still recite my favourite cold weather poem, hoping it will bring more. At one time it seemed to herald several cold days; now all it usually brings is fog.

> Come, lovely Morning, rich in frost
> On iron, wood and glass . . .

W.H. Davies was an underrated poet, but as I read his winter words I can see the frost on the windows and feel the cold on my cheeks as I breathe in that cold, clear, healthy air. I mean healthy air, for that is another bonus of a long hard winter: it seems to kill off the germs of colds and flu. The traditional cures can still be tried, however, without the ailments; hot wine and whisky – taken as a medicinal precaution, of course.

Amazingly some people still imagine we have cold winters. The weather forecasters apologize at every frost, forgetting that some of us actually want them. Last year English Nature amazed me too. Commenting on the decline of kingfishers in my area they blamed a 'cold snap' two or three years ago that somehow escaped my notice. What escaped their notice was the fact that the kingfishers disappeared in high summer, thanks to mink. Somebody ought to have a quiet word with the government's 'wildlife advisers' about the damage being done to our indigenous wildlife by the menace of mink.

My childhood winters were wonderful, but frustrating – frustrating when asthma coincided with the freeze-up and confined me to the farmhouse. Once my wheezing turned to pneumonia; it was freezing hard when I went into hospital; it was freezing when I came out and it was still freezing when I put on my skates.

At the village school frost was always greeted with delight. With an open sky and the temperature plummeting as dusk fell, the 'big boys' would get buckets of water from a nearby pump and sling it into the playground. In the morning there would be a great sheet of clear, solid ice and we would make a slide as long as a cricket pitch. Some of the older boys, whose fathers worked on the farms, had handed-down hob-nailed boots and would speed along out of control. There are many ways to slide, standing up, crouching down and on the seat of your pants; it was fun, fast and dangerous, an ideal sport for the Winter Olympics. My efforts became too spectacular and resulted in a whole day off school after crashing head-first into the ice, causing a bump on my forehead the size of a bantam's egg. I wonder if it has had any lasting effect? As soon as the swelling was down I was back sliding.

After three nights of frost the entertainment would move to the village pond. After school virtually all the children would migrate to the ice, again to slide. There I managed to improve my performance by falling through the ice completely. It was not deep enough to be a danger, but it did manage to freeze the parts that are better off warm. Now of course a health and safety officer would want salt put down in the school playground and I never see children sliding on the pond. I suppose incomers to the village somehow see it as a danger; it can only be a matter of time before some busybody demands that the village pond is filled in.

Once the frost was really established, the adults stirred too. They would dig out their 'fen runners', traditional skates that could be strapped on to boots or shoes. Boots were preferred because of the support they gave to ankles. Being on the edge of the Fens the skating tradition was strong and during my parents' childhoods several fields were deliberately flooded for skating. The sewage farm was also popular, until a boot went through the ice. Even today at Earith, in the Fens, a field is still flooded when frost is in the air and many locals, me included, keep looking up into the evening sky, hoping for stillness, starlight and cold.

It is another sign of the regularity of freeze-ups that the skates came in all shapes and sizes, from smallest to largest. Had ice been infrequent, children would not have been given skates, they would have been too wasteful and expensive. I had my first strap-on pair almost as soon as I could walk. My mother taught me, pushing a small chair in front of me for support. When I crashed to the ground she would pick me up and dust me down and I would immediately start again. Our skating was not carried out on deliberately flooded land, but on water meadows that flooded naturally, several times each winter. Alas, not only have the frosts decreased, but, as I have said, the water meadows were drained.

During a dry winter the skaters went on to the brook itself, with lanterns warning of thin ice or overhanging boughs. Now the 'improved' brook flows too quickly and the water is rarely able to freeze. 'Improved' is not the word I would have chosen to describe the damage caused by drainage, but it seems to be the word favoured by water engineers in an attempt to justify their vandalism over much of lowland Britain.

Skating went back so far in our family that it was remembered that one of my grandfathers actually learnt to skate on blades of bone. My grandmother was ever-present whenever there was ice. She skated until she was over eighty, finally breaking an arm while skating alone. She bandaged her injury up herself and did not tell anybody of the damage until the break had healed. My father has skated into his late seventies, finally retiring after falling over and bringing twenty following skaters down on top of him. I wish he had kept on, it was very entertaining.

When snow came, brooms were fetched to sweep the ice, but when the snow froze on to the ice, making it unskatable, interest turned to other sport. My favourite was sledging down the railway bridge on a small metal stepladder that doubled as a sledge. We thought it almost matched the Cresta Run; today any child trying to follow suit would be run over by a bus.

Several times the village was cut off by snow drifting off the fields in arctic conditions and blocking the roads. It was a much-enjoyed 'hardship'. The farmhouse always looked beautiful in snow, with a slight daily thaw creating giant icicles hanging from the thatch. Skating and sledging were not the only traditional activities of a cold winter. Carol-singing also seemed to go better in frost and I cannot believe that the authors of old carols would have written similar words in today's climate.

> In the bleak midwinter
> Frosty wind made moan,
> Earth stood hard as iron,
> Water like a stone;
> Snow had fallen, snow on snow,
> Snow on snow,
> In the bleak midwinter,
> Long long ago.

The sound of singing travelled further in the cold. Old Mr Carter wore mittens as he scraped his frozen violin and we would sing heartily to keep warm. At the end of the evening hot mincepies and drinks would finish the job. It was almost like a scene from *Under the Greenwood Tree*. Thomas Hardy was an accurate recorder of the natural cycle. I am sure his carol-singers would have been far different in a world full of ozone depletion, car exhausts and warm winters.

Life on the farm and in the fields changed during times of cold. All the water pipes were lagged with straw and sacking well before winter, but inevitably some pipes froze solidly. Then the mornings were spent with buckets of hot water and rags trying to move the ice. Potatoes and mangold-wurzels were safe in their clamps and there would be a daily collection of mangolds and kale if the old Fordson Major could be started. The tractor was always a problem in cold weather and had to be started by swinging a handle. We still have an old Fordson Major on the farm to show schoolchildren an early tractor. It takes me all my time to swing it once; swinging it time and time again shows that my father was a better man than I am; it must have been his breakfasts: traditional fry-ups preceded by porridge, just right for old tractors on cold mornings.

But frost and snow actually gave one big advantage. All the mud of the farmyard froze solid so that we could walk quickly and easily over it, a problem since overcome with lorry loads of concrete. In the fields the winter landscape was one of peace and tranquillity, although the footprints of foxes often told a different story. The landscape took on a Christmas card aspect – that was before Dutch Elm Disease removed our most prominent landscape feature. Now, a winter scene of treeless land, without ice or snow would be a waste of a card.

The worst winter I can remember was in 1963, when ice and snow seemed to last from Christmas until spring. The land was like iron but we quickly got into our cold-weather routine and it caused few problems. For nature it was a disaster, however, and after the thaw much wildlife had disappeared. Birds and animals weakened by pesticide poisoning had been finished off by the cold; it really was a silent spring. Barn owls, kingfishers, green-woodpeckers, sparrowhawks and kestrels had all vanished, as had the otter. Now, thirty years later and after most of the chemicals responsible have been banned, only the barn owl is still absent.

According to my now non-skating father, 1947 was even worse. All I can remember of it as a small boy is of snow and ice and skating. I can recall the thaw, however; it came so quickly that our small brook turned into a raging torrent. Rain and meltwater ran quickly off the still deeply frozen ground and the resulting floods were the worst in living memory. From the farmhouse we could hear the roar of the water as it squeezed under the small road-bridge, over a quarter of a mile away – something that has not been heard since.

Before that, an elderly aunt believes that the winter of 1929 was worse still. Then, an uncle skated all the way from Cambridge to Ely on the Cam. But to her it was the warm winters which were unusual as cold was a normal part of winter.

Today some people claim that the weather remains unchanged, while others believe that global warming is coming. I believe that they are both wrong; global warming is not coming – it is here already. I hope I'm wrong.

49

Ho, Ho, Ho

Another Christmas is over. This one has been different, however, as Father Christmas really did visit the farm – twice. He came to our old cowshed, complete with six live reindeer, and local families flooded in to see the sight. Disaster almost arrived with him, together with a charge of indecent exposure. As the first child arrived, Santa began to walk over to him with a friendly 'Ho, ho, ho'. Sadly for him I was soon convulsed with a genuine 'Ho, ho, ho', for as he walked, his strides suddenly became jerky and restricted and he nearly fell on his face. His jolly red trousers had fallen down and wrapped themselves tightly around his jolly white ankles.

He greeted the children sitting down after that, not wishing to expose his ample boxer shorts to the world for a second time. A

Father Christmas wearing boxer shorts? The discerning child would have realized something was not quite right. Surely the real Santa wears thermal long-johns, to protect himself from the North Pole's icy blasts.

The reindeer had come from Scotland and were part of the Cairngorm reindeer herd. Each year Alan and Tilly Smith take a group of their reindeer to numerous shopping centres, as part of their exercise in diversification. Every now and then they drop in at the farm for a few days' rest between appearances. While with us this year, we decided to diversify, too, with a real, rotund Father Christmas, raising money for the Countryside Restoration Trust. In real life this particular Father Christmas sells biscuits; from his shape I think he eats almost as many as he sells.

The reindeer's presence completely destroyed the myth of Rudolph's red nose, as they are the only deer species to have a furry nose; so much for all those cartoons of a naked nose, glowing with cold.

I normally disagree with transporting animals long distances. But, incredibly, the six reindeer, fresh off the hills, get out of their horse-box totally unstressed, almost as if they enjoy the experience. It shows what several thousand years of semi-domestication can achieve. It also shows the advantage of travelling in a draught-proof lorry, with plenty of room.

I went with Alan, a native Highlander, into the Black Hole – London. It was only his second time on the Underground. I have always wanted to visit London with a Masai tribesman, straight out of the bush. Visiting London with Alan was not much different. Most of the time his eyes were wide open in total amazement: 'Why are these people [commuters] behaving like robots?' he asked. 'Why are there so few English here?' and 'Why does the driver [in the Underground] drive so close to the wall?'

Riding back to Cambridge by train it was my turn to be amazed. I was accosted by a man wearing a badge proclaiming 'Revenue Protection Inspector'. Wasn't he a 'ticket collector'? What a strange world we are living in. I wonder what a 'station master' is now called: 'Director of Off-Road Transportation Centre', I suppose.

To prove the world is now totally mad I have to mention Hemel Hempstead. The week before Alan and Tilly's reindeer visited its shopping centre, 20,000 people had turned up to see Mr Blobby. Twenty thousand people to see an anonymous man wearing an inflatable pink suit. I wouldn't cross the road to see Mr Blobby – education and television have a lot to answer for.

While at Hemel Hempstead Alan learnt something useful too; he overheard a male onlooker say to his wife: 'I don't know why all these people have turned up to see these – you can see them in the New Forest anyday.' Reindeer in the New Forest? They would be the warmest reindeer in the world; unfortunately Hemel Hempstead's home-grown deer expert did not know the difference between reindeer and fallow deer. I wonder if he knows the difference between chalk and cheese. I worry about people who have to live in Hemel Hempstead; it's almost as bad as Milton Keynes.

Christmas is usually a happy time on the farm, but this year we had a shadow of sadness – my brother John's dog, 'Husky', died. Dogs are an important part of farm life; they live with us, work with us and play with us, and when they go they are deeply missed. He was a lovely, big, bouncy dog, a cross between an Alsatian and a border collie – we think. Although only eight years old, a month ago his bouncing stopped; his kidneys failed and almost before we realized that he was ill he had gone.

He had been a real part of the farm; when didecoys arrived on the road outside, his blood-curdling bark stopped them in their tracks; yet when a school party came he would be gentle and his patience was never-ending. He would play with water from a hose just like a puppy and his ratting was unsurpassed. As a cattle dog his bravery had to be restrained as he wanted to hang on to every tail in sight, but at the first gunshot, while out rough-shooting with John, he would run homewards with his tail between his legs.

I still laugh when I think of the day he surreptitiously relieved himself against the leg of an elegant travelling salesman. The torrent gushed so warm and long that the male model had to dance around, shaking his foot, to prevent his shoe from filling.

He loved antagonizing the geese, running backwards and forwards to face a gauntlet of hisses, pecks and wings. One day he snapped his jaws as he ran, biting off the old goose's tail as clean as a whistle. I could not believe my eyes. The whole tail just lay in the mud, complete with the oily gland to waterproof the old girl's feathers; there was hardly a drop of blood in sight.

Bedraggled, tailless Beatrice is still with us, avoiding water like the plague. Sometimes in winter I wonder if I should catch her and rub her down with olive oil – or even dripping (not goose dripping – that would be a bit unfair, both for the goose and for me, as I still love bread and dripping). But she survives and on cold, wet days I shut her up to keep her warm and out of the wind chill.

So, Husky is deeply missed; one chapter ends, but another one has already begun, as a little black labrador puppy called Tess has come to help, hinder and make her mark.

One of my most pleasing Christmas presents this year was the biography of Peter Scott, by Elspeth Huxley. Peter Scott was one of my childhood heroes; Elspeth Huxley is one of my modern-day heroines. At the age of eighty-six she tells me that she has at last retired. But then she told me that three books ago; I hope she is wrong again this time too.

50

Ode to Milton Keynes

I wanted to write a chapter on Milton Keynes, that architectural, social and environmental abomination, surrounded by ring roads and traffic islands. This is the only thing that would come out:

> New town,
> Straight road,
> Wide road,
> All clear,
> Speed up,
> Roundabout,
> Slow down,
> Engine roars,
> Change gear,
> Left right,
> Straight road,

Winter light,
Accelerate.
BMW,
Close behind,
Faster still,
Roundabout,
Slow down,
Brakes squeal,
Hooter blares,
Left right,
Straight ahead,
Burn up.
Exhaust fumes,
Overtake,
Exchange glares,
Roundabout,
Change gear,
Slow down,
Tyres burn,
Wear and tear,
Left right.
Open road,
Late for work,
Wrinkled brow,
Faster still,
Roundabout,
Slow down,
Turn left,
Grate the gears,
Speed up,
Slow down.
Large box,
Design award,
Where I work,
Turn right,
Stop the car,
Lock the door,
Petty theft,
Clock on.
Hot and dry.
Dust and Noise,
Tea break,
Fill in forms,
Lunch hour,

Check the car,
Stretch my legs.
Dry and hot,
Noise and dust,
Laugh with Jock,
What's the time?
Darkness falls,
Another day,
Start my car,
Straight road,
Wide road,
Full of cars,
Lights glare,
Slow down,
Roundabout.
Slower still,
Full stop,
Left right,
Fast away,
Roundabout,
Slow down,
More exhaust,
Engine hot,
Fuel's low,
Left right.
All clear,
Engine roars,
Slow down,
Lorry sways.
Over there,
Concrete cows,
Roundabout,
Turn right,
Little box,
Where I live.
Lights out,
Wife gone,
Broken home,
Design award,
Darkness all,
New town,
Grand design,
Milton Keynes.

51

Back to Basics

Nineteen-ninety-four has started in a disastrous way. My problems began on New Year's Day and it has been downhill ever since. I woke up on 1 January with a splitting headache and it took me over an hour of agony to get out of bed and crawl to the bathroom. To put my shirt on, I had to leave it spreadeagled at the top of the stairs and creaked six steps down so that it was level with my head. I was not boasting the world's greatest New Year hangover – my back had gone again.

New Year's Eve had looked so full of promise. After recent rain, rain and yet more rain, the clouds vanished and the sun set in a pure, clear sky. The stars were crystal clear in the darkness: the Plough, Orion's Belt and the Seven Sisters. Because of street lights and an irrational fear of darkness, many people forget just how beautiful an English winter night can be. Darkness can be restful and soothing too, good for the soul.

It seemed a fine time to clean out the pigs; finish the old year how I intended to continue the new. I have never been enthusiastic about working nine to five. I always work when I want to, or have to, whether that is six o'clock in the morning, or eleven o'clock at night. It happened to be six o'clock in the evening.

I actually like cleaning the pigs out; it is good for the pigs; it expands the lungs; it tightens the stomach muscles; it is good for you. Bramble went to his usual place, up in the dry hay bales to watch from afar; it was worth a grandstand view. After heaping the good organic sludge into the corner of the stye, as stage one, I then went to throw it into the nearby muck-spreader. The fork went into the heap; my body swung back, bearing a huge forkful of 'gardener's delight', and then, with beauty and precision, I swung forwards and upwards to clear the side of the spreader.

My muck fork and I had the unison and symmetry of Torvill and Dean.

As the fork went upwards in a graceful curve, suddenly everything stopped. My back had gone. I had seized up in agony. Well, to say everything stopped is a slight exaggeration; my body had stopped, my lungs had stopped and the fork had stopped, but the momentum of the exercise meant that the muck kept going. It was a beautiful sight; an incompleted arc meant that the evil-smelling mire rose gracefully, slowed, stopped; it even seemed to hover; then it began to fall. Using the laws of gravity only as a forkful of muck can, it completed its own arc, landing fair and square on the top of my head.

How can these disasters happen to me so regularly? There I was bent almost double, with pig shite glistening in the moonlight, dripping from my head – I was like a late, sparkling Christmas decoration. The six pigs watched in amazement; the donkey was astonished, and, as for Bramble, I swear it is the first time I have ever seen a dog fighting to suppress a smile. I looked like a down-trodden peasant; I felt like a down-trodden peasant; I smelt like a down-trodden peasant – I was a down-trodden peasant. What a way to start the new year.

Of course, I have to confess that my back is not the only problem, for my front seems to have a mind of its own as well. In years gone by on feast days and holidays I unashamedly ate all that was available: turkey, Christmas pudding, pork pie, pickles, cakes, mince pies, cheese straws, trifles and all the rest disappeared without fuss or discomfort. The next day I was ready for more.

Now everything I eat hangs around, mainly over my belt and under my chin. Pie, pudding, cake, port, wine and scrumpy all turn almost immediately into one thing: fat. My body is like a machine designed to convert all food instantly into flab. My stomach bulges; my weight increases, but my appetite remains the same.

It is terrible, but I love food, seasonal food, and winter food. There was no escape from Christmas pudding; there is no escape from meat pudding, and already Pancake day is looming large on the horizon. I suppose it could be argued that I am merely providing myself with natural insulation against the cold, like the seals of the Weddell Sea. The difference being that the seals of the Weddell Sea do not have to clean pigs out on New Year's Eve.

I am sure that my expanding front can damage my back; it is like walking about with bags of sugar strapped to my midriff. I am now heavier than I have ever been before: twelve stone. My New Year's resolution was simple: a diet. It is still going to start tomorrow.

I did not creak into my doctor's surgery with my back as I did not want a prescription of coloured pills and an appointment to see a consultant at Addenbrooke's hospital in 1997, where the dead, dying and damaged are now charged to park their cars. (I wonder if Mrs Bottomley has to pay a parking fee at the House of Commons?) Instead I went to an osteopath: a couple of careful twists, pulls and a trample, and my back is now as right as rain. I won't mention my lungs – they are another story.

I now realize why osteopaths do not come under the inaccurately entitled National Health Service. You can see them almost immediately and they cure you. A friend now refuses to go to the doctor. He says that they are so keen to get you out of the surgery with a handful of pills that it is hardly worth going. He says he knows of so many wrong diagnoses 'that you may as well stay at home and die in peace, without any chemical delay or inducement'.

His only problem is that he believes some doctors are so harassed that they cannot even diagnose death correctly. From all those brain-dead people, allowed to be loose on the streets, who flock to see Mr Blobby, he could be right.

52

Digging for Victory

The Countryside Restoration Trust continues to astonish me. Not only do memberships and donations still arrive with virtually every post, but offers of help and gifts of assorted country items also keep Eric the postman busy. One of his deliveries was a root of flowering rush; another was a packet of snake's head fritillary seed.

A fortnight ago several helpers bypassed Eric; they came in person to plant a hedge. The aim was to divide the long meadow of the Trust's first twenty-two acres into two. The brookside will be turned back to water meadow and this year the rest will be environmentally friendly cereals. The dividing line will be the new hedge; by the time I reach my three score years and ten and am due to roll off my bean-bag, it should look good.

Twenty 'Friends', aged from seven to seventy-four arrived to put in the hedge, over a quarter of a mile long. The weather was awful; the field was a quagmire, but they came with forks, spades and clean boots. They made a remarkable cross-section of society from lorry-driver to farmer, from secretary to college bursar and from nurse to biscuit salesman. Only those within easy reach of Cambridgeshire had been invited, but even so two young ladies arrived from Shropshire, including one from Harper Adams agricultural college. In view of the conservation illiteracy of most agricultural colleges, it was heartening to see such an enthusiasm for planting trees.

About 1,800 saplings were planted, including hawthorn, blackthorn, dogwood, privet, wild rose, field maple, oak and ash. They have since been joined by crab apple and wild pear from that wonderful old conservation visionary, Miriam Rothschild.

The mud was so thick that the seventy-four-year-old crawled on all fours and at one time I thought she was in grave danger of planting herself; the seven-year-old soon got bored and went fishing. One volunteer was Jill Barklem, author and illustrator of the beautiful Brambly Hedge children's books – she wanted to help create a real Brambly hedge.

At the end of a long, hard, damp day, there were no moans or groans, just smiles. A surveyor commented: 'I spend all my week building roads and seeing hedges ripped out – it was so satisfying to put one back.' Another simply said: 'It was a real privilege to do something good like that.' A local's observation was more basic: 'I'll see you up the pub later.' He never made it; he fell asleep in front of his fire and woke up just in time to go to bed. The attitude of the hedge-planters can best be summed up by the old proverb: 'He that plants trees loves others beside himself.'

The field is not the only thing changing, as the brook has also been improved, in a way that will be appreciated by the otters. When the brook was 'cleaned out' in 1971, it was straightened for the sake of 'efficiency' and a whole meander was cut off and filled in with spoil. Now, following a request by the CRT, the National Rivers Authority has dug out the meander again, with imagination and skill. Where the brook was straightened they have built two 'riffles' of reject gravel, which have in effect become two dams; as a consequence the water has backed up behind them, raising the level of the brook by several feet for hundreds of yards. Each riffle had eighty tons of flint tipped into it, diverting water around the restored meander to create an island. On the island old logs and branches have been heaped, which when covered with brambles will make another excellent otter holt. So, before our eyes, in a remarkably short time, a landscape is being healed, restored and created.

A few days after the hedge-planting and the NRA's excellent work I could not believe my eyes. The water of the brook had gone black, as had the flint, the banks and the vegetation; then came the news from upstream: a 'fail-safe' sewage pumping station belonging to Anglian Water had failed, and shown itself to be unsafe; sewage had been discharged into the brook. I was angry; I could not believe it; virtually the entire length of the brook had been contaminated with sewage. The flints of the new riffles were covered with dark-brown slime; there was an unedifying smell and the signs of otters at the holt disappeared. Despite the mess Anglian Water did not notify landowners below the spill, including the Trust, and told me that the whole thing was a 'minor incident'. When a local farmer polluted the brook with slurry a few years ago he was fined, quite rightly, several thousand pounds. I await with interest to see if Anglian Water receives the same treatment.

What gives the incident a bizarre twist is the fact that each year Anglian Water runs a 'Caring for the Environment' competition. Last year the prizes were presented by, yes, my old friend Mr Gummer. Perhaps Anglian Water should enter their own competition this year, then John Gummer could award them the booby prize.

Fortunately the volume of water dispersed the sewage within four to five days and the otters are again back at the holt; but the incident has shown just how quickly new threats to their welfare can arise. One other threat is also emerging on the horizon. The Planning Committee of South Cambridgeshire District Council, not known for its perception or vision, has just given permission for a new town of 3,000 houses to be built around the headwaters of the brook. If that projected blot on the landscape has 'fail-safe' drainage systems as efficient as those already in place, then it is surely time that the nice Mr Gummer called in the absurd scheme and placed it firmly in the dustbin where it belongs.

Our work on the new land of the CRT has coincided with the establishment of six new Environmentally Sensitive Areas by the Ministry of Agriculture, in which farmers will be paid to conserve wildlife as they farm. The boast is that ten per cent of farmland will then be covered by ESAs. Sadly it is an example of 'island conservation' yet again. It does give protection to a few special areas, but what about the other ninety per cent of the general countryside where most of us live? In four or five years' time the CRT's land will already begin to be attractive and sensitive, well away from any ESA. Recently farmers all over Britain received their IACS payments, annual handouts made under the lunatic CAP reforms. This money has no environmental strings attached whatsoever. The sooner all agricultural payments are linked to wildlife and landscape benefits the better. Conservation would then cease to be a choice, but a responsibility. The sort of changes the CRT is already putting into effect on its small piece of farmland would become possible all over Britain, involving hundreds of thousands of acres.

53

Rain, Rape, Arson and Pillage

Something very strange happened the other day at dusk. I was feeding the hens when a shadowy figure appeared by our small duck pond and released a white duck from a sack. The white duck sat on its rump perplexed; the shadowy figure ran off into the night. It was a case of duck-dumping – or more accurately drake-dumping. Why somebody should assume that we wanted their unwanted white drake is beyond me. The last thing we wanted was a solitary white drake.

The geese and our Khaki Campbell drake didn't want it either and soon it was heading for the wide open spaces beyond the farm: fox country. Although we did not want the poor bird, we didn't think it fair to let it commit suicide either, as one night out would have left a pile of white feathers and a fat contented fox, so we had to mount a duck-rescue operation, running, panting and diving until Donald was safely behind bars. He has settled in now, but the question remains, why should someone fed up with their own livestock, dump it on a farm and run. Sadly, countrywide, all sorts of stock are treated in the same way when irresponsible owners want to be freed from their pets.

Some of our Cochins had a much stickier end the other night. Cochins are large hens with extremely small brains. I moved our little flock from one henhouse to one nearer the farmyard to save the daily wade through winter mud.

I shut them in for a week, opened the hatch, and they immediately returned to their old henhouse. Consequently I made a small run until they learned to go in and out of their new accommodation. The run was then removed, and they still went in and out with no problems – success.

One evening I failed to anticipate the sluggish movement of the

203

Cochin brain. I returned to the farm late after moving the sheep; darkness had already fallen. I shut the hatch of the Cochins' home without looking inside; yes, I had shut them out – they were sitting in their old shed with the door wide open.

At eight o'clock, mayhem broke loose; hens were screaming 'rape, arson and pillage'; one of our friendly neighbourhood foxes was doing its rounds. Feeling full of fun it had decided to try to kill all the Cochins, instead of making do with one. Dead and dying birds were littered everywhere and it looked as if several feather-filled quilts had been emptied into the orchard. I found one hen skulking, frightened, but alive; the three other hens had vanished. One large cockerel expired as I reached it, while the four others were on their backs, feet up, croaking the croak of the unwell and mortified.

My anti-hunting nephew was also mortified; it was an unfortunate lesson in fox behaviour. If only scientists would invent a dart that would induce foxes to eat cucumber sandwiches. Three of the four injured cockerels survived; now they will not leave their new henhouse at all; they have learnt something at last.

I still take the reasoned but unfashionable view that fox-hunting is the best way of controlling foxes. It doesn't wipe them out and, by stirring them up, it makes them less likely to visit farms where there are barking dogs. We are too near the M11 for hunting to take place and I have come to the conclusion that the local foxes actually visit us just to listen to the dogs barking.

In the north of Nottinghamshire, a hunt was in full progress recently. Hounds flushed a fox from a spinney and it made off across a large field of late stubble. The pack followed in full-cry, two hundred yards behind.

The driver of a rattling blue van saw the excitement and screeched to a halt. He flung the rear doors open and a large lurcher shot out like an arrow from a bow. It ran fast and straight, overtaking the hounds easily and catching the fox. It was all over in an instant and the lurcher trotted back to its master, head held high. The driver, a Nottinghamshire miner, was just restarting his wreck when the Master rode up in a state of high dudgeon: 'What did you do that for?' he asked sternly.

The miner was not impressed: 'I thought I would show you that you only need one dog to catch a fox, as long as its a good-un,' he replied, before driving off into the sunset.

Two weeks ago I had to make a quick dash to Kenya to record a couple of *On Your Farm* programmes for Radio 4. It was hot, dry and dusty. The papers were full of stories about drought and the onset of starvation. My last day coincided with the start of the International Cricket Conference's competition to find the three minor countries to take part in cricket's World Cup. As soon as Holland took to the field the clouds began to build up and at midday the heavens opened – the drought was over, unbelievably, it was 'rain stopped play'. So the answer to Africa's rainfall problems seems simple: not dams, irrigation schemes or aid programmes, but cricket – send your old cricket bats to Oxfam now.

54

A Badger in Love

How do you tell when a Badger is in love? This is not a deep and meaningful question related to the life and times of Brock the Badger, it is simply a query about the romantic health of my old friend Badger Walker. I am worried about Badger; he wears that distant, dreamy look, normally associated with adolescents in spring. More importantly he has started to recite poetry.

He was supposed to leave his sett the other day to visit the farm for our annual day of traditional hedge-laying – to mark the end of winter. 'I'll see you at breakfast,' he had said. He arrived, bleary-eyed, half-way through the morning, mentioning that he had stopped off on the way to see – we had better call her – 'Daisy'.

Now, at eleven o'clock in the morning, he wanted breakfast: toast and two pots of tea. The telephone rang; incredibly it was Tony Fitzjohn, that African backwoodsman, who had met Badger on an earlier hedge-laying day [*A Peasant's Diary*]. 'You'll never guess what Tony,' I informed him, 'Badger's in love.' The great Mr Fitzjohn, himself newly in love, was astonished. 'Really,' he said. 'Ask him how many legs she's got?' I thought he was a bit unfair.

After talk and more toast Badger wanted to see the Trust land and the new hedge; he eyed it knowingly: 'That'll be a good hedge – I want to be the first person to lay that. The trouble is, by then you'll want a high hedge – if the Countryside Commission gets its way all the hedges will be flattened in a few years' time.' He had a point I suppose. Through the Countryside Commission's almost excellent Stewardship Scheme, payments are made to farmers for coppicing and laying hedges, and the CC encourages this. So Badger thinks that in those areas where high, wild hedges meet Stewardship, the landscape will become trimmed, neat and tidy. I hope he's wrong and we will talk to the CC in an attempt to keep some of our Stewardship hedges high.

By now it was twelve-fifteen and time to phone Daisy. At twelve-thirty we actually started hedging; at twelve-forty-five we stopped for dinner at the Hoops. At two Badger wanted to look round the nearby church. I am told that love induces an interest in ecclesiastical structures and altars in particular. At two-forty-five it was time to phone Daisy. At three-fifteen he wanted to visit my father and mother and at three-thirty he wanted to watch the Cheltenham Gold Cup on television. A visit to the otter holt was followed by an appreciation of mating toads in the pond; work was resumed at four-thirty. At five-thirty Daisy had to be phoned, followed by a pause for tea which stretched into supper. Finally as the tawny owls called, Badger claimed he had to rush home, pressing the redial button of his mobile phone as he went.

It must have been the shortest length of hedge ever layed by two grown men in one whole day. From my Baptist upbringing I should have been appalled at a day-long rebellion against the work ethic; sad to say I enjoyed it. Next year we will try again; by then Badger could even be singing and I will try to arrange for Daisy to be sitting thirty yards along the hedge by nine o'clock in the morning.

A meeting with Badger is always entertaining. Some months ago I was given a cassette of British songbirds. A knowledge of birdsong can be such an aid to identification. So I play it in my car on long journeys and short journeys and know it almost inside-out; one of the long journeys was to see Badger on his home ground in Derbyshire, to watch badgers. Walking by the side of a hedge Badger suddenly stopped at an unfamiliar birdsong. 'What's that,' he asked. 'I don't know,' I replied, 'but the next one's a chiffchaff.'

After reporting the return of the otters to Daisy, it was Badger's turn to be asked a question: 'How do you make an otter holt?' she asked. 'That's easy,' he replied. 'Stand on its tail.'

Apart from being an expert hedge-layer, Badger's greatest claim to fame is that he was a close friend of that wonderful old writer and artist 'BB' – Denys Watkins-Pitchford, who died in 1990 after a long, happy and productive life. In his later years, although separated by over a generation, Badger was his travelling companion and confidant; he was his driver, his porter, and his arms bearer. BB's last dawns of goose-shooting were enjoyed with Badger at his shoulder. He loved wildfowling and at over eighty, with tubes still in place for kidney dialysis, he continued to visit his favourite estuaries. In theory he went to shoot geese; in reality he went for one last look at those wild open spaces, to breath salt air and to experience the ragged skeins of whitefronts, greylags and pink-feet – wild wanderers of our winter skies.

In his prime BB wrote many outstanding books, and Badger has first editions of every one – including those printed abroad. Quite why Badger wants books in Japanese is beyond me – but all Badger behaviour is full of surprises. My favourite BB books are *Wild Lone, Brendon Chase* and *The Quiet Fields*. In addition of course he wrote that children's classic *The Little Grey Men*, long before anyone had ever heard of John Major.

His other great love was butterflies and in a wood near his Northamptonshire home he successfully introduced that finely named butterfly, the purple emperor. In one of his last summers I had the good fortune to go with BB and Badger to the wood, and there in a shaft of sunlight I saw his beloved butterfly for the first time. It was Badger who gave the old man mobility as his health failed and in appreciation he gave Badger a manuscript – dedicated to him – his last, still unpublished book.

Recently another book has appeared: *BB A Celebration*, about the life of BB. In it there is no mention of Badger, or of Badger's memories of the great man. Sadly the *Celebration* is incomplete.

I like horses, but I will not be visiting the Grand National today. It is too far away, too crowded and surrounded by too much hype. If I am honest, I think the jumps are too high. In any case I prefer point-to-points; traditional jump racing organized by assorted local hunts. They are small and friendly events, where a broad section of the rural community meets to exchange news and views (usually known as gossip). They are also places where money is lost; my most recent donations to the Bookies' Pension Fund occurred at the nearby Cottenham Point-to-Point.

In the first race I backed form, and lost. In the second race I backed

the jockey, and lost. In the third race I backed the best-looking horse, and lost. In the fourth race I backed the horse with the prettiest stable girl, and lost. Finally, in desperation, I backed the jockey with the silliest name. This dubious privilege fell to a certain Miss Belcher, riding a horse at thirty-three to one. I was astonished: from the off the amazing Miss Belcher streaked to the front. After the first circuit she was still well in the lead. Almost round the second circuit her horse was resembling Pegasus. At the final jump the wonderful Miss Belcher was going to make me rich. In fact Miss Belcher had other ideas – at least gravity had – at speed, with untold grace and beauty, Miss Belcher did a swallow dive into the mud. She had given me a clean sweep: I had lost every race. So my Baptist upbringing had struck again: I shouldn't have been gambling anyway.

55

Estuaries in the Mire

To the naturalist, sportsman and countryman, an estuary is a very
special area. It can be one of the few remaining oases of peace and
tranquillity in an increasingly frenetic, unfriendly world. It is a place
where land and fresh water meet the sea; nature can be heard and
felt and for a few brief moments the visitor can imagine wilderness,
freedom and that time when the world was young and unspoilt by
Man. It is a place of water and tide, mud and wind, harshness and
gentility, life and death – all under wide-open skies, which at dusk
and dawn can be fired by an awesome natural beauty. There are
feelings of remoteness mixed with wildness, where wingbeats and
the distant call of geese stir feelings as old as Man himself. It is in
such places that it is still possible to feel at one with nature, part
of nature – not in perpetual conflict with nature.

The wide skies help to form these feelings – as the moon gradually
ousts the sun on a winter evening, the office, nine-to-five and
Neighbours on television seem like aberrations from an alien
planet. These wild places have been described in music, poetry
and prose. In Henry Williamson's books of *Tarka the Otter*, and
Salar the Salmon, the words recreate the wonder of real places, for
once visited by people with vision and feelings, the memories of
estuaries settle permanently in the memory.

Another writer, too, wrote of estuaries with such skill that from
his pages come the smell of salt, the sound of the tide turning and the
sibilating wingbeats of passing wildfowl. BB was a master craftsman
who described the places he loved; that love still lives on in his books
such as *Tide's Ending* and *Dark Estuary*.

The estuary is haunting at all seasons of the year. At high summer
with the samphire ready to pick and redshank whistling in warning.
On such days the saltmarsh is apparently endless as it shimmers in

210

a haze of heat. By winter the landscape has changed into a hundred shades of grey and brown, but thousands of wings give movement and life as wildfowl and waders fly.

Sadly fewer people seem to be appreciating such sights today as the urbanization of Britain continues. It is a movement that is frightening: a whole generation is now growing up who seems divorced from nature, the countryside and real life. Wildlife is seen as a television documentary in the Third World; the world this generation inhabits is primarily one of new roads, houses, superstores, entertainment complexes and instant pleasure. Countryman and natural man are being replaced by homogenized and stereotyped man. Now, when an estuary is seen from the local car park or picnic centre, the beauty, wildlife and wilderness are not noticed; all that registers is mud – miles of it, thousands of acres of it, useless, dirty, pointless mud. Sadly, the businessman, planner and politician see slightly more than mud – they also see money; these wastelands can be transformed into productive land for houses, factories, airports, waste sites, marinas – for yuppies, and barrages. The wheeler-dealers see a holiday home in the Bahamas, a 'Merc' at the door and an OBE for job creation as their rewards. It used to be 'where there's muck there's money'; now it's 'where there's mud there's money', lots of money, and various opportunists are eyeing up our estuaries, regardless of the wildlife and environmental implications.

As a result nearly all of Britain's major estuaries are now under threat, both long term and short term. Virtually all of them are Sites of Special Scientific Interest, as they hold some of the largest wintering populations of wildfowl and waders in Europe – yet their 'special', 'protected' status seems to count for nothing. Already

one such estuary has gone regardless of its wildlife importance. Cardiff Bay is having a barrage constructed in one of the most disgraceful developments ever allowed in Britain – a case of a First World country knowingly, and brazenly, destroying a whole eco-system. There was no great economic reason for this act of legalized vandalism, just the yuppification of Cardiff's waterfront for the benefit of a few political and business egos. Many of those closed minds who backed the marina argued that the birds would still have water; their brains could not apparently grasp that the wealth of an estuary is in its mud and the animal life in it – a knot or a curlew can obtain food from uncovered mud; they fly away from marinas surrounded by pretty lights, overpriced boats and restaurants where tired decision-makers eat lasagne – and chips.

The scale of the threat is huge, the time of threat is now. Yet as the concrete-mixers churn, the government fiddles and its conservation record will soon rank among the worst in Europe. I have been a paid-up member of the Conservative Party for years, but unless it puts the 'conserve' back into 'Conservative', it will not be getting my vote at the next election. Instead, it has been left to organizations such as the RSPB and Friends of the Earth to fight long and hard against this madness, but so far few people seem very interested in 'mud'.

Yet Britain's coastal wildlife is spectacular. Its coastline itself extends for over 11,000 miles, which is almost the equivalent of half the circumference of the earth at the Equator. Almost twenty-five per cent of that shoreline is low-lying, containing estuaries that support well over a million and a half wintering waders and anything up to a million wintering wildfowl. These figures make Britain one of the most important areas in Europe for wildlife and gives some of the most exciting wildlife sights in the world.

These last words are not meant to be just another cliché. I mean it. I travel regularly off the beaten-track in Africa and have looked for tigers in India, but still the thought of going to an English estuary in winter gives me a greater sense of anticipation than going to the Masai Mara in Kenya; to me the Masai Mara is like the South Downs with wildebeest. (I have to confess, though, that some parts of Northern Kenya could pull me away from English mud).

I first appreciated the attraction of salt creek and mud bank as a boy. Then an uncle had a small farm on Mersey Island in Essex. Once away from the boats and holiday-makers it became a different world: of redshank, snipe, flowers and the rhythms of nature. Spring holidays in Devon also took us to the small but beautiful estuary of the River Otter at Budleigh Salterton. There I saw my first bar-tailed godwit and dunlin so close that they seemed almost to have lost their fear.

It was ten years ago that I fully appreciated the importance of our estuaries. It was then that I had the good fortune to write *The Wildlife of the Royal Estates*, a book which took me to two of the most important estuaries in Britain – the Wash and Morecambe Bay.

The Sandringham Estate in Norfolk goes right down to the Wash and one morning in winter it showed its wealth of wildlife. With a dawn start, the day was unforgettable. I wrote: 'It was high tide and as I made for the marshes the full moon was bright and being reflected in a shimmering path of silver over the Wash. There were many gulls and shelducks on the water and their brilliant white was more than matched by the thousands of wavelets each reflecting concentrated moonlight.

'Oyster-catchers piped and teal whistled as a male hen harrier hunted over rough grassland, steel grey with ink black tips to his wings. He flew off, startling roosting birds. Knot flew in great masses, thousands of them, dark against the bright sky. As the moonlight evaporated under the brilliant sun, the cold air became full of geese. Two flocks of Brent geese moved inland to feed, while a great V of high flying pink-feet flew in the opposite direction, out on to the Wash, calling as they went. They were followed by a long ragged skein at "hedge-hopping" height; as if some had been left behind by the first movement of birds. They had been feeding by the light of the full moon and were intending to roost during the day. A large group of wigeon were in the Duke's sanctuary, some grazing and others resting on the water. Redshank too were feeding, and another flew in calling melodically; their call in the wind is the music of wetland, marsh and muddy creek. It is the sound of solitude, wild places and freedom, and it strikes a distant chord, gently stirring, soothing and releasing those emotions normally locked deep within the soul.'

Over 220,000 waders visit the Wash during the winter and spring, as well as more than 25,000 wildfowl. In the eastern Wash close to Sandringham they include 35,000 knot, 12,000 oystercatchers, 8,000 dunlin, 5,000 bar-tailed godwits, 3,000 grey plovers, 1,500 curlew, 7,000 shelducks, 5,000 widgeon, 2,500 mallard and, 2,500 pintail. In addition there will often be over 10,000 geese and 500 teal.

Morecambe Bay too is spectacular and the royal link comes from the fact that the Duchy of Lancaster owns much of the foreshore. At its peak the bay attracts over 250,000 wading birds and again the sites can be astonishing. While visiting Morecambe, I met John

Wilson, the RSPB warden from nearby Leighton Moss. He took me on to Morecambe's mud to explain why it is so vital to wintering birds. In fact the estuary is three times more fertile than top-quality farm land because of all the nutrients carried in by the rivers and sea. In the wetter areas there are thousands of marine snails, which average about 3,000 per square yard. The smaller waders love them, as do shelducks, sieving them busily with their large scarlet bills. The snails are so small that it must take thousands to satisfy such a large duck. The Baltic tellin, a small shellfish with beautiful rose-pink shell, averages around 4,000 per square yard; the small tellins are taken by knot, while the larger ones are loved by oystercatchers.

Most waders eat sandhoppers that live in small U-shaped burrows, 6,000 to the square yard. In addition there are mussels, cockles and various other molluscs and crustaceans that bolster the food supply still more. At the same time tens of thousands of worm casts reveal the presence of lug worms; rag worms are also plentiful, but they leave no tell-tale heaps of sand. The two larger worms live at greater depths, beyond the reach of knot, dunlin and redshank; instead they fall prey to the long curved beak of the curlew, and the slightly upturned slender bill of the bar-tailed godwit. So mud is not just something to build on, flood, or turn into a waste-tip – it is a whole kingdom teeming with life on which countless wintering, migrating and resident birds depend. Instead of simply wanting to exploit mud, we should have a sense of responsibility towards it, and the things that depend on it for their survival.

Needless to say both the Wash and Morecambe Bay are threatened, typifying the shadows now falling on virtually all our estuaries. The Wash has a selection: estuarine barrage proposals for water supply, port and urban expansion, dredging, shellfish – and bait-digging, fresh and sea water pollution, recreational pressure, military training and a rising sea level.

Morecambe Bay is facing a similar list of absurdities – a tidal barrage scheme, sea defences, extraction of sand for dock development, urban-industrial development, recreational pressure including proposals for a marina, shell-fishing and bait-digging, long sea outfall for untreated sewage, changes in grazing regimes, river pollution, and a rising sea level yet again.

Out of 123 estuaries surveyed by the RSPB (eighty per cent of Britain's total), eighty were considered to be under some degree of threat, with thirty estuaries in imminent danger of permanent damage; forty-nine were threatened by recreational pressure, thirty-three by marinas, twenty-nine by pollution, twenty-nine by land claim, twenty-two by barrages, seventeen by bait-digging, seventeen by industry, fifteen by cockle-fishing and fourteen by port expansion.

All types of estuary, large and small, are affected. For example, the River Severn faces several proposed barrages, an airport, a motorway, a second road bridge, additional pollution and the usual sea level rise, while the Medway is threatened with power station development, port extension, dredging disposal, waste disposal and marina expansion. Even the mid-Essex coast faces changes in agricultural practice, recreation, coastal erosion, proposed airport development and other built development.

It is a depressing tale of financial opportunism, planning ineptitude, and lack of concern, and that lack of concern goes from local councillors to the very top of the political ladder. In 1992 the Commons Select Committee on the Environment recommended coastal zone protection and co-ordinated planning – yet two years later nothing has been done. While the Secretary of State for Agriculture, now supremo of the Department of the Environment, John Gummer, was red-hot at implementing European directives that I mentioned earlier caused havoc to small slaughter houses and butchery businesses; his current department seems incapable of grasping, or implementing the Council of the European Communities Directive 79/409/EEC of 2 April 1979, on the Conservation of Wild Birds, that should give our estuary bird populations all the protection they need. Alas, government implementation of EC directives appears to be extremely selective.

It is also obvious that our coastline is the responsibility of a whole list of organizations and quangos, each with their own vested interests. Surely it is time that there was a National Coastal Policy organized and implemented by a single organization, such as the NRA?

However, I continue to believe that the biggest threat to our estuaries, our wildlife and our countryside in general, remains that blinkered, urban disaster area, the House of Commons. Most MPs come from urban backgrounds and they seem uninterested in country matters, the fate of our estuaries included. Many too seem to be simply career politicians, only concerned with short-term advantage. Developing estuaries gives just that – short-term advantage in brief job creation and economic activity. What is needed to save our estuaries, and our diminishing countryside are committed politicians who actually believe in things, people who believe in the importance of our natural heritage and our responsibilities for handing them on in good condition to future generations.

56

Furious about Foxes

I am writing this diary in a state of fury; a fox has just had one of
my lambs. I am not furious with the fox, however, although I am
annoyed; I am furious with all those fox apologists who claim that
foxes do not take lambs. They sometimes amend this line of fantasy
by saying, 'Yes, foxes do take lambs, but their victims are always
weak, dead or dying.' What nonsense! This lamb was fit, well and
very much alive. And why shouldn't foxes take lambs? They take
wild brown hares which are fitter, faster and heavier than lambs.

The poor little fellow was the eldest and largest of twins. He was
born at eight o'clock in the morning; by four in the afternoon he
was skipping. When I checked the sheep again just after midnight
he was fine; at dawn he had vanished into thin air and there was a
disgusting smell of fox. The mother bleated forlornly for her son
all day long and that evening I put them all under cover.

The ewes had been lambing in a small paddock, surrounded by
sheep-fencing, close to the farmhouse. To the fox this was evidently
no problem. This is the first lamb I have lost in the five or six years
I have been keeping sheep – but it is annoying, as foxes are creatures
of habit and opportunity. Once they get the taste for something they
will often come back for more. Normally I have the lambing ewes
in the cow yard, after the cattle have been turned out into the fields
for summer. This year the appalling weather meant that the cows
were still in.

Two nights later the fox returned; in the morning there was a
little pile of white feathers. Yes, the white duck dumped in the
farmyard a few chapters ago had bitten the dust. On an evening
of torrential rain the brainless bird had refused to go into its run.
I had got soaked and frozen trying to get it to safety, but it knew
best; so did the fox. I suppose that as I was getting soaked, running

216

round in ever-decreasing circles, those people who blame fox losses on farming negligence were warm, dry and in front of their fires.

My condition has not been helped either by an anonymous letter telling me that the bad behaviour of foxes is greatly exaggerated and not their fault (the letter-writer knows – he or she has seen a video). Apparently the video was of a fox killing hens in a henhouse. The letter-writer claims that the fox's behaviour was abnormal as it was in a confined space and triggered by all the flapping. What the video did not show is how the fox came to be filmed in the first place, who produced it and why the cameraman did not stop the fox. I suspect that it was a video designed to give a partial point of view. There are several of these about at the moment being sent to schools and countryside groups. I suppose some of them are made to mislead rather than to inform.

In fact 'surplus killing' by foxes is not simply confined to henhouses or enclosed spaces. I have seen foxes killing hens out in the open: it was a game with fluttering balls of feathers – so much for the main thrust of the video nasty. In addition, of course, sometimes ground-nesting wild birds are killed in large numbers, a fact my letter-writer seemed to ignore completely.

One of the most notorious cases of fox felony occurred at the famous tern colony of Skolt Head in Norfolk. Significantly it was not videoed by any fox apologist. When Bob Chestney, the old warden, retired, his ex-employers – English Nature – ordered that his methods should not be followed. Chestney controlled predators, including foxes, for the benefit of his beloved terns. As he went out, the foxes moved in and the terns left; one of Britain's most important wildlife sites became almost deserted.

Fortunately sanity returned. It has now been realized that you cannot have foxes and ground-nesting birds. Some of the wardens even went on a pest control course with the British Association for Shooting and Conservation, to learn how to shoot and snare foxes, and now the terns are coming back. For years I have considered the links between gamekeepers and wildlife wardens to be much closer than some conservationists like to admit – this incident seems to confirm it. Gamekeepers preserve pheasants and grouse by managing habitat and controlling predators such as crows, magpies and foxes; now an increasing number of wildlife wardens are doing the same thing to preserve birds under pressure. Last year the RSPB lost both little terns and avocets to foxes. This year, as I understand it, they are being much harder on predators. The facts are that avocets and little terns have few suitable sites in which to breed. Foxes, crows and magpies, on the other hand, can breed virtually anywhere, and so their control in areas of wildlife, game or farming importance does not put the main populations at risk. So, sanity is breaking out at last. Who knows, in five years' time, the conservationists may also be taking a more sensible look at sparrowhawks. I hope by then it will not be too late for the snipe of the Ouse Washes who are in rapid decline, partly thanks to the local sparrowhawks.

I was recently invited to take part in a BBC television *Open Space* programme, to be shown in May, on country sports. Earlier the producer had made a film about Britain's Black Conservatives. Following one black, refined, hunting Conservative to a hunt, she heard him regaled by an angry hunt saboteur. 'Have you forgotten slavery already,' the young lady bawled. 'A hundred years ago these people would have been hunting you.' 'My dear,' the black hunter replied calmly, 'five hundred years ago I would have been eating you.'

57

Rip-Off

Oh dear, I wish I hadn't mentioned sparrowhawks again in the last chapter, as I have had another flood of letters – in the eyes of many they are becoming as troublesome as magpies. A farmer's wife in Shropshire tells me that not only has her bird-table been cleared by sparrowhawks, but also her whole garden, while a farmer in Devon describes how they try to take his young house martins as soon as they leave the nest. Another reports how a sparrowhawk was chasing a pigeon which flew in such panic, straight through the glass of his bedroom window. The poor pigeon was dead on the floor, and so what did the sparrowhawk do? Try to get at the corpse through the hole in the window of course.

Just last week I had a sparrowhawk near-miss. A blackbird was on a collision course with my windscreen with a hawk breathing down its neck. I shut my eyes and braked hard – the blackbird swerved away and the sparrowhawk flew up and back in the direction it came from. It was a lucky escape for all three of us.

Another reader has phoned to ask how sparrowhawks actually catch snipe in the Ouse Washes; in his opinion snipe fly too fast and too far. Apparently there are two pairs of sparrowhawks hunting the Washes which specialize in snipe. They appear to have changed their normal hunting patterns and are flying almost like harriers. They are quartering the ground and paying particular attention to clumps and tufts of grass and rush. If a snipe is flushed, while nesting or feeding, the sparrowhawk drops on it as it takes off and before it has picked up speed.

The removal of the two pairs of sparrowhawks would solve the problem, as there are plenty of sparrowhawks elsewhere. But the conservation establishment has decreed that populations of birds of prey must be left alone, regardless of the consequences, in this case

219

regardless of the plummeting numbers of snipe. It is another case of a public relations exercise taking priority over practical and proper conservation.

Before too long I predict that another raptor will be causing havoc and that serious control measures will be called for. Goshawk numbers are exploding and it is an even larger, more efficient killer than the sparrowhawk. In Finland the bird is already controlled – 3,000 birds are shot by the government each year, to protect more vulnerable and endangered species. Watch this space.

It is always a relief, coming to the end of lambing, for it is a tiring time. Once the last ewe has lambed safely it means that I can go to bed before midnight and lie-in after dawn. We averaged two lambs per ewe this year which is not bad considering the season. A lot of shepherds were not so lucky and I feel really sorry for all those who have lost lambs in large numbers this year, from Bodmin Moor to the north of Scotland. The ewes have simply not been able to get themselves in condition, or stay in good condition, in a winter that has been long, cold and damp. This has meant weaker lambs, and many thousands have succumbed in the cold and wet.

No sooner had lambing stopped than I had to go the Television Centre to do some recording for *One Man and His Dog*. It was a two-day visit to the big city – the Black Hole. When I claim to be a naïve, innocent country peasant, some people think that I am deliberately exaggerating. I am not, as my Black Hole experience shows.

The BBC booked me, and the other new boy to the programmes, Gus Dermody, in at the Hilton Hotel, in Kensington. Unsurprisingly each room has a telephone. In my house I too have a telephone. Now I thought telephones were for using, so at six-thirty in the morning I phoned a friend in Nairobi to enquire about Richard Leakey and elephant poaching. I spoke for about fifteen minutes, and in the simple world in which I live I expected to pay about ten pounds. When I enquired how much I owed, the charming receptionist pointed out that with the hotel's commission the call came to a modest £111. She kindly explained, with a smile, why hotel telephones are charged at a different rate to those found in peasant hovels, and I didn't understand a word of it. The Kensington Hilton is always awash with Japanese visitors; with them all phoning home the hotel must be making a fortune. The Hilton described it as their 'pricing policy'; in my view somebody in my local pub gave it a much more appropriate two words – he called it a 'rip-off'. It is a good job ET didn't visit the Hilton; he would not have been able to afford to 'phone home'.

Sadly, my tribulation was not over. For the duration of the two days in London, my beloved Daihatsu Fourtrak had been parked at British Rail's lovely, unguarded, Royston Station, and British Rail has not yet realized that some people have to work longer than nine to five and their vending machines only give parking tickets for a maximum of twenty-four hours. That's right, on my return, there was something large, yellow and metallic on one of my wheels; a BR customer encouragement wheel-clamp. Then insult was added to injury. I phoned the clamping company in a rage, complaining of the clamp. The reply still amazes me. 'No you haven't got a clamp,' a buffoon informed me. 'The clamper is not in your area today.' 'Could you explain what that large metal object is doing attached to my wheel then?' was the gist of what I asked in exasperation. 'I don't know,' the Brain of Britain replied. 'It can't be one of ours.' It was one of his, and it cost me £40 to be released from this non-existent wheelclamp. If things continue to go on like this I soon won't be able to afford to do *One Man and His Dog*.

'Phone the station first and tell them, before parking', say British Rail. Can anybody tell me how to call a BR station and get the phone answered? Perhaps I should phone via the Hilton.

58

A Dog's Who's Who

Bonio
A bone-shaped biscuit loved by all dogs of taste and breeding. No, the manufacturers have not given me any money during the writing of this book – Bramble just happens to like them.

John Gummer
This man could never be mistaken for a dog unless there are any unfortunate beasts which look thin, balding and shifty. I have met him several times during the writing of this book and he continues to amaze me. As a man he is pleasant, amusing and good company. As a politician he defies description. During the course of this book he travelled from Secretary of State at the Ministry of Agriculture, Fisheries and Food (MAFF) to Secretary of State at the Department of the Environment. In his religion he travelled even further, leaving the Church of England to become a Roman Catholic, over the issue of women priests. This I found very odd as most Catholic priests, including the Pope, seem to dress up as women anyway.

Gillian Shephard
During the course of this book she became the new Secretary of State at MAFF. Early on she was described to me as 'Gummer in a skirt' – what a horrifying thought. She obviously comes from ancestors who had severe learning difficulties – they certainly could not spell. One of her first acts as Secretary of State was to appoint a special adviser, a consultant in industrial policy with a special knowledge of the steel industry – obviously just the job for MAFF.

Daihatsu Fourtrak
My wonderful vehicle that for this book managed to remain unstolen the whole time. Daihatsus are often owned by working farmers. Ninety-five per cent of four-wheel drive vehicles never see mud or go off the road, they are owned because of the poser-syndrome. Ninety-five per cent of Daihatsus see mud and go off the road.

Bovine Spongioform Encephalitis – BSE
It makes cows behave in a very strange way. It affects the nervous system. The beast sways, froths at the mouth and staggers around in an erratic manner. Its brain is obviously affected. The sickness is more commonly known as mad cow disease.

Mr Blobby
A pink fat inflatable suit worn by an anonymous man. His eyes roll and his vocabulary never progresses beyond 'Blobby, Blobby, Blobby'. Promoted by the BBC, Mr Blobby represents the Corporation's highest cultural achievement for many years. Wherever he goes he attracts onlookers in large numbers and gives a new meaning to the phrase 'brain dead'.

Mr Nicholas Soames MP
Minister of Food. Bears a remarkable resemblance to Mr Blobby.

Twyford Down
A wonderful area of once unspoilt downland. To show its commitment to 'biodiversity' and the 'global environment', the 'green' Conservative government put a motorway through the middle of it. It was also a Site of Special Scientific Interest (SSSI) which should have given it protection. It must be assumed that the government and its civil servants think SSSI stands for Site of Special Scientific Indifference.

Mr John MacGregor MP
Minister of Transport who actually seemed to think that the motorway through Twyford Down was an environmental improvement. This illusion, or delusion, explains why Mr MacGregor's hobby is conjuring. At one move of the hand he can cover an SSSI with concrete – remarkable.

Mr John Major MP
Said to be Prime Minister. A good friend and fellow countryman from the north thinks that he would make a very good valet.

The New Forest
One of Britain's oldest surviving forests. With roads, development and pollution, developers, planners and politicians are trying to divide it up into a number of wooded traffic islands between acres of tarmac.

Mrs Virginia Bottomley MP
Secretary of State for Health. A politician with a highly developed sense of humour. She claims the National Health Service is working better than ever, that waiting lists are getting shorter and all the staff are happy. At the time of writing this Who's Who I was expecting to attend an appointment to see a specialist about my knees. After waiting for twenty-five months, my appointment was cancelled by Addenbrooke's hospital on the day of the appointment. Mrs Bottomley doesn't have to wait twenty-five months for appointments, neither does she have to pay parking fees at her place of work – the House of Commons – unlike the nurses, and patients, at Addenbrooke's hospital.

London
A huge consuming city out of touch with anybody and anything not in London. Those living in London pay themselves considerably more than anywhere else in Britain. Anything that happens in London is considered to be news. Anything that happens outside London is considered to be of marginal importance. The only redeeming features about the place are that in the event of global warming and sea-level rise, much of London will be flooded. In the event of nuclear war, London will be hit first.

Semi-Detached Suburban Mr James
(a) A very good sixties pop song. (b) Four million commuters who live around London.

The National Rivers Authority
A quango that could be important in cleaning up and conserving our river systems and wetlands if we had a government interested or committed to conservation and the countryside.

The Conservative Government
A remarkable body that has managed to take the 'Conserve' out of its own name.

Gordon Beningfield
My very good friend and fellow Trustee of the Countryside Restoration Trust. The greatest wildlife and landscape artist of our age.

Rodger McPhail
Another artist and very good friend of mine. The second greatest living artist of our time.

Will Garfit
Yet another artist and very good friend of mine. The second equal greatest living artist of our time.

Torvill and Dean
The greatest British sports personalities of our time – they can dress up and dance on ice.

One Man and His Dog
The best programme ever to have been seen on British television.

Backword

For me this book has been something of a landmark. Not only is it my twentieth book – admittedly some of them have been very small – but it is the first one that I have delivered late: very late. The reason is simple and has nothing to do with laziness, misfortune or losing the manuscript; the delay has been caused entirely by the astonishing interest in the Countryside Restoration Trust. Letters have continued to flow in nearly every day and without the help of Ken Gifford, the Treasurer, and his wife Pat, and also my part-time secretary Margaret, the book would have been later still, or remained incomplete.

But although the book is finished, and I hope each reader enjoys it, the life it describes goes on, and the work of the Countryside Restoration Trust goes on. As I write this the Trust's field has been planted with hay meadow mixture; arrangements are being made to erect barn owl and little owl boxes, as well as a hanging basket for hobbies. Then we aim to try to buy a whole farm, an over-intensive prairie farm to restore it to the type of farm and the type of countryside described in this book. If anyone wants to give us land, then we would consider taking that on too.

So if you want to help, or find out more, write to The Countryside Restoration Trust, Barton, Cambridgeshire, CB3 7AG.